The Author

George Cantor has worked as a reporter and commentator in Detroit print and broadcast media since 1963. An award-winning newspaper columnist and sportswriter, he is the author of nine books on travel, including *The Great Lakes Guidebook*, *Where the Old Roads Go*, and from Visible Ink Press *Historic Black Landmarks*, *North American Indian Landmarks*, and *Pop Culture Landmarks*. He makes his home in West Bloomfield, Michigan.

D0067558

Historic Festivals

A TRAVELER'S GUIDE

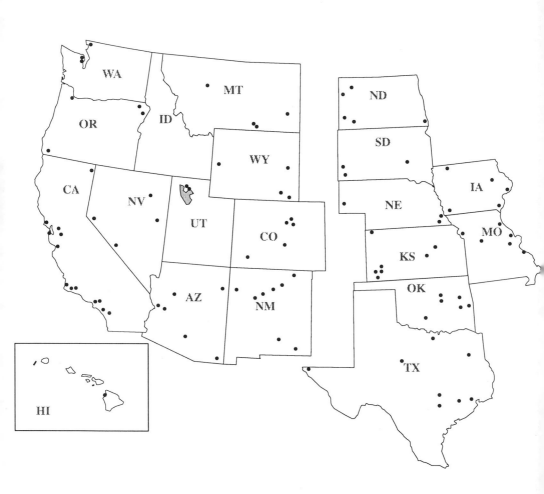

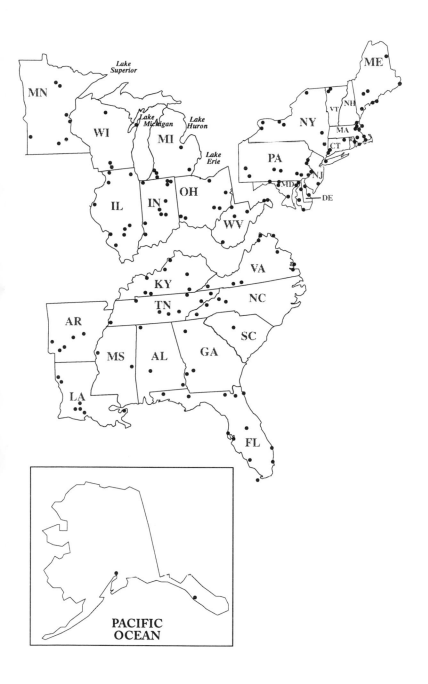

Historic Festivals

A TRAVELER'S GUIDE

GEORGE CANTOR

with foreword by
ARMANDO MORENO
President of the International Federation of Festival Organizations
Sherman Oaks, California

DETROIT • NEW YORK • WASHINGTON, D.C. • TORONTO

HISTORIC FESTIVALS

A Traveler's Guide

George Cantor

The Library of Congress has cataloged the Gale Research Inc. edition as follow:

Cantor, George, 1941–
    Historic festivals : a traveler's guide / George Cantor ; with foreword by Armando Moreno.
    p. cm.
    Includes index.
    ISBN 0-8103-9150-3
    1. United States—Guidebooks. 2. United States—Anniversaries, etc. I. Title.
E158.C247 1995
394.2'6973—dc20
    95-36742
    CIP

Published by Visible Ink Press™
a division of Gale Research

Visible Ink Press is a trademark of Gale Research

ISBN 0-7876-0824-6

Cover and Page Design: Pamela A. E. Galbreath; Map Designer: Sherrell Hobbs; Editors: Marie Ellavich and Rebecca Nelson; Acquisitions Editor: Christine Nasso; with thanks to: Jolen Gedridge, Camille Killens, Andrea Kovacs, and Jessica Proctor

COVER ILLUSTRATION: James Denk

10 9 8 7 6 5 4 3 2 1

Most Visible Ink Press books are available at special quantity discounts when purchased in bulk by corporations, organizations, or groups. Customized printings, special imprints, messages, and excerpts can be produced to meet your needs. For more information, contact Special Markets Manager, Gale Research Inc., 835 Penobscot Bldg., Detroit, MI 48226. Or call 1-800-776-6265.

To the memory of my grandparents,
a festive crowd if ever there was one.

Contents

❖ GREAT LAKES & OHIO VALLEY

❖ GREAT PLAINS

❖ WEST & PACIFIC

Images appearing in *Historic Festivals: A Traveler's Guide* were received from the following sources:

Carriage Parade Horse Race. Courtesy of Winterthur: **12**; Windjammer Day. Courtesy of Booth Bay Harbor Region Chamber of Commerce: **14**; Chester Greenwood Day. Reproduced by permission: **15**; Maine Lobster Festival. Courtesy of Paul "Gil" Merriam: **19**; Tea Party Festival. Courtesy of Kent County Chamber of Commerce: **23**; Chesapeake and Ohio Canal Boat Festival. Courtesy of John D. Millar: **25**; The Waterfowl Festival. Courtesy of The Waterfowl Festival, Inc.: **27**; Boston Tea Party. Reproduced by permission of Ewing Galloway, Inc.: **30**; Sheepshearing Festival. Courtesy of the Museum of American Textile History: **35**; Harvest Home and Thanksgiving. Courtesy of Plymouth Plantation, Inc., Plymouth, Mass.: **36**; Cranberry Harvest Festival held in South Carver, Mass. Courtesy of Agnew, Carter, McCarthy, Inc.: **39**; Iroquois Indian Festival. Courtesy of Iroquois Indian Museum: **45**; Stone Houses Day. Courtesy of Reverend Charles E. Stickley: **47**; Dankfest. Courtesy of Historic Harmony, Inc.: **58**; Kutztown Folk Festival. Courtesy of Ann Burrows: **61**; Battle of Germantown. Courtesy of Cliveden of the National Trust: **63**; Mummers Parade, Philadelphia. © David H. Wells. Reproduced by permission of The Image Works, Inc.: **65**; Groundhog Day. Reproduced by permission of Wide World Photos: **67**; Tennis Week. Courtesy of Michael Bazp, the Tennis Hall of Fame: **71**; W. C. Handy. Reproduced by permission of Wide World Photos: **85**; Mardi Gras. Courtesy of Alan Whitman: **87**; Hope Watermelon Festival. Courtesy of Hope-Hempstead County Chamber of Commerce: **90**; Hemingway Days. Reproduced by permission: **99**; Spanish Night Watch. Courtesy of The Committee for the Night Watch: **102**; The Jeanie Auditions. Reproduced by permission: **107**; Kentucky Guild of Artists and Craftsmen's Fair. Courtesy of Kentucky Department of Travel Development: **114**; Shaker Festival. Courtesy of Shaker Museum at South Union: **120**; Shrimp and Petroleum Festival. Reproduced by permission: **126**; Mardi Gras Parade. © Archive Photos. Reproduced by permission: **129**; Grandfather Mountain Highland Games. Courtesy of Grandfather Mountain: **136**; Mule Day. Courtesy of Mule Day Office: **141**; George Washington's Birthday. Courtesy of Alexandria Convention & Visitors Bureau: **149**; Chincoteague Pony Penning Day. Courtesy of Chincoteague Chamber of Commerce: **150**; Old Fiddlers Convention. Courtesy of Tom Jones: **152**; August Court Days. Courtesy of J. Patterson: **154**; New Market Battlefield Historical Park. Courtesy of Virginia Military Institute, a registered National Historic Landmark accredited by the American Association of Museums: **156**; Yorktown Battlefield. Courtesy of National Park Service, Colonial National Historical Park: **158**; Broom Corn Festival.

Courtesy of Arcola Chamber of Commerce: 167; Old Canal Days. Reproduced by permission: 171; Grand Levee at the Statehouse. Courtesy of Illinois Historic Preservation Agency: 175; Auburn-Cord-Duesenberg Festival. Courtesy of Auburn-Cord-Duesenberg Festival: 177; James Whitcomb Riley Festival. Courtesy of James Whitcomb Riley Festival Association, Inc.: 179; Forks of the Wabash Pioneer Festival. Courtesy of Mary DeLaney: 181; Early Indianapolis 500. © Archive Photos. Reproduced by permission: 182; Circus City Festival. Courtesy of Circus City Festival Inc.: 184; Covered Bridge Festival. Courtesy of Allan Miller: 185; Valparaiso Popcorn Festival. Valparaiso Popcorn Festival Inc.: 187; Battle Creek Cereal Festival. Courtesy of Battle Creek Cereal Festival: 190; International Freedom Festival. Courtesy of Joe Cracchiola, Detroit Edison Photography: 192; Tulip Time Festival. Courtesy of Tulip Time Inc.: 195; Colonial Fort Michilimackinac Pageant. Photo courtesy of The Mackinaw Area Tourist Bureau: 196; Fasching. Courtesy of The Concord Singers: 202; Defeat of Jesse James. Courtesy of *Northfield News:* 203; Annie Oakley. © Archive Photos. Reproduced by permission: 209; Apple Butter Festival. Courtesy of Stephen J. Shaluta, Jr.: 213; Election Day, 1860. Courtesy of Harpers Ferry National Historical Park: 215; West Virginia Oil and Gas Festival. Courtesy of West Virginia Oil and Gas Festival: 217; Stonewall Jackson Heritage Jubilee. Reproduced by permission: 218; Green County Cheese Days. Courtesy of Studio Haus: 221; Swiss Volksfest. Courtesy of New Glarus Chamber of Commerce: 223; Houby Days Festival. Courtesy of Cedar Rapids Area Convention & Visitors Bureau: 232; Glenn Miller Festival. Courtesy of Glenn Miller Birthplace Society: 234; Bix Beiderbecke. © Archive Photos. Reproduced by permission: 235; Wah-Shun-Gah Days. Courtesy of Council Grove Chamber of Commerce: 237; Dodge City Days. Courtesy of Dodge City Area Chamber of Commerce: 238; Beef Empire Days. Courtesy of Beef Empire Days & F Stop Photo: 239; Tom Sawyer Days. Courtesy of Hannibal Visitor's Bureau: 245; Scott Joplin. UPI/Bettmann. Reproduced by permission: 251; Arbor Day Parade. Courtesy of Nebraska City Chamber of Commerce: 255; Frontier Army Days. Courtesy of the North Dakota Tourism Department: 258; Will Rogers. Reproduced by permission of The Granger Collection: 263; Corn Palace Festival. Courtesy of Mitchell Chamber of Commerce: 271; Chisholm Trail Roundup. Courtesy of Delbert Bailey: 274; Fiesta San Antonio. Courtesy of Al Rendon: 277; Fur Rendezvous. Courtesy of Anchorage Convention & Visitors Bureau: 289; Gold Rush Days. Courtesy of Wickenburg Chamber of Commerce: 295; Navajo Nation Fair. Courtesy of Dawn Ferguson: 297; Jumping Frog Jubilee. Courtesy of Carol Cook, Jumping Frog Jubilee: 299; Gilroy Garlic Festival. Courtesy of Bill Strange: 301; Pasadena Tournament of Roses. Courtesy of Jocelyn Engel, Pasadena Tournament of Roses: 305; Chinese New Year. Reproduced by permission of Wide World Photos: 307; Old Spanish Days. Courtesy of Jeffrey Cords: 309; World Championship Pack Burro Race in Fairplay, CO.

Reproduced by permission of Gary E. Nichols, Park County Tourism Office: **313**; Kona Coffee Festival. Courtesy of Current Events: **318**; Charles Russell Art Auction. Courtesy of The C. M. Russell Auction of Original Western Art: **320**; Little Big Horn Days. Courtesy of Karen Simpson: **322**; Western Folklife. Courtesy of S. R. Hinrichs: **326**; Pony Express. Reproduced by permission of Ewing Galloway, Inc.: **327**; Carlsbad Caverns National Park. Courtesy of National Park Service: **331**; Chief Joseph of the Nez Perce. The Bettmann Archive. Reproduced by permission: **341**; Starlight Parade. Courtesy of Portland Rose Festival Association: **344**; Union Pacific Railroad. Reproduced by permission of Ewing Galloway, Inc.: **347**; Jackalope Days. Courtesy of The Douglas Budget and Douglas Area Chamber of Commerce: **353**.

Enriching the Future
by Understanding the Past

by Armando Moreno
President of the International Federation of Festival Organizations
Sherman Oaks, California

I am delighted to introduce *Historic Festivals: A Traveler's Guide* to readers. This book comes at a time when culture, education, and tradition are widely discussed, and it is certain that festivals, in particular those that are historic, are among the events where these matters are explored and celebrated.

The word "festival" derives from the Latin *festivas*, meaning a celebration focusing on a particular event. This meaning holds true today. A festival's theme is often drawn from a particular village or town—from the town's ethnic heritage; a historical event that occurred there and became locally, regionally, or nationally important; an era that brought prosperity to the region; or a specific crop or industry that shaped the lives of the people there. Festivals focus on community.

In the United States, a country of unprecedented levels of ethnic and cultural diversity, festivals often represent an exploration of the roles that people and events have played in forming our unique American cultural heritage. Individuals such as Daniel Boone, Chief Joseph, Johnny Appleseed, Annie Oakley, Stonewall Jackson, Will Rogers, and even Elvis Presley are celebrated for leaving their mark not only on a community, but on the nation. Local events with larger repercussions are also the focus of festivals—whether it be a moment that affected national military history, such as Boston's remembrance of the evacuation of the British during the Revolutionary War, or an important moment in civilian affairs, such as the first claim filed under the Homestead Act, which is honored by a special day in Beatrice, Nebraska.

Some communities have preserved their place in history by passing their ancestors' stories and traditions from one generation to the next and celebrating them today with both ritual and contemporary cultural expressions. This can be observed in festivals as diverse as Dodge City Days in Kansas; Thanksgiving in Plymouth, Massachusetts; Gold Rush Days in Wickenburg, Arizona; Steamboat Days in Burlington, Iowa; and the Shaker Festival in South Union, Kentucky. These events often include re-creations of folk traditions, which are centered on the idea of togetherness and inspired by music, dance, art, stories, crafts, costumes, and food. Through such activities, historic festivals help us learn more about our similarities and differences, as well as about the range of cultural expressions in the United States.

Participating in festivals stimulates communication and increases an understanding of the diverse peoples and cultures in the United States. In these pages, we find numerous cultures preserving their unique heritage—from Native American celebrations such as Philadelphia, Mississippi's Choctaw Fair, and Anadarko, Oklahoma's American Indian Exposition, to ethnic festivals of immigrant communities such as Danish Days in Solvang, California, the Swiss Volksfest in New Glarus, Wisconsin, and the National Basque Festival in Elko, Nevada. This intermingling of traditional, ethnic, and contemporary elements contributes to the perpetuation of a culture that is experiencing a resurgence or a renaissance.

The arts, too, benefit from our tradition of festivals, which support artists by providing a place for them to exhibit and demonstrate their work. Historic festivals also encourage artists to be informed by history. Festivals foster the preservation of artistic traditions and work for their future as well as their contemporary expressions. Musical festivals range from the Baroque, as seen in Bethlehem, Pennsylvania's Bach festival, to the newer and particularly American sounds of the Bluegrass Music Festival, the Glenn Miller Festival, the Scott Joplin Ragtime Music Festival, and the New Orleans Jazz Festival. Artwork and crafts are showcased in festivals such as the Kentucky Guild of Artists and Craftsmen Fair, the Kutztown Folk Festival, and the C. M. Russell Auction of Original Western Art. By making the arts their focus, festivals become a bridge between people and organizations, linking them with the broad resources that are available to them.

Festivals have many positive characteristics: they strengthen our multicultural heritage, inform educators and the media about the role of the arts in their community, and make government agencies and private patrons of the arts aware of the achievements—and function—of culture and the arts. Festivals are an exceptional means of communication, through which we are able to share experiences. Festivals that celebrate history embrace the ways of the past, tying them to the issues we face today, helping us not only to foster traditions but to retain our identity.

Historic Festivals: A Traveler's Guide welcomes readers to learn more about the coast-to-coast events that celebrate American history. Teachers and students of history and social studies, the people who organize festivals, artists who participate in festivals, tourism officials, travel agents and those who promote festivals will find this a valuable resource. And all travelers will discover the modern-day enthusiasm of festivals and the history they recall.

June 1995

The first place I ever visited on assignment as a travel writer was Ste. Genevieve, Missouri. Actually, I had assigned the visit to myself, since I was also the newly-appointed travel editor. I chose this place for my initial trip after seeing it featured on a PBS series about American history. I had never heard of it before, but the segment about its French heritage intrigued me. So I flew into St. Louis and made the drive south to the old town along the Mississippi River. At the time, it was more accurately described as *within* the Mississippi River. The spring of 1973 was a time of terrible flooding and much of Ste. Genevieve was inundated, although not the historic section. As I visited the old structures and talked to people, two remarks stayed in my memory.

A guide at one of the old homes expressed surprise that any travel writer would be doing a story about the place. "Why, everybody already knows about Ste. Genevieve," she said. And she was quite serious.

The other statement came after I had asked another guide if much of the town still was French. "No, we're almost all of German descent here," she said. "We just feel it's important to remember the place's past."

It was good to return to Ste. Genevieve in compiling this book on historic festivals. Because I think that the sentiments I heard there years ago are the book's foundation. Above everything else, these events celebrate a sense of place. This history, this way of life is what distinguishes this town, this place, from every other place around it. Our past is what makes us who we are. In a world of ever-widening homogeneity, these communities hold fiercely to the qualities that make them unmistakably unique.

"Everybody knows about us." That's the voice of assurance, of confidence in the significance of this place's past as something worth celebrating.

"It's important to remember the place's past." That's the voice of continuity, a recognition that a community severs the link with its past self at the risk of its future.

Both of these qualities are cause for celebration, wherever they survive. In these pages is a guide to the places where they not only survive, but are exalted.

George Cantor
June 1995

Northeast

Connecticut

Delaware

Maine

Maryland

Massachusetts

New Jersey

New York

Pennsylvania

Rhode Island

Vermont

Washington, D.C.

Connecticut
1. Barnum Festival, Bridgeport
2. Oyster Festival, Norwalk
3. Shad Derby, Windsor

Delaware
4. Return Day, Georgetown
5. Winterthur Point-to-Point Races, Talleyville

Maine
6. LaKermasse Festival, Biddeford
7. Windjammer Day, Boothbay Harbor
8. Chester Greenwood Day, Farmington
9. Potato Feast, Houlton
10. Blueberry Festival, Machias
11. Maine Lobster Festival, Rockland
12. Log Day, Skowhegan

Maryland
13. Chesapeake Appreciation Day, Annapolis
14. Preakness Celebration, Baltimore
15. Tea Party Festival, Chestertown
16. National Hard Crab Derby, Crisfield
17. Chesapeake and Ohio Canal Festival, Cumberland
18. Old St. Joseph's Jousting Tournament and Horse Show, Waterfowl Festival, Easton
19. Alsatia Mummers Parade, Hagerstown
20. Lotus Blossom Festival, Lilypons

Massachusetts
21. Evacuation Day, Patriots' Day, Bunker Hill Day, Boston Tea Party Reenactment, Boston
22. St. Peter's Fiesta, Gloucester
23. Sheepshearing Festival, North Andover
24. Harvest Week, Thanksgiving, Plymouth
25. Haunted Happenings, Salem

26. Massachusetts Harvest Cranberry Festival, South Carver
27. Patriots' Day March, Mustering of Minutemen and Fife and Drum Muster, Sudbury

New Jersey
28. Miss America Pageant, Atlantic City

New York
29. Toy Festival, East Aurora
30. Iroquois Indian Festival, Howes Cave
31. Stone Houses Day, Hurley
32. Canal Festival, Medina
33. St. Patrick's Day, San Gennaro Festival, Halloween Parade, Thanksgiving Day Parade, New York
34. Seaway Festival, Ogdensburg
35. Lilac Festival, Rochester
36. Convention Days, Seneca Falls

Pennsylvania
37. Bach Festival, Christmas in Bethlehem, Bethlehem
38. Memorial Day Festival, Boalsburg
39. Dankfest, Harmony
40. Chocolate Festival, Hershey
41. Kutztown Folk Festival, Kutztown
42. Rose Festival, Mannheim
43. Battle of Germantown Reenactment, Philadelphia
44. Elfreth's Alley Fete Day, Philadelphia
45. Mummers Parade, Philadelphia
46. Groundhog Day, Punxsutawney
47. National Pike Festival, Uniontown
48. Reenactment of the Delaware River Crossing, Washington Crossing

Rhode Island
49. Tennis Week and Music Festival, Newport
50. Gaspee Days, Warwick
51. International Quahog Festival, Wickford

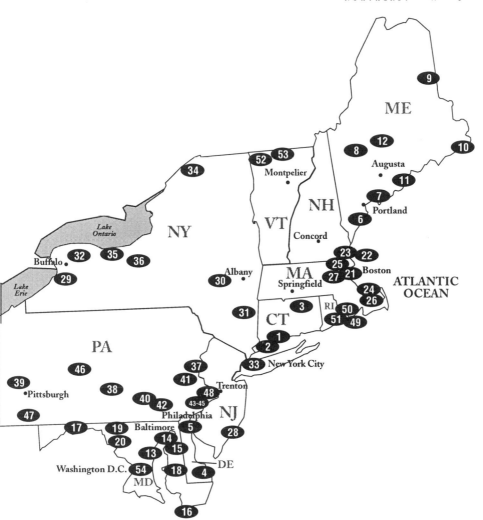

Vermont

52. Dairy Festival, Enosburg Falls
53. Maple Sugar Festival, St. Albans

Washington, D.C.

54. Cherry Blossom Festival

❄ January

New Year's Day: **Mummers Parade,** Philadelphia, Pennsylvania

❄ February

2: **Groundhog Day,** Punxsutawney, Pennsylvania

Presidents' Day weekend: **Chocolate Festival,** Hershey, Pennsylvania

◆ March

17: **Evacuation Day,** Boston, Massachusetts

17: **St. Patrick's Day,** New York, New York

◆ April

First two weeks: **Cherry Blossom Festival,** Washington, D.C.

Third Monday: **Patriots' Day,** Boston, Massachusetts

19: **Patriots' Day March,** Sudbury, Massachusetts

Dates vary: **Maple Sugar Festival,** St. Albans, Vermont

◆ May

Sunday of the first full weekend: **Winterthur Point-to-Point Races,** Talleyville, Delaware

Second and third weekends: **Bach Festival,** Bethlehem, Pennsylvania

Second week: **Lilac Festival,** Rochester, New York

Week before the third Saturday: **Preakness Celebration,** Baltimore, Maryland

Third Sunday: **Sheepshearing Festival,** North Andover, Massachusetts

Third weekend: **National Pike Festival,** Uniontown, Pennsylvania

Third weekend: **Shad Derby,** Windsor, Connecticut

Saturday before Memorial Day: **Tea Party Festival,** Chestertown, Maryland

Weekend closest to the 30th: **Memorial Day Festival,** Boalsburg, Pennsylvania

Memorial Day weekend and the week following: **Gaspee Days,** Warwick, Rhode Island

❄ June

First weekend: **Dairy Festival,** Enosburg Falls, Vermont

First weekend: **Elfreth's Alley Fete Day,** Philadelphia, Pennsylvania

Second Sunday: **Rose Festival,** Mannheim, Pennsylvania

17: **Bunker Hill Day,** Boston, Massachusetts

Late June: **Windjammer Day,** Boothbay Harbor, Maine

Last full week: **LaKermasse Festival,** Biddeford, Maine

Last weekend: **St. Peter's Fiesta,** Gloucester, Massachusetts

❄ July

First week: **Kutztown Folk Festival,** Kutztown, Pennsylvania

Weekend closest to July 4: **Barnum Festival,** Bridgeport, Connecticut

First weekend: **Canal Festival,** Medina, New York

Second Saturday: **Stone Houses Day,** Hurley, New York

Second full weekend: **Chesapeake and Ohio Canal Festival,** Cumberland, Maryland

Second week: **Tennis Week and Music Festival,** Newport, Rhode Island

Weekend closest to July 15: **Lotus Blossom Festival,** Lilypons, Maryland

Weekend closest to July 19: **Convention Days,** Seneca Falls, New York

Third weekend: **Seaway Festival,** Ogdensburg, New York

August

First Saturday: **Maine Lobster Festival,** Rockland, Maine

First Wednesday: **Old St. Joseph's Jousting Tournament and Horse Show,** Easton, Maryland

Third weekend: **Blueberry Festival,** Machias, Maine

Fourth Sunday: **Toy Festival,** East Aurora, New York

Fourth weekend: **Dankfest,** Harmony, Pennsylvania

Last weekend: **Potato Feast,** Houlton, Maine

Last Saturday: **Log Day,** Skowhegan, Maine

September

Labor Day weekend: **Iroquois Indian Festival,** Howes Cave, New York

Labor Day weekend: **National Hard Crab Derby,** Crisfield, Maryland

Weekend after Labor Day: **Oyster Festival,** Norwalk, Connecticut

Weekend after Labor Day: **Miss America Pageant,** Atlantic City, New Jersey

Week before September 19: **San Gennaro Festival,** New York, New York

Last Saturday in September: **Mustering of Minutemen and Fife and Drum Muster,** Sudbury, Massachusetts

October

First Saturday: **Battle of Germantown Reenactment,** Philadelphia, Pennsylvania

Begins first weekend: **Harvest Week,** Plymouth, Massachusetts

Sunday closest to Columbus Day: **International Quahog Festival,** Wickford, Rhode Island

Second weekend: **Massachusetts Harvest Cranberry Festival,** South Carver, Massachusetts

Second Saturday after the third Monday: **Alsatia Mummers Parade,** Hagerstown, Maryland

Last weekend: **Chesapeake Appreciation Day,** Annapolis, Maryland

Weekend nearest Halloween: **Haunted Happenings,** Salem, Massachusetts

31: **Halloween Parade,** New York, New York

November

Thursday following the first Monday of November (even-numbered years only): **Return Day,** Georgetown, Delaware

Second weekend: **Waterfowl Festival,** Easton, Maryland

Fourth Thursday: **Thanksgiving,** Plymouth, Massachusetts

Fourth Thursday: **Thanksgiving Day Parade,** New York, New York

December

Between Thanksgiving and New Year's Day: **Christmas in Bethlehem,** Bethlehem, Pennsylvania

First Saturday in December: **Chester Greenwood Day,** Farmington, Maine

15: **Boston Tea Party Reenactment,** Boston, Massachusetts

25: **Reenactment of the Delaware River Crossing,** Washington Crossing, Pennsylvania

Connecticut

❖ Barnum Festival: Weekend closest to July 4.

He was the impresario of the implausible, the earl of the erratic, the haroun of humbug. And while taking time off from all that, Phineas T. Barnum was also mayor of Bridgeport.

A century has gone by, and yet in a culture thoroughly inundated by the values of entertainment Barnum is still recalled as the greatest showman of all time. He introduced attractions and events as diverse as Tom Thumb's wedding, Jumbo the elephant, and coloratura soprano Jenny Lind to the American public. He was also a master of logistics, practically inventing the transport system that enables a road show to function.

Barnum was born in Bethel, Connecticut, and first achieved a dubious sort of fame by turning up in New York City with an aged black woman and claiming that she was George Washington's nurse. Since this would have made her something like 160 years old, the odds against it were long. But with her as the main attraction, Barnum formed his first company and toured the country.

He used the proceeds to buy a museum in New York in 1841, where he exhibited assorted oddities and several outright frauds. But after reading a news report about a young man named Charles Stratton, who had stopped growing at the height of twenty-nine inches, he hit the jackpot. Renaming Stratton Tom Thumb, Barnum toured North America and Europe with him for years, astonishing everyone from Queen Victoria on down. The success he experienced with Stratton enabled him to sign Lind for the incredible sum of $1,000 a performance and the publicity that occasioned only added to his legend.

Barnum may not actually have said that "there's a sucker born every minute." But in this age of supermarket tabloids reporting on space aliens

P. T. Barnum's hometown remembers the showman who was once the mayor of Bridgeport.

and Elvis sightings and movie star revelations, who are we to say he was wrong if that's what he thought. Barnum was far more serious as a politician and is credited with securing harbor and railroad improvements that were critical to Bridgeport's industrial development.

The great showman died in 1891, but each summer his hometown remembers him with a four-day splurge that goes heavy on the hoopla.

✳ **Location:** Various locations throughout this city on Interstate 95, about 60 miles northeast of New York City. ✳ **Events:** Special exhibits at the Barnum Museum, 820 Main Street, where many historical items associated with the man are on permanent display. Parade, street fairs, concerts, art show. Most of the events have either a circus or carnival theme. ✳ **Contact:** Barnum Festival Committee, c/o Holiday Inn, 1070 Main St., Ste. 208, Bridgeport, CT 06604, (203) 367-8495; Bridgeport Chamber of Commerce, (203) 335-3800.

NORWALK

◈ **Oyster Festival:** Weekend after Labor Day.

There were few foods encountered in colonial America that made as great an impression on visiting gourmands as oysters. Native Americans had learned the secret of cultivating them in natural beds just off the shoreline on Long Island Sound, and the first settlers picked up the knack from them. Norwalk became an early leader in the industry.

Oysters were an American staple, a feature of late suppers in fashionable homes. They were served up stewed in cream, fried, or baked in various sauces. They were larger than any oysters Europeans had ever experienced. Writer William Thackeray upon eating his first one said the sensation was like "swallowing a baby." Oyster cellars in inland cities proliferated much as fast food outlets do today.

The problem was that oysters did not travel very well. The familiar adage about not eating them in the months with no "r" in their names stems from the fact that those—May through August—are the hot-weather months, when spoilage was a major problem. The development of the tin can after the Civil War took care of that, although there was still resistance to eating canned oysters for many years afterwards because of false reports that the soldering was poisonous in heat.

Between 1870 and 1890, Norwalk is credited with shipping out three-quarters of the oysters exported to Europe from the United States. It was the most efficient of the producers, the first to introduce steam dredging to work the beds. Growing pollution of the Sound retarded the industry for a while, but in recent years oystering has made a strong comeback in local waters.

✳ **Location:** Norwalk is about 50 miles northeast of New York City. ✳ **Events:** Food booths, boat races, crafts displays, nautical exhibits at the Maritime Center, which is located on the Norwalk River at 10 North Water Street. ✳ **Contact:** Norwalk Chamber of Commerce, Norwalk Seaport Association, 132 Water St., Norwalk, CT 06854, (203) 866-2521.

WINDSOR

 Shad Derby: Third weekend in May.

This is one of the oldest towns in the Connecticut River valley, dating from 1633 when a small band of settlers from the Plymouth Colony arrived and drove off the previously entrenched Dutch. Scouting parties had issued glowing reports on the fertility of the riverside soil, and within a year the colonists were growing wheat and onions. In 1640 they began cultivating tobacco, which remained the major crop for 300 years.

But the settlers discovered that the river brought other benefits, too. Late in spring, the shad began their run up the valley to spawn in the shallow creeks of the Connecticut's tributaries. The fish, a member of the herring family, was prized not only for its flesh but also for its roe, which was made into a domestic caviar.

Farmers would place nets across the streams during the run, supplementing their incomes nicely with this seasonal gift from the sea. But the netting resulted in wasteful overkill and severely depleted the stock of shad. The fish had almost died out when regulations were changed, permitting the shad to replenish itself. This spring celebration pays tribute to the salt water bounty that makes its way this far from the sea.

✳ **Location:** Windsor is virtually a suburb of Hartford, north of the city by way of Interstate 91. ✳ **Events:** Fishing competition, beauty pageant, parade, waterfront bazaar. ✳ **Contact:** Shad Festival Bureau, P.O. Box 502, Windsor, CT 06095; Windsor Chamber of Commerce, P.O. Box 9, Windsor, CT 06095, (203) 688-5165.

GEORGETOWN

❖ **Return Day:** Thursday following the first Monday in November, in even-numbered years.

No one is quite sure when this odd custom, observed only in Sussex County, began. The best guess is the presidential election of 1832, the first one held after the state passed a reform bill that allowed voters to cast ballots in local polling stations rather than coming in to the county seat.

In this sparsely populated area of southern Delaware, there was no daily newspaper to carry the election results. So the local custom developed of driving into Georgetown two days after the election and hearing the results read from the courthouse steps.

Nowadays election results are broadcast almost as soon as the polls close. But that didn't seem reason enough to stop a tradition like Return Day. In fact, it has been an official half-holiday in the county since 1965, and the crowds that flock to Georgetown are thicker than ever. It has become an occasion for politicians, winners and losers, to congratulate or console each other and to start the next campaign with the voters.

✱ **Location:** Georgetown is on U.S. 113, about 35 miles south of Dover.
✱ **Events:** Traditional food booths near the courthouse, ox roast, political speeches, parade. ✱ **Contact:** Georgetown Chamber of Commerce, (302) 856-1544; Sussex Co. Return Day, Inc., P.O. Box 55, Georgetown, DE 19947.

Technology may have eliminated the need to gather at the courthouse to learn of election results, but the citizens of Georgetown still enjoy the political celebration. (Courtesy of Sussex County Return Day, Inc.)

TALLEYVILLE

◆ Winterthur Point-to-Point Races: Sunday of the first full weekend in May.

The rolling fields of the northern section of Delaware have been known as fox-hunting country since colonial times. The Talley family, for whom the town of Talleyville is named, was famous for its hunts, which gathered in families from across the surrounding countryside.

This was the area in which the du Ponts, at one time regarded as the wealthiest family in America, built their estates. The grandest of them was Winterthur, erected in 1885 by Col. Henry F. du Pont. He furnished it as a museum of the history of American decorative arts, the rooms being furnished in the style of the late seventeenth to mid-nineteenth centuries. A museum is what it is today.

Each spring Winterthur celebrates the hunting enthusiasms of an earlier generation. The steeplechase is an event that was derived from fox-hunting days. These cross-country horse races, with a course drawn across a number of natural obstacles, are guided between various points by landmarks, such as church steeples.

The traditional steeplechases at Winterthur recall a favorite pastime of the area's colonial forebears. (Courtesy of Winterthur)

✳ **Location:** Winterthur is on Delaware 52, about 6 miles northwest of Wilmington. ✳ **Events:** Steeplechases, pony races, parade of antique carriages. An admission is charged to the races. ✳ **Contact:** Winterthur Museum, Point-to-Point Office, Winterthur, DE 19735, (302) 888-4600.

Maine

❖ LaKermasse Festival: Last full week in June.

Maine grew up along its rivers, and because they were so wide and so deep what usually happened is that separate towns developed on either side. Biddeford is divided from Saco by the Saco River, and each place grew up in its own way.

Saco is more residential and predominantly Yankee. Biddeford turned into a textile center, the home of Pepperell Mills, and three-quarters of its people are of French-Canadian descent. A similar situation developed in the cities of Lewiston and Auburn, on either side of the Androscoggin River, with Lewiston becoming a French-Canadian town.

Maine's long border with Quebec and the French-speaking area of New Brunswick profoundly influenced the character of the state, from the look of its churches to the sound of its accents. When the French-speaking Acadians were expelled from their homes in Canada by the British in 1755, many of them were transported to Louisiana, where they became known as Cajuns. But many more escaped and simply slipped across the border into what was then the Massachusetts Bay Colony. Their presence was established for over a century when they were joined by another great influx of French-Canadians, drawn by the well-paying jobs in milltowns like Biddeford. The shaping of Maine's culture is celebrated in this festival.

✳ **Location:** Biddeford is about 16 miles south of Portland on the Maine Turnpike. ✳ **Events:** Parades, traditional foods and crafts, street dancing. ✳ **Contact:** Biddeford Chamber of Commerce, Atten. LaKermasse Festival, P.O. Box 289, Biddeford, ME 04005, (207) 282-1567.

Once a familiar sight on the coast of Maine, a regatta of windjammers gathers in Boothbay Harbor each summer for this festival. (Courtesy of Boothbay Harbor Region Chamber of Commerce)

BOOTHBAY HARBOR

❖ Windjammer Day: Late June.

The age of sail was the era of New England's commercial dominance. Crews from this region manned the finest ships afloat, the clippers, that ran all the way to China and made rich men of their captains. With ready access to both the wood for making them and the water to sail them on, Maine took the lead in this industry. Its shipyards were regarded as the best in the world.

While a few of the old shipbuilding ports continue to turn out fine vessels, the tall ships, mainly, are just a memory. But each summer the windjammers return to this harbor, among the finest in the state. Boothbay turned out a wealth of two-masted schooners at its shipyards, and well into the twentieth century they were a familiar sight transporting pulpwood along the coast.

Now Boothbay Harbor is a summer resort. The sailboats that come here are vessels built for recreation. The homes built by the clipper captains are bed-and-breakfast inns and souvenir stores. Many people know the picturesque harbor as the location for the movie version of *Carousel*. But this festival brings back memories of earlier days in Boothbay Harbor.

Chester Greenwood invented, among other things, the earmuff. (Courtesy of Greater Farmington Chamber of Commerce)

✳ **Location:** Boothbay Harbor is on Maine 27, about 12 miles south of U.S. 1 from Wiscasset. ✳ **Events:** Windjammer regatta, seafood festival, art fair, parade, concerts. ✳ **Contact:** Boothbay Regional Chamber of Commerce, P.O. Box 356, Boothbay, ME 04538, (207) 633-2353.

FARMINGTON

❄ Chester Greenwood Day: First Saturday in December.

In the winter of 1873, a 15-year-old local boy wanted to go ice skating on a nearby pond. But the whistling Maine wind made it too hard on his ears. So Chester Greenwood, struck by an inspiration, fastened two fur pieces together with a metal band and invented the earmuff.

Greenwood patented his invention four years later and, until his death in 1937, manufactured them in Farmington. Greenwood was actually an inventor of wide-ranging interests. He was granted more than one hundred patents, and the Smithsonian Institution voted him one of America's top fifteen inventors of all time.

Among his other brainstorms were self-priming sparkplugs, airplane shock absorbers, steel archery bows, spring steel rakes, and a mechanical mousetrap. But his earmuffs were enough to secure his place in the warm memories of his hometown.

✳ **Location:** Farmington is on U.S. 2, about 35 miles north of Augusta. ✳ **Events:** Parade, old-time vaudeville shows, invention displays. ✳ **Contact:** Farmington Chamber of Commerce, 30 Main St., Farmington, ME 04938, (207) 778-4215.

H O U L T O N

❖ Potato Feast: Last weekend in August.

The Aroostook is a part of Maine so remote that in 1839 the state almost went to war with New Brunswick over it. Gov. Edward Kent accused Canadian lumbermen of ignoring the border and coming over to his side to do their logging. The Canadians argued that the border was poorly defined and, besides, it was the Maine loggers who were interloping on New Brunswick.

The state militia was sent into the area; they built a stockade at Fort Kent, marched up and down for a while, and then went home in the spring. Tempers cooled and by 1843 there was a permanent treaty fixing the border. That made it safe for the Maine forests to be thoroughly decimated by American loggers.

After that was accomplished, however, there was the problem of finding a new way for residents of the area to make a living. The soil was fine for potato growing, but the region was so remote from the rest of the country that the lack of access to markets made widespread cultivation impractical. When the Bangor and Aroostook Railroad reached Houlton in 1894, it was finally connected to the rest of the United States. Potato growing went so well that within fifty years it was estimated that about fifty percent of the national crop was grown within a three-county area here. Now Maine is out-spudded by Idaho and Washington, but the Aroostook area still grows ninety percent of the state crop.

Houlton is the largest city in the area, and when the potatoes start coming in everything stops for the festivities.

✳ **Location:** Houlton is on Interstate 95 and the intersection of U.S. 1 and 2, about 135 miles north of Bangor. ✳ **Events:** Food booths serving up potatoes in all manner of preparations, parades, crafts booths. ✳ **Contact:** Houlton Chamber of Commerce, 109 Main St., Houlton, ME 04730, (207) 532-4216.

MACHIAS

◈ Blueberry Festival: Third weekend in August.

No one can say that Maine Yankees don't have a sense of humor. According to the dictionary one of the definitions of the word "barren" is fruitless. Nonetheless, "the barrens" is what Maine calls an area in which ninety percent of the nation's blueberries are grown.

Blueberries were a desperation crop, chosen because they could be cultivated in thin, sandy soil. That was all that remained in Washington County in the 1870s. Maine's lumbermen had finished their work here and moved on, leaving a devastated landscape behind. But new canning techniques, developed to feed troops in the recently-ended Civil War, were just coming into commercial use. That enabled local farmers to ship the fruit long distances and gave blueberries a foothold in the state's economy.

The barrens stretch out across Washington County, over a 200-square-mile plateau. Machias, the county seat, is named for the rushing river than runs through the middle of town. In Algonquian, the name means "bad little falls" because it was an annoying stretch of water for canoes.

✳ **Location:** Machias is on U.S. 1, about 90 miles east of Bangor. ✳ **Events:** Food booths featuring blueberries in a variety of dishes, parade, Yankee crafts. ✳ **Contact:** Machias Chamber of Commerce, P.O. Box 606, Machias, ME 04654-0606, (207) 255-4402.

◈ While You're There:

The University of Maine operates an experimental farm, Blueberry Hill, near the town of Columbia Falls, 16 miles west of Machias. It offers free tours.

Machias is the oldest settlement in Maine east of the Penobscot, and its Burnham Tavern dates to 1770. When local men learned in the spring of 1775 that the British were sending a schooner here to secure a wood supply, they planned a preemptive strike in a meeting at the tavern. Sailing from Machias Harbor, they captured the *Margaretta* on June 12, in the first naval engagement of the Revolutionary War. Its success encouraged Congress to fund a permanent navy. The old tavern is still open to visitors.

ROCKLAND

❖ Maine Lobster Festival: First Saturday in August.

Maine may be the only state in the country that lists an animal as its top tourist attraction. It is unlikely that you will ever pick up tourist literature about Maine that does not include a picture of one of these crustaceans. Maine and lobsters are bound up in the American imagination like no other example of geography and food.

By the late nineteenth century, lobsters had become an American symbol for gourmandizing. Expensive restaurants in many parts of the East were referred to as "lobster palaces." It has consistently been a costly food item because of the expense of shipping them. Lobsters do not travel well, and the premium always has been on speed.

In addition, lobsters run through an annual pricing cycle. In winter they can cost three times as much at the dock than during the summer months. They are not easy to find even during the best of times. They hide out on ledges and around shipwrecks, and the equipment needed to trap them is expensive. Lobsters also have many natural enemies—including each other. In captivity they have their claws banded. Otherwise, they would go after one another for dinner.

Rockland has long been one of the top lobster ports in Maine and each summer the Penobscot Bay town offers tourists a chance to salute their favorite shellfish with this festival.

✳ **Location:** Rockland is on U.S. 1, about 80 miles northeast of Portland. ✳ **Events:** Community dinners and lobster bakes in huge tents, parades, street entertainers. ✳ **Contact:** Rockland Festival, P.O. Box 552, Rockland, ME 04081; Rockland Chamber of Commerce, (207) 596-0376.

At this festival you can feast on the favorite crustacean of Maine—the lobster. (Courtesy of Rockland Festival)

SKOWHEGAN

❖ **Log Day:** Last Saturday in August.

The Kennebec River was the great highway to the heart of Maine during colonial times. At its outlet to the sea was the great shipbuilding town of Bath. Traders from the Plymouth colony established an outpost upriver at the site of the future state capital, Augusta, in 1628. Benedict Arnold and his troops followed the Kennebec into the uncharted north on the ill-fated expedition against Quebec City in 1775.

The Kennebec was also the highway for logs. The timberlands of the Kennebec Valley were prized for centuries. The British set apart certain forests to harvest for the navy's masts, a policy that caused no end of resentment among local residents and helped foster a revolutionary spirit.

Log drives along the Kennebec were a familiar sight for more than one hundred years. Even when most of the logging industry had moved on to the Great Lakes after the Civil War, extensive timber stands remained in Maine, their value enhanced by conservation practices. The peak year of monetary return for Maine lumber, in fact, was 1909. But log drives continued on the Kennebec for another sixty-seven years. The final run through Skowhegan is memorialized in this late summer celebration. The town is still the location of a paper and pulp industry, but the wood arrives by other means.

✳ **Location:** Skowhegan is at the junction of U.S. 2 and 201, about 15 miles north of Interstate 95. ✳ **Events:** Lumberjack competitions, parade, fireworks, community bean dinner. ✳ **Contact:** Skowhegan Chamber of Commerce, P.O. Box 326, Skowhegan, ME 04976, (207) 474-3621.

Maryland

✦ Chesapeake Appreciation Day: Last weekend in October.

Chesapeake Bay is the soul of Maryland. Annapolis, its capital, and many more of its historic cities lie along its shore. This long, curved arm of the Atlantic, with its countless coastal indentations and islands, brought the state's first settlers and remains an anchor of the Maryland economy. It is one of America's finest sailing areas and also holds some of its richest fishing grounds.

The bay has developed distinctive kinds of craft. The most widely used is the skipjack, which is the working boat of the Chesapeake oystermen. It is single-masted, and usually has a large jib and triangular mainsail. It is named after a kind of fish because of the shared ability to skip rapidly across the top of the swells.

At this autumn celebration, skipjack boatmen stage races at Sandy Point State Park. It is intended as a tribute to the bay's bounty and the men who gather it.

✳ **Location:** Sandy Point is 7 miles east of Annapolis, on U.S. 50, at the western edge of the Chesapeake Bay Bridge. ✳ **Events:** Sail races, seafood cookouts, traditional bay crafts. ✳ **Contact:** Sandy Point State Park, (410) 974-2149; Maryland Waterman's Association, 8105 A Virginia St., Annapolis, MD 21401, (410) 268-7722.

BALTIMORE

 Preakness Celebration: Week before the third Saturday in May.

The Preakness is known as the second jewel in American horseracing's Triple Crown, even though it is older than number one, the Kentucky Derby. The first Preakness went off at Pimlico Racetrack in 1873, two years before the first Derby in Louisville. But because of three years in the 1890s when the race was not run here, the Derby is actually the senior affair.

The Preakness is where the suspense builds, however. It is where the winner of the Derby, held two weeks before, comes under enormous pressure to take the next step towards the Crown. Only eleven have made it all the way, from Sir Barton in 1919 to Affirmed in 1978. But the Preakness is a race of possibilities, and that gives it a special aura.

Pimlico Race Track is named for a district in London, the name of the area's original colonial land grant. A beloved part of Baltimore lore, the race is now preceded by a week-long celebration of Maryland's history.

✳ **Location:** Pimlico is in the northwestern part of Baltimore, 2 miles west of the Jones Falls Expressway, at Park Heights and Belvedere Avenue. The celebration goes on throughout the city. ✳ **Events:** Hot air balloon race, parade, concerts. ✳ **Contact:** Preakness Celebration, World Trade Center, 401 East Pratt St., Ste. 311, Baltimore, MD 21202, (410) 837-3030.

CHESTERTOWN

 Tea Party Festival: Saturday before Memorial Day.

Boston was not the only port that seethed over tea. In many places throughout the colonies, indignation ran high when Parliament reaffirmed its right to tax imports to America and handed the tea monopoly to the East India Company. Several of them followed Boston's example of December 1773 and held tea parties of their own.

In Maryland, resentment towards Parliament's high-handedness ran almost as deep as it did in Massachusetts. When the brigantine *Geddes* arrived in Chestertown five months after Boston acted, the people of this community knew what was expected of them. After an emergency meeting of citizens, the ship was boarded on May 13, 1774, and the cargo dumped into the Chester River.

The residents of Chestertown reenact their lesser-known tea party of May 13, 1774. (Courtesy of
Kent County Chamber of Commerce)

Chestertown didn't stop there. Parliament had decided to punish
Boston for its rash act with the Boston Port Act. This legislation, the first
of the "Intolerable Acts" that brought war ever nearer, closed Boston to all
commerce until the city compensated the East India Company for its
dumped tea. The law went into effect thirty-three days after Chestertown's tea party. This town reacted by immediately sending off provisions
to be smuggled into Boston. Maryland then decided to boycott all British
imports and to refuse to allow the collection of any debts owed to Britain
in the colony until the Boston Port Act was rescinded. Such defiant ges-
tures were made in several colonies, but Maryland actually lived up to this
one, virtually drying up all trade with England. As in Boston, the tea party
was so important to Chestertown that the place feels compelled to reenact
it annually.

✳ **Location:** Chestertown is on Maryland 213, about 35 miles north of the eastern end of the Chesapeake Bay Bridge. ✳ **Events:** Costumed reenactment of the tea party, colonial era crafts and foods, entertainment. ✳ **Contact:** Kent County Chamber of Commerce, P.O. Box 146, Chestertown, MD 21620, (410) 778-0416.

CRISFIELD

 National Hard Crab Derby: Labor Day weekend.

They say the waterfront area of this town is built entirely on oyster shells. People have been shucking oysters here for so long the shells are part of the place's foundation. On Tangier Sound, in the extreme southwestern corner of Maryland's Eastern Shore, Crisfield has the strongest sea flavor of all the Chesapeake Bay towns.

For generations the residents here have supported themselves from the bay. Early in the twentieth century, Crisfield boasted that it shipped more crabs than any other port in America. On its waterfront, visitors can still watch the processing of seafood in sheds that have stood on the site for decades. Most are brick instead of wood now, but the sites are unchanged.

The town was isolated from all land connections until John Crisfield brought his railroad here in 1868. That enabled the place to ship out its perishable product to market much faster than was possible by boat and turned Crisfield into a major seafood center. This celebration is the largest of its kind on Chesapeake Bay and regarded as one of the premier seafood festivals in the country.

✳ **Location:** Crisfield is on Maryland 413, about 35 miles southwest of Salisbury. ✳ **Events:** Seafood booths, crab races, crab picking and boat docking contests, beauty pageant, fireworks, parade, entertainment. ✳ **Contact:** Crisfield Chamber of Commerce, P.O. Box 292, Crisfield, MD 21817, (301) 968-2500.

CUMBERLAND

 Chesapeake and Ohio Canal Festival: Second full weekend in July.

His experiences in the French and Indian War convinced George Washington that the best route from Virginia to the new lands in the Ohio country was along the military road he had traveled. It followed the course

The arrival of railroads ended activity on the Chesapeake and Ohio Canal, but Cumberland residents commemorate its nineteenth-century importance. (Courtesy of Chesapeake and Ohio Canal Boat Festival)

of the Potomac River to its northernmost loop and then proceeded northwest until it reached the Ohio River at Wheeling. The settlement at that northern loop grew into Cumberland, and through it poured the westbound commerce of the nineteenth century.

The road Washington followed eventually became the National Pike, the first federal highway project. He also envisioned a canal built along the same route and that proved a little tougher to arrange. Washington was the head of an early company formed to build such a canal, but nothing ever came of it. Not until 1828 did work on the Chesapeake and Ohio Canal begin, and by that time the Baltimore and Ohio Railroad also was laying track towards Cumberland. The canal won a legal battle over the right-of-way through the narrow neck of land at Harpers Ferry. But still the railroad won the race, its first train arriving in 1842, more than eight years before the canal opened for business.

Its impact on the area was brief. Within thirty years of its opening, the canal was out of use, unable to compete with the economics of the rails. By the 1930s, it was weed-choked and abandoned. But the right-of-way was then acquired by the National Park Service, which turned it into a recreation area and historical park for much of its length between Washington, D.C., and Cumberland.

✳ **Location:** The festival takes place 5 miles south of Cumberland, at the Canal Park, on Maryland 51. ✳ **Events:** Rides on a canal boat replica through the old locks, horse and buggy rides, canal walking tours, ox roast, street dancing. ✳ **Contact** C & O Canal Festival, 14602 North Bel Air Dr. SW, Cumberland, MD 21502, (301) 729-3136.

EASTON

◈ **Old St. Joseph's Jousting Tournament and Horse Show:** First Wednesday in August.

◈ **Waterfowl Festival:** Second weekend in November.

Things are done a little bit differently on Maryland's Eastern Shore. More than almost any other part of America, it is a place where old traditions and customs seem to hang on. Cut off from land access to the rest of Maryland for generations, the Eastern Shore continues to be a place in close intimacy with its past and the natural life around it.

Part of that past is an affinity for jousting. This echo of medieval times and chivalry survives here as an annual event, not just as a sideshow in one of the Renaissance fairs that have sprung up around the nation. Several Southern states held tilting tournaments in the years before the Civil War, when that region thought of itself as the embodiment of lost gallantry. But while it died out elsewhere, this staple of movie epics is still part of life here.

It is not the deadly event of the past, in which one of the participants usually wound up with a broken neck or an impaled gut. This version is an exercise in fine horsemanship, and while flowery speeches about chivalry are part of the ritual, the only thing the riders are trying to spear are small rings. In some tournaments earlier in the twentieth century, women were the competitors. But this traditional event, the oldest such tournament in the state, is strictly a male affair.

Easton is also in the heart of some of the country's finest duck-hunting country. The Chesapeake retriever was bred to work in the specific conditions of this area. The Eastern Shore is situated on North America's great migratory flyway. The spectacle of waterfowl flocking across the skies in early spring and autumn is one of the great sights of the Easton region. Maryland was a pioneer in the passage of conservation laws to protect its waterfowl. This festival is Easton's celebration not only of the hunting of birds but an appreciation of their continuing role in the historical development and life cycle of the region.

✳ **Location:** Easton is located on U.S. 50, about 20 miles south of the eastern end of the Chesapeake Bay Bridge. The jousting tournament takes place northeast of town, near Cordova, at St. Joseph's Church, on Church

The waterfowl that migrate across Easton, Maryland, twice a year are honored through exhibits of antique decoys, carvings, and paintings. (Courtesy of Waterfowl Festival)

Lane, near Maryland 309. ✳ **Events:** The Jousting Tournament features a horse show, medieval pageant and coronation of a queen, country picnic. The Wildfowl Festival spotlights the work of artists who display their carving and paintings. There are also exhibits of antique decoys and Chesapeake food specialties. ✳ **Contact:** Jousting Tournament, 30300 Chapel Station Dr., Cordova, MD 21625, (410) 822-6915. Waterfowl Festival, P.O. Box 929, 40 South Hampton St., Easton, MD 21601, (410) 822-4567.

HAGERSTOWN

◆ Alsatia Mummers Parade: Second Saturday after the third Monday in October.

The organization began as something of a joke. A group of men got together in Hagerstown in 1911 and started a social club. They named it after a district in London, which was then notorious for its thieves.

While no thieves signed up for membership in the Alsatians, the club was a fairly broad cross-section of the community. In its tenth year, looking for a worthwhile community project, the group held a Halloween parade, in an effort to hold down a growing problem of holiday vandalism.

The parade was very successful and has been repeated every year since, except for the World War II period when blackouts intervened. It is among the oldest such events in the country. The parade features marching bands and floats from all across the Middle Atlantic states. There are 10,000 participants, and more than 150,000 spectators pour into the little town to enjoy the festivities.

✳ **Location:** Hagerstown is at the intersection of Interstates 70 and 81, about 25 miles northwest of Frederick. ✳ **Events:** Parade through the middle of town, entertainment. ✳ **Contact:** Alsatia Club, 141 West Washington St., Hagerstown, MD 21740, (301) 739-2044.

LILYPONS

 Lotus Blossom Festival: Weekend closest to July 15.

She was the greatest gate attraction of her time in opera. After French-born Lily Pons made her debut with New York's Metropolitan Opera in 1931, her name guaranteed a sellout. She once drew 300,000 spectators to a concert in Chicago's Grant Park and virtually revived the opera *Lakme* all by herself, so audiences could thrill to her singing of "The Bell Song."

A small woman, barely over five feet tall, she brought glamour and chic to opera at a time when it was dominated by large men and women. She even enjoyed a brief movie career in the 1930s, although her French accent made most of her dialogue incomprehensible. But the audience didn't come to hear her talk. They wanted to hear her voice.

At the height of her fame, the owner of a 100-acre tract dedicated to raising pond lilies and ornamental fish decided to incorporate as a town. He called the place Lilypons. The soprano was honored and made frequent visits to the town named for her, being named mayor of the place in 1941. Miss Pons died in 1976, but Lilypons is still a going concern. This festival comes at the peak of the blooming season.

✳ **Location:** Lilypons is east of Maryland 85, about 13 miles south of Frederick. ✳ **Events:** Lilies and lotus blossom displays, crafts, entertainment, food booths. ✳ **Contact:** Lilypons Water Gardens, P.O. Box 10, 7000 Lilypons Rd., Buckeystown, MD 21717, (301) 874-5503.

Massachusetts

◈ **Evacuation Day:** March 17.

◈ **Patriots' Day:** Third Monday in April.

❖ **Bunker Hill Day:** June 17.

❖ **Boston Tea Party Reenactment:** December 15.

In the decade of the 1770s, as political and emotional bonds were formed that turned thirteen separate colonies into a nation, Boston was the heart and the mind of revolution. As in no other place, agitation against British rule reached fever pitch here. The firebrands of Massachusetts made war inevitable and tugged the rest of the colonies onto the path of rebellion.

The great events that led to war were played out in this city. The conflict began on its outskirts. The first great battle was fought within sight of its streets. And the first great triumph, the evacuation by British troops, was cheered here, too.

These four historical celebrations commemorate events that occurred within just twenty-seven months of each other, between December of 1773 and March of 1776. Yet they shaped the city for the next two centuries and their echoes still sound in Boston's definition of itself.

Last on the yearly calendar but first chronologically is the Boston Tea Party. In the recounting of acts that led to war, this is always given as a watershed. The Tea Party set forces in motion on both sides of the conflict that simply could not be controlled or turned around.

The tax on tea was three years old in 1773, and during that time there had been little problem collecting the three-penny levy at customs. Some tea was smuggled in from Holland, but most of the colonists

The Boston Tea Party in 1773 signalled the beginning of revolution in the American colonies.

(Ewing Galloway)

accepted the tax. Then Parliament, in the face of rising agitation in the colonies, made the mistake of reaffirming the tax and giving a monopoly over tea imports to the financially struggling East India Company. That clearly indicated to the colonists that their complaints about taxation were going to be ignored and Parliament was intent on asserting its authority.

There was resistance to the new act everywhere, but under the agitation of Samuel Adams feeling ran highest in Boston. By the evening of December 15, there were three British ships in Boston Harbor waiting to unload. An assembly of the Sons of Liberty was called in the Old South Meeting House. In an address that summed up all the grievances against England, Adams concluded: "Gentlemen, there is nothing more this meeting can do to save the country." At those words, several dozen men, who had disguised themselves as Indians, ran from the hall and headed to the harbor. Boarding the ships, they dumped the tea in the harbor.

Historians still aren't sure exactly who carried out the raid, but they seemed to include a broad cross section of Boston—from laborers to merchants. The issue had united them. So on every December 15, Bostonians from every walk of life put on costumes and reenact the defiant gesture that helped win their freedom.

Revere's Ride Commemorated

By April 1775, conditions had deteriorated so badly in Massachusetts that Prime Minister Lord Dartmouth decided that he had to make a pre-emptive strike against the colonists. He had taken office as a moderate, but Dartmouth firmly believed in the primacy of Parliament and that belief informed his actions. He ordered Gen. Thomas Gage, military commander in Boston, to seize colonial stores of weapons in Concord and Worcester. His letter arrived on April 14 and Gage, knowing that he would be sending troops into a hornet's nest, picked out the best soldiers from each unit in his command for the assignment. That turned out to be a mistake. Led by officers they didn't know, these troops had no will to stand and fight when attacked by American militia and guerrillas.

Word of Gage's preparations leaked out and the gathering of small boats to carry British troops across Back Bay was evident to everyone in Boston. Gage was ready to move in four days, but by that time the colonials were watching his every move. When British troops started their advance to Concord, Paul Revere and Charles Dawes were off on their famous ride to alert the countryside.

The commemoration of events at Lexington and Concord is discussed below (see Sudbury). But in Boston, the symbolic reenactment of Revere's ride is observed each Patriots' Day with the running of the Boston Marathon. Since its inception in 1897, with fifteen men in the field, the marathon has become a combination of prime athletic event and patriotic celebration, unlike any other in America. It is now the world's oldest continuously held footrace and attracts a field of thousands of men and women. The starting point in Hopkinton on race day is one of the great spectacles in American athletics.

Shortly after the retreat from Concord, Gage decided to fortify Dorchester Heights, which commanded the city of Boston. But before he could make that move, colonial forces entered Charlestown, across the Charles River from Boston, and built breastworks atop Bunker and Breeds Hills. Their hope was to keep the British bottled up in the city. Parliament had expressed its dissatisfaction at Gage's performance by sending three other generals to assist him in military preparations. Gage now deferred to Gen. William Howe in the planned June attack on the heights in Charlestown.

The New England troops were well entrenched, but Howe treated them disdainfully, ignoring textbook military tactics to intimidate them with a sheer show of numbers. The colonials, waiting until the advancing

British columns were clear targets, inflicted a terrible slaughter on some of Howe's best troops. The British commander wrote later that he experienced "a moment I had never felt before," as the possibility of defeat confronted him.

But officers managed to rally the battered forces and they swept across the American positions when the defenders ran out of ammunition. The colonials were forced to retreat from both hills and then from Charlestown itself, but the retreat was orderly and never gave way to panic. The British had lost 1,054 dead and wounded, while the American casualties totaled 411. The British generals knew that they could not sustain losses like that with their supply lines stretched across the Atlantic. Bunker Hill was the first sobering realization that the Americans would fight well and that this revolution would not be easily quelled. The battle was technically an American defeat, but it is marked by celebrations on its anniversary in June.

British Evacuation of Boston

George Washington arrived to take command of the colonial army in July, and for the next seven months the situation in Boston remained static. The British were, in effect, under siege in the city. As winter went on, the colonial commander decided to carry out Gage's original plan and fortify Dorchester Heights.

The campaign began with a tremendous artillery bombardment on March 1, 1776. For the next four days, the Americans and British lobbed shells at each other, with the Americans picking up the pace on the night of the 4th. The barrage masked the movement of colonial troops onto the heights, and when Howe awoke on the 5th he found himself under their guns. Moreover, his naval commander informed him that his ships would be blasted right out of Boston Harbor if he remained there. Howe, haunted by the memory of the carnage at Bunker Hill, decided to evacuate instead of attack. On the morning of March 17, the British troops and their supplies were hastily loaded onto the support ships and left Boston forever.

It was a major psychological advantage for Washington's army, although the British would go on to occupy New York and Philadelphia for several more years. But Boston was free and Evacuation Day is still a cause for celebration, especially since it also falls on St. Patrick's Day, a grand event in itself in Irish Boston.

✳ **Location:** The observances are general throughout the Boston area. The Boston Tea Party, which took place at what was then called Griffin's Wharf, is reenacted at the nearest approximate site, which is on Congress Street at the Harbor Walk. Hopkinton, the starting point of the Boston Marathon, is west of the city, just southeast of the intersection of Inter-

state 495 and the Massachusetts Turnpike. Bunker Hill is reached by following the signs from the exit on northbound Interstate 93. Or, better yet,
by taking a cab. ✳ **Events:** High points of the Tea Party and Bunker Hill
celebrations are the costumed reenactments of two of the most famous
events in American history. For the marathon on Patriots' Day and the
Evacuation Day-St. Patrick's Day celebration, it is the carnival atmosphere
that imbues the entire city. Boston is a young city because of the number
of universities in its immediate area and during these festivals it gets even
younger. ✳ **Contact:** The best clearinghouse of information on all these
events is the Greater Boston Convention and Visitors Bureau, Prudential
Tower, Ste. 400, P.O. Box 990468, Boston, MA 02199-0488, (617) 536-
4100. The best source of information on the Tea Party is the Boston Tea
Party Ship and Museum, Congress St. Bridge, Boston, MA 02210, (617)
338-1773. Visitors actually get to throw tea overboard here.

❖ While You're There:

Bunker Hill and the Boston Tea Party Museum would be visited
during the course of attending these re-creations. Also figuring in these
events were the Old South Meeting House, where Samuel Adams
inflamed the Tea Party participants, still standing at 310 Washington
Street downtown; the Old North Church, where the warning lanterns that
alerted Revere and Dawes at the start of the ride were hung, at 193 Salem
Street in the North End, and the Paul Revere House, just a few blocks
away, on North Square. All of these sites are on the Freedom Trail, the
self-guided walking tour to many of the greatest places in Boston's history.

GLOUCESTER

❖ St. Peter's Fiesta: Last weekend in June.

This town is the symbol of seafaring New England to much of the
world. It was immortalized by Rudyard Kipling's "Captains Courageous,"
a tribute to the men of the fishing fleets that once sailed some of the most
dangerous waters in the Atlantic, the Grand and Georges Banks.

Since the first fishing boat put to sea here in 1623, it is estimated
that more than 10,000 Gloucester men have been lost on the ocean. The
Fishermen's Memorial on the harbor, a bronze statue of a captain at his
ship's helm, is a moving tribute to them. Every Memorial Day it is decorated with flowers.

But in the following month comes a more festive tribute to Gloucester's fleet. The Feast of St. Peter is an annual celebration of the seafaring life, joined in enthusiastically by the city's Portuguese and Italian communities, who now make up the bulk of its sailors.

* **Location:** Gloucester is at the eastern terminus of Massachusetts 128, about 35 miles northeast of Boston. * **Events:** Blessing of the Fleet by the cardinal of Boston, parade, religious processions in the streets, fireworks. * **Contact:** Rose Aiello, 7 Cherryhill Rd., Gloucester, MA 01930, (508) 283-1664.

NORTH ANDOVER

◊ **Sheepshearing Festival:** Third Sunday in May.

In the towns of the Merrimack River Valley, the Industrial Revolution accelerated the pace of American life. Samuel Slater is credited with smuggling the design of the spinning machine out of England in his head. The mill he opened in Pawtucket, Rhode Island, in 1793 is usually given as the start of industrialization in the United States. But textile mills really began to dominate the Massachusetts economy in the next generation.

A wealthy Bostonian, Francis Cabot Lowell, duplicated Slater's feat, and in the 1820s he returned from England after memorizing the details of the power loom. The adaptation of steam power to the textile industry enormously increased production capacity and along each falls of the Merrimack woolen towns grew up. The most famous were Lowell, the paradigm of the New England mill town, and Lawrence, one of the first totally planned company towns in America. The northern portion of Andover, Shawsheen Village, which adjoins Lawrence, was another American Woolen Company town.

Since the basic material for the industry was wool, the town holds an annual celebration of that material and the animal that bears it.

* **Location:** North Andover is about 25 miles north of Boston. Take Interstate 93 north to Route 495, then continue north to the North Andover exit. The festival is held on the Green, on Massachusetts 28. * **Events:** Sheepshearing exhibition, spinning competition, crafts fair, sheepdog demonstrations, fleece judging, music, food booths. * **Contact:** North Andover Department of Public Works, 384 Osgood St., North Andover, MA 01845, (508) 687-7964.

Festival-goers take a final look before the sheepshearing begins. (Courtesy of Museum of American Textile History)

PLYMOUTH

◈ **Harvest Week:** Begins first weekend in October.

◈ **Thanksgiving:** Fourth Thursday in November.

Thanksgiving is the most American of holidays, although its double origins go back to the start of written history. Days of thanksgiving were a general feature of all religious communities and could be called at any time of year. Harvest festivals have been held since the human race first took to farming.

The Thanksgiving of the Pilgrims was the religious sort, coming too late in the year to make sense as a harvest celebration. Its basic details make up the fabric of America's self-image, taught to schoolchildren in the first grade: People seeking freedom came to a new world. Because

The people of Plymouth, Massachusetts, celebrate Thanksgiving with a historic flair. (Courtesy of Plimouth Plantation, Inc.)

they felt chosen by God for a destiny unlike other nations they were compelled to give thanks. In the late autumn of 1621, having come through starvation, disease, and terrible isolation in the year after their landing, those who survived held a feast.

In recent years, Native Americans have been given an increasingly prominent role to play in the celebration, as friends and equal participants. The Wampanoag could have attacked the Pilgrims at any time, which would likely have destroyed the tiny settlement. But their own numbers were diminished by disease and they looked to the Europeans as potential allies against traditional enemies. So they gave them assistance in the early years. It was a brief amity, though, lasting only until the English settlers were strong enough to take away the Wampanoag lands after a terrible war of attrition. For the Indian guests, Thanksgiving was more like a Last Supper.

It took more than 200 years, however, for Thanksgiving to become a celebration for all Americans. It was always a distinctly New England holiday, in the manner of most harvest festivals. Not until 1777 did Congress attempt to reinvent it as a national celebration, as part of the nation-building process, designating November 1 as a Thanksgiving Day. Twelve years later, George Washington moved it to the last Thursday of the month. (The Pilgrims' feast is thought to have occurred in early December.)

Between the Revolution and the Civil War, national acceptance was slow. The federal government's holiday declarations were not binding on the states. Some observed it, some didn't. Moreover, this was still an agricultural country and people were tied to the cycle of the land and the habits of their neighbors. Harvest Week was an important part of this annual cycle, much more universally observed than the designated Thanksgiving. But changes in travel and technology, and especially the growth of the public schools, began creating a sense of nation that was more accepting of holidays that transcended mere local meaning.

Lincoln Declares National Holiday

The final step came in 1863. In the midst of the Civil War, President Lincoln issued a proclamation fixing a national day of thanksgiving on the last Thursday of November. (It was changed again to the fourth Thursday by President Roosevelt in 1939. Businessmen were unhappy because it didn't fall until November 30 that year, shortening the Christmas shopping season.) Lincoln meant to address Northern patriotism by fixing the Pilgrims' experience as the legitimate root of the nation, rather than that of the Virginia colony which had been established eleven years previously. Thanksgiving Day became one of the instruments that helped bring about a healing after the war, and its observance as a truly national holiday dates from that era.

At the Plimouth Plantation, a Harvest Week celebration, concentrating on the bounty of the land, is observed in October. This is still the time of the Canadian Thanksgiving celebration and it was the time of year that such observances were most commonly held in colonial America. In Plymouth itself, however, Thanksgiving Day is observed with ceremony and solemnity at November's end.

✴ **Location:** Plymouth is about 40 miles south of Boston, by way of Massachusetts 3. The Plantation is 3 miles south of the city, on Highway 3A. ✴ **Events:** Harvest Week has the sorts of games, crafts, and foods that the first colonists would have known. Thanksgiving in Plymouth features a reenactment of the Pilgrims walking from church to Cole's Hill, where the first colonists were buried, near the traditional site of the first feast. ✴ **Contact:** Plimouth Plantation, P.O. Box 1620, Plymouth, MA 02362, (508) 746-1622.

❖ While You're There:

Pilgrim Hall is one of the oldest museums in America, opening in 1824. It preserves the personal belongings of many of those who came over on the Mayflower, enabling us to see these highly mythologized figures as real people who used simple chairs and forks and cradles.

SALEM

◈ Haunted Happenings: Weekend nearest Halloween.

It's hard to shake a reputation. Go out and kill a few witches and a town gets pegged for life as a spooky sort of place.

Salem was one of the great New England seaports during the era of the clipper ships. Its federal-era architecture is among the best in the country. Yet the very name of the place conjures up images of the infamous witch trials of 1692, in which twenty presumably innocent people were executed in an outburst of hysteria unlike any other in American history. Some historians have tried to explain it as a disguised land grab, in which key property holders were deliberately targeted by their enemies. Others simply regard it as religious frenzy. But it has inspired writers from native son Nathaniel Hawthorne to playwright Arthur Miller, who found in the witch trials a parallel to the career of Sen. Joseph McCarthy and wrote *The Crucible*. Such political persecutions are still referred to as "witch hunts" in this country.

Eventually, Salem decided to go along with the story. This celebration began in 1982. The city of witches now uses Halloween to exorcise its past in a light-hearted tribute to the country's spookiest holiday.

✱ **Location:** Salem is about 15 miles northeast of Boston, by way of Massachusetts 1A. ✱ **Events:** Haunted house tours, costume parade, psychic readings, seances, historical tours. ✱ **Contact:** Salem Halloween Committee, P.O. Box 8139, Salem, MA 01971-8139, (508) 744-0013.

❖ While You're There:

The Witch House, at 310 1/2 Essex Street, where the accused were examined, was the home of one of the judges in the trials. The Salem Witch Museum, at 19 1/2 Washington Square North, is a multi-media examination of the trials. The House of the Seven Gables, built in 1668, in which Hawthorne set his own tale of justice gone wrong and wizards executed, is off Salem Harbor, at 54 Turner Street.

SOUTH CARVER

◈ Massachusetts Harvest Cranberry Festival:
Second weekend in October.

It is a reasonable assumption that cranberries were served at the first Thanksgiving feast at Plymouth (see above). The fruit was well known to

The harvesting of cranberries from the bogs of eastern Massachusetts is just the beginning of a three-day event that glorifies this delicious, bright red fruit. *(Courtesy of Cranberry Harvest Festival)*

the local Indians. The British settlers who ate them to ward off scurvy called them fenberries because they were grown in swampland. Not until later did they borrow the Dutch name for them. It derived from the shape of the stamen, which to their eyes resembled the beak of a crane, or "kran."

Whatever the Pilgrims called them, they certainly did not serve them up as cranberry sauce. That wasn't invented until after World War I when the Ocean Spray Cooperative developed the dish as a way to expand sales. In those years, cranberries were strictly a seasonal item, selling only around Thanksgiving. The sauce, and further expansion into muffins and juices, turned the crop into a year-round proposition.

Cranberries are grown extensively in New Jersey and the Pacific Northwest. But in the public mind, they are forever linked with Massachusetts. This town in the bogs south of Plymouth is the center of the state's cranberry belt. The Edaville Railroad, a narrow-gauge line which was built to haul cranberries from the scattered bogs to a central shipping point, now serves as a sightseeing attraction. The town itself was named for John Carver, first governor of the Plymouth Colony.

✳ **Location:** South Carver is about 10 miles south of Plymouth on a county road reached from U.S. 44. ✳ **Events:** Train tours of the cranberry bogs, views of harvesting, food booths, crafts displays, country fair, entertainment. ✳ **Contact:** Massachusetts Harvest Cranberry Festival, P.O. Box 730, East Wareham, MA 02538, (508) 866-3811.

SUDBURY

◈ **Patriots' Day March:** April 19.

◈ **Mustering of Minutemen and Fife and Drum Muster:** Last Saturday in September.

"Listen, my children, and you shall hear / Of the midnight ride of Paul Revere." Hardly a schoolchild in America can have avoided reciting, at least once, the opening stanza of Henry Wadsworth Longfellow's poem about Revere's ride. Revere never made it this far into Middlesex County. He was picked up by British patrols outside of Lexington, had his horse confiscated, and had to walk back to Boston. But the alarm that he spread reached Sudbury.

David How, an innkeeper and colonel in the local militia, quickly gathered his minutemen at dawn of April 19. He marched them up to Concord, seven miles up the road, in time to take part in the famous fight at the stone bridge.

The inn that How owned was built as a private residence in 1702. He had added two rooms and operated it as the How Hotel. But eighty-eight years after How marched from his inn to attend to more urgent matters in Concord, it became a national landmark. Longfellow used it as the setting for his 1863 collection of verses, *Tales of a Wayside Inn*. Each poem in the volume is in the form of a story told by one of the guests at the old inn. The best-known was the tribute to Revere.

The Wayside Inn was restored by Henry Ford in the 1920s, but had to be completely rebuilt after a disastrous fire in 1956. Because of the shutdown resulting from the blaze, the Wayside Inn lost its claim of being the oldest continuously operating hotel in America. That title now goes to the Beekman Arms, in Rhinebeck, New York, which has been receiving guests since 1766. But its connections with the Revolution, both first-hand through its former owner and second-hand through its poem, make the inn a focus for these patriotic observances.

✳ **Location:** Sudbury is about 20 miles west of Boston, on U.S. 20. The Wayside Inn is in nearby South Sudbury. ✳ **Events:** On Patriots' Day, costumed minutemen gather on the Sudbury Common and then make the march up to Concord for the anniversary tribute to the war's opening fight. For the Minutemen and Fife and Drum Muster, units from all over New England gather at the Wayside Inn to play the military music of colonial times. There are also demonstrations of colonial skills and a crafts fair. ✳ **Contact:** Wayside Inn, Wayside Rd., Sudbury, MA 01776, (508) 443-8846.

New Jersey

ATLANTIC CITY

◆ Miss America Pageant: Weekend after Labor Day.

All the promoters wanted to do was make summer one week longer, persuade the crowds to remain in Atlantic City beyond the traditional Labor Day close of the season. What they did was create an institution.

Atlantic City has changed completely, from the country's most popular beach resort to a rather blowsy gambling town. Standards for what makes ideal face and form have been altered a dozen times. The Miss America pageant has been reviled by feminists, parodied by comics, imitated by competitors. Yet it remains securely a piece of Americana. People who scoff at and ignore other such competitions still read about Miss America, and the stories about the pageant remain front-page news in most papers in the country.

It began in 1921 as almost an afterthought, just another in a series of promotions. The next two years, in fact, the same young woman, Mary Campbell, of Columbus, Ohio, won the title, the only repeat performance in the pageant's history and unthinkable under current rules. It was all just fun and froth, and when the contest was briefly discontinued in the late 1920s, it wasn't missed by many.

But as Atlantic City felt the bite of the Depression, the competition was revived in 1933. It was formalized, given some style, elevated to a show that considered factors beyond mere beauty. And it caught on. A few winners—Bess Myerson, Lee Meriwether, Marilyn Van Derbur, Vanessa Williams—went on to successful show business careers. But most returned to a life of only local celebrity after their season in the spotlight. The pageant has also become a barometer of changes in the national attitude. African Americans have won and, in 1994, a deaf woman was crowned Miss America, far cries from the splashing flappers of the 1920s.

✳ **Location:** The Miss America Pageant is held at the Convention Center, on the Boardwalk between Mississippi and Florida Avenues. ✳ **Events:** Parade, entertainment, schedule of appearances by the contestants. ✳ **Contact:** Miss America Pageant Organization, P.O. Box 119, Atlantic City, NJ 08404, (609) 344-5278.

New York

❖ Toy Festival: Fourth Sunday in August.

In the early years of the twentieth century, this village was the home of America's Arts and Crafts movement. An entire campus dedicated to reviving and improving traditional crafts was built by Elbert Hubbard, a wealthy advertising executive who was convinced that this was the way to insure quality in the face of mass production. Hubbard, who became famous by writing the inspirational tract, "A Message to Garcia," called his organization the Roycrofters, and it was an influential force in American design and architecture around World War I.

Hubbard went down on the *Lusitania* in 1915 and, although his son carried on for another twenty-three years, the heart of the movement sank with the ship. The Roycrofters closed up in 1938, almost simultaneously with the arrival of other people concerned with small, well-made crafts, Fisher-Price Toys.

This company built its reputation as the designer of simple but sturdily made toys for toddlers. In 1984 it was said that 99 percent of American homes with a child under the age of six had at least one Fisher-Price plastic or wooden product. While the company is now part of a larger conglomerate, its main production facility remains here and East Aurora celebrates each summer with this festival.

✳ **Location:** East Aurora is about 25 miles southeast of Buffalo by way of New York 400. ✳ **Events:** Parades, costumed characters entertaining children, new toy displays, food booths. ✳ **Contact:** Toy Festival Committee, P.O. Box 238, East Aurora, NY 04152, (716) 652-8444.

Visitors join Iroquois dancers in honoring the traditions of the six tribes of the Iroquois Confederacy. (Courtesy of Iroquois Indian Museum)

❖ While You're There:

Many of the old Roycroft buildings were reopened in the late 1970s and offer traditional crafts for sale in their shops.

HOWES CAVE

❖ Iroquois Indian Festival: Labor Day weekend.

The Iroquois Confederacy was already fifty years old when Columbus made his first landfall in America. Two gifted leaders had persuaded the five most powerful Native American tribes in what would become New York to unify for their shared economic and military benefit. The idea originated with Dekanawida and was initially met with ridicule. But he struck an alliance with a gifted orator named Hiawatha, a Mohawk who lived among the Onondaga. Together they convinced those two tribes along with the Oneida, Cayuga, and Seneca to combine and form the Five Nations. (In the eighteenth century, the Tuscarora would join the confederacy as the sixth nation.)

Throughout the colonial era, the Iroquois were a major force that had to be considered in the plans of the European powers. Implacable enemies of the French, they tipped the balance against the French empire in Canada by fighting with the British in the wars of the 1750s. But the Iroquois miscalculated during the Revolution. Their loyalty to the Crown won them the hatred of the Americans. All but a small remnant were removed from their lands after the war and followed the British retreat into Canada.

Some historians claim to see the germ of the American federal system in the Iroquois Confederacy. Its cultural legacy is still a powerful force in New York, Ontario, and Quebec. The Iroquois Museum, established here in 1992 in the shape of a traditional longhouse, tells the story of the six tribes and their culture through exhibits and living history demonstrations. This traditional festival is part of the effort to bring that culture alive.

✳ **Location:** The Iroquois Indian Museum is north of Interstate 88 from the Central Bridge exit, about 35 miles west of Albany. ✳ **Events:** Traditional foods, dances, and crafts in the setting of a harvest festival. ✳ **Contact:** Iroquois Indian Museum, P.O. Box 7, Howes Cave, NY 12092, (518) 296-8949.

H U R L E Y

 ### Stone Houses Day: Second Saturday in July.

This village was settled by families from the nearby town of Kingston in 1661. They called it Nieuw Dorp, a Dutch name for a very Dutch place. The town leaders were named Van Dusen, Elmendorf, Houghtaling. And the houses they built were made of stone.

Hurley has the greatest concentration of stone houses in the country, and quite a bit of history is attached to them. For two months in 1777, this was the capital of New York. A British expedition up the Hudson River had seized and burned Kingston, which was then the colonial capital, and the government retreated here. It set up shop in the spacious Van Dusen House, built in 1723. The capital didn't stay long, just enough for the senate to meet a few times and for a British spy to be

Visits to the stone houses of Hurley are accompanied by historic tales of this former colonial capital of New York. (Courtesy Stone Houses Day)

captured and hanged. Then it moved along and Hurley was left to its pleasant stone obscurity.

The Elmendorf House, dating from the last decade of the seventeenth century, is the oldest of the stone structures. During Hurley's capital days it operated as the Half Moon Tavern. The DuMond House is now called the Guard House, because it was here that Lt. Daniel Taylor was imprisoned before meeting a spy's death on an apple tree nearby.

Mattys Ten Eyck was locally famous for delivering an interminable welcoming address from the shelter of his house's front porch to George Washington, who was standing in the rain. It is believed that the famed antislavery crusader Sojourner Truth lived at the Gerardus Hardenberg House when she herself was a slave as a child.

Hurley opens its houses and retells the stories during its special day.

✳ **Location:** Hurley is on U.S. 209, about 3 miles west of New York Thruway Exit 19. ✳ **Events:** Tours of the houses, antique show, fair, community dinner. ✳ **Contact:** Stone Houses Day Committee, Hurley Reform Church, P.O. Box 328, Hurley, NY 12433, (914) 331-4121.

MEDINA

 Canal Festival: First weekend in July.

The idea of building a canal across New York, from the Hudson to the Great Lakes, along the Mohawk River and through chains of inland lakes, had intrigued politicians and engineers since colonial times. There were fears that without such a link, the new settlements beyond the Appalachians in the West might eventually split off and form a separate country. A canal along this route, the only break in the wall of mountains anywhere in the East, would open this highway of commerce.

The original plan envisioned the canal terminating at Lake Ontario, near Oswego, New York. But there were political considerations involved. The Holland Land Company owned vast tracts of territory in western New York and it needed the canal to open them up. The company was a major player in New York politics, and it kicked in a gift of 100,000 acres to the state as an enticement. Moreover, there was concern that if trade were channelled into Lake Ontario, the well-developed Canadian cities on the lake's northern shore would siphon off a good share of the action. But a Lake Erie terminus would keep the major part of it in the United States.

Surveyor James Geddes made his route recommendation in 1809 and outlined how the canal could be extended to Lake Erie. It would run 363 miles, drop 565 feet, contain 84 locks, and bridge 18 streams by aqueduct. At the time, the longest canal in America ran 26 miles, so this was an undertaking beyond the wildest dreams of ambition. Before work could actually begin, the War of 1812 intervened, turning some of the Erie Canal's proposed route into a battleground. But in 1817, canal fever revived. Even after being turned down in its plea for assistance from the federal government, New York decided to go ahead on the project. Eight years later, the first boat left the basin at Buffalo Creek on Lake Erie, heading for the Hudson, and a new era began in American history.

The Great Western Canal, as it was then called, remained the commercial lifeline to the Great Lakes through the Civil War era. It created great cities along its path—Syracuse, Rochester, Buffalo—and turned remote outposts like Cleveland and Detroit into booming ports, shipping western farm produce to the waiting markets of the East. The canal solidified New York City's position as the financial and commercial center of the nation and its most important port. It created a canal folklore, and the cry "Low bridge, everybody down" entered the American vernacular.

Much of the original route of the Erie Canal is now covered over by the cement of growing cities or crumbling in disuse. Some of it was converted into the New York State Barge Canal and is still of commercial importance. Medina lies in the old Holland Land Company grant and owes its existence to the coming of the canal. So the midsummer celebration of old days on the Erie Canal is a reminder of its birth.

✳ **Location:** Medina is about 20 miles north of New York Thruway Exit 48A, by way of New York 77 and 63. It is about 45 miles west of Rochester.
✳ **Events:** Canal-side food booths, pioneer crafts, rides on the canal, entertainment. ✳ **Contact:** Medina Chamber of Commerce, P.O. Box 21, Medina, NY 14103, (716) 798-4287.

❖ While You're There:

For a taste of what a trip on the Erie Canal was like in the 1840s, the mule-drawn packet boat, Miss Apple Grove, a replica of an actual canal craft, makes two-hour trips from the dock on New York 31E.

NEW YORK CITY

◈ St. Patrick's Day: March 17.

◈ San Gennaro Festival: Week before September 19.

◈ Halloween Parade: October 31.

◈ Thanksgiving Day Parade: Fourth Thursday in November.

The "melting pot" is regarded as an unfortunate phrase in the era of multiculturalism. But at the start of the twentieth century it was seen as the highest social benefit for immigrants, a way of acculturating to American values while retaining as much of an ethnic identity as they wished in their private lives. New York was the very cauldron of the melting process. It liked to boast that it had more Irish than Dublin, more Italians than Florence, more Jews than Jerusalem. All found their place and became Americans on the streets of the big city.

Another thing New York has always done well is hold a parade. The Fifth Avenue parade was established as such a tradition that even by the 1920s merchants were complaining to the city that their frequency was a major disruption to business. Under the city's official host, Grover Whalen, in the 1920s and 1930s, New York brought the art of the ticker-tape parade for visiting heroes, potentates, and celebrities to a pinnacle of refinement. But when New York's minority groups combine with the city's love of parades, that remains something special, almost a signature of what this city means.

The St. Patrick's Day Parade grew to prominence after the massive immigration of Irish in the 1840s. By the 1870s, as the group rose to local political power, it became an important barometer of standing. Favored politicians were invited to participate and those left on the sidelines could count the votes marching away from them. It is still a hot issue. In the 1990s, the parade turned into a tug-of-war between organizers and Irish gay rights groups who were refused inclusion on the grounds that it was a religious event.

St. Patrick's Cathedral, at Fifth and 50th Street, has been the focus of the parade, as it has been ever since its opening in 1879. The reviewing stand is placed right in front of the cathedral as the green-clad brigades go marching by.

Parades Salute Cultural Heritage

New York's Italian community has its own Fifth Avenue parade on Columbus Day. But the more typical Italian celebration takes place downtown, on the streets of Little Italy. The San Gennaro Festival, which is centered on Mulberry Street, is the best-known Italian street celebration in the country.

There is music, food, games, dancing (although not too much of that because the crowds swarm so tightly that there is barely room to walk), and processions of the saint. The streets in Little Italy are narrow as it is, but this celebration packs them to capacity.

In many American cities, Halloween has occupied a special place on the calendar of the gay community. Because it was the one night of the year when it was all right, if not encouraged, to walk around in outlandish costumes, it became a time when one could dress in drag without police harassment. As the Gay Pride movement gathered force in the 1970s, gay men and women seized upon this holiday as an expression of their creativity and the exercise of their rights.

The Halloween parade through the streets of Greenwich Village has grown from a lightly attended curiosity to one of New York's major holiday attractions. The area around 6th Avenue and Houston is lined with tens of thousands of spectators, cheering at the creative getups marching past. Television news crews send the images to stations across the country. Residents of the area say that it is the one night of the year that Greenwich Village actually lives up to its reputation of being a small town within the city.

Macy's Launches an American Tradition

The Thanksgiving Day Parade has become one of the most successful commercial promotions in American history. Sponsored by Macy's to start off the Christmas shopping season, the parade down Broadway to the store on 34th Street has become a national holiday symbol.

The first parade marched off in 1924 over a much longer route. It began all the way up at 145th Street, as compared to 77th Street in recent years. An estimated 10,000 spectators turned out. The parade now attracts 2 million along the route and another 80 million on national network coverage.

Macy's parade is known for the show business celebrities who ride on the floats and stop to perform along the way. The giant balloons, which have been a parade staple since 1927, are made for the department store at the Goodyear Corporation hangars, home of the famed blimps, in Akron, Ohio. The parade is still the product of store employees, who make most of the floats and supply the personnel for the march. As the official press kit helpfully points out, it is the true "Miracle on 34th Street."

✳ **Contact:** Information on all the New York City events can be obtained through the New York Convention and Visitors Bureau, 2 Columbus Circle, New York, NY 10019, (800) NYC-VISIT.

OGDENSBURG

❖ **Seaway festival:** Third weekend in July.

Just as the vision of the Erie Canal haunted the dreams of planners for decades (see Medina), the possibility of a seaway down the St. Lawrence River tantalized engineers and political leaders in both the United States and Canada for centuries. The St. Lawrence had been the first great path of exploration by Europeans into the heart of the North American continent. But between Montreal and Lake Ontario, a series of rapids made further progress by water difficult, if not impossible. Most early explorers to the West took the Ottawa River and then portaged to Lake Huron. So the southern Great Lakes, although much further east, were the last to be explored.

By the end of the seventeenth century a canal had been built around the Lachine Rapids. But 250 years later, twenty-two small and inefficient locks still made it difficult for ocean-going vessels to enter the Great Lakes. Canada began work on modernizing and enlarging its portion of a seaway in 1952, and two years later the U.S. Congress voted to participate. In 1959, in ceremonies attended by Queen Elizabeth II and President Eisenhower, the seaway was formally dedicated. After expenditures of $410 million by both nations, the number of locks had been reduced by one-third, travel time from Duluth to Montreal had been cut by twenty hours, and freighters from around the world became a familiar sight in Midwestern cities like Milwaukee and Toledo.

The seaway also had some unforseen consequences. Ocean life, such as the sea lamprey, adapted to fresh water with devastating effect on the Great Lakes' fishes it preyed upon. Saltwater zebra mussels also thrived in the lakes and managed to clog up water intake systems in several locations. But the seaway worked a revolution in world trade and, with its associated electric power projects, proved worth the long wait. Ogdensburg, which once lay at the base of the impassable International Rapids, the most formidable of the barriers on the river, is now the home of a seaway marine terminal.

* **Location:** Ogdensburg is about 40 miles east of the Thousand Islands Bridge, on New York 12 and 37. * **Events:** Canoe race, fishing derby, fireworks, parade, drum and bugle corps competitions, concerts on the water. * **Contact:** Seaway Festival, c/o Ogdensburg Chamber of Commerce, P.O. Box 681, Ogdensburg, NY 13669, (315) 393-3620.

ROCHESTER

 Lilac Festival: Second week in May.

The first white settler in Rochester was Ebenezar Allan, who may very well have come to this wilderness in 1782 because no one else wanted anything to do with him. A Loyalist in the Revolution, he was also a self-confessed murderer and polygamist. He did, however, build a gristmill at the falls of the Genesee River, giving the place the foundation for its first major industry.

By 1840, the mills of Rochester, strategically situated on the Erie Canal, were grinding out 300,000 barrels a year and the town was calling itself the Flour City. Then things changed. Minneapolis, closer to the country's new grain belt, wrested dominance in milling from Rochester. Many local investors began turning to indoor nurseries, instead. In one of the great slogan switches in promotional history the erstwhile Flour City then billed itself as the Flower City.

Flowers have remained a central feature of Rochester's life ever since. Highland Park was donated to the city in 1887 by one of the most successful of the early nursery companies, Ellwanger and Barry. They covered its 108 acres with a variety of plants, but the most extensive were lilac bushes. There are now 1,200 of them in the park, and in May they bloom with over 600 different kinds of lilacs. The city has observed this festival since the 1890s, and it has become one of the leading floral celebrations in the country.

* **Location:** Highland Park is just south of downtown by way of South Avenue. * **Events:** Nature walks, illuminated gardens, entertainment, flower shows. * **Contact:** Lilac Festival Committee, 171 Reservoir Ave., Rochester, NY 14620, (716) 256-4960.

SENECA FALLS

❖ **Convention Days:** Weekend closest to July 19.

They came to this little town in the Finger Lakes in the summer of 1848, men and women dedicated to the idea that, in the words of a keynote speaker, "Women have the right—or ought to have the right—to vote and hold office." The sentiment was revolutionary. The people who signed the declaration of the first Women's Rights Convention were excoriated in the press and ridiculed by ministers and politicians. Many of them demanded afterwards that their names be removed from the document. But the movement went forward, although not many at the convention would have dreamed that it take another three-quarters of a century before their goal was achieved.

Elizabeth Cady Stanton was the moving spirit behind the meeting. She was a resident of Seneca Falls and the words in the speech quoted above were those of her husband, although it is possible she wrote them for him. She was a gifted and persuasive writer and helped shape the arguments that eventually won over a majority of the country to her views. In those years, the causes of women's rights and abolition of slavery were very closely allied. Meetings for one cause frequently attracted adherents to the other. It was after attending an antislavery meeting in London, but being relegated to the balcony and not allowed to participate because of her gender, that Mrs. Stanton was moved to organize this meeting.

Her greatest local ally was Amelia Jenks Bloomer, wife of the local postmaster. In later times she would have been saluted for her sense of public relations. The uniform she advocated for suffragists, a knee-length skirt worn over trousers, attracted such wide publicity that her name became attached to it for all time. She saw it as a symbolic casting-off of male-imposed dress restrictions. But when the clothes got more attention than her ideas, she stopped wearing bloomers.

Susan B. Anthony didn't arrive in Seneca Falls until 1851, but it was her alliance with Mrs. Stanton that energized the women's rights movements for the next fifty years. An accomplished organizer, Anthony, who came from nearby Rochester, imposed order to the ideas that flowed from Stanton's pen. All of these remarkable women are memorialized in this annual celebration and in the National Women's Hall of Fame, also located here.

✳ **Location:** Seneca Falls is on U.S. 20, just south of the New York Thruway Exit 41 and about 55 miles southeast of Rochester. ✳ **Events:** Parade, plays, and movies based on this history of the women's rights movement, outdoor parties, crafts festival. ✳ **Contact:** Seneca Falls County Tourism, (800) 688-7188; Seneca Falls Historical Society, Cayuga, NY 13148, (315) 568-8412.

❖ While You're There:

The Women's Rights National Historical Area includes a museum that chronicles the development of the movement and also preserves the home of Elizabeth Cady Stanton. One block away is the Hall of Fame, with displays saluting the achievements of American women.

Pennsylvania

◈ **Bach Festival:** Second and third weekends in May.

❄ **Christmas in Bethlehem:** Between Thanksgiving and New Year's Day.

There has been music in the air in Bethlehem ever since the Moravians arrived here from Germany to establish a religious colony. The group was founded in Bohemia by John Hus in the fifteenth century. They were a target during the centuries of religious wars that followed and suffered tragic losses. Finally, a Saxon nobleman, Count von Zinzendorf, offered them refuge in 1722 and nineteen years later agreed to underwrite a new home for them in America.

The count, a convert to the religion, accompanied the group, and on Christmas Eve, 1741, they reached their new home in Pennsylvania. Gathering for holiday ceremonies, they sang a hymn to hail the birth of Jesus and decided to name their new community Bethlehem.

The Moravians included music as an essential part of their religious service. Trombone choruses were used to herald special events, a tradition established on Easter, 1754, and continued to this day. They were especially enthusiastic about the works of Johann Sebastian Bach. Many of his choral compositions were published and performed in this remote town before they were heard in much of Europe. A musical college, to encourage both religious and secular music, was set up here in 1744.

The Bach Festival, which traces its origins to 1882, is one of the country's major musical events. The enthusiasm and doggedness of one remarkable teacher, Dr. J. Fred Wolle, is responsible for its location here. A choir leader with the Moravian Church, he organized the city's Bethlehem Choral Union. After a trip to Germany in 1884, where he heard a performance of Bach's *St. John Passion*, he decided to dedicate his life to bringing the work of the master to his hometown. Four years later, the Bethlehem group performed the work and went on to give annual performances of other great Bach compositions. But when Wolle began rehearsal on Bach's Mass in B Minor the choir rebelled, saying that it was too complex to master. Wolle resigned, insisting that he would lead no other work. In 1900, the choir was reorganized as the Bethlehem Bach Choir and performed the Mass that year. That is usually given as the start of the festival. Wolle continued as its director until his death in 1933.

Bethlehem also has one of America's most colorful and inspiring Christmas observances, involving the entire city. It runs for more than a month, beginning at Thanksgiving and finishing up on New Year's Eve. Its main features are a Christmas market, held in heated tents; candlelight concerts that feature early Moravian and Christmas music; bus tours of the city's illuminations; walking tours of the historic district; a Christmas Pageant on the second weekend of December and a Caroling Festival on the first Saturday in December. The celebration recalls both the season and the city's historic roots, with its founding on Christmas Eve.

✳ **Location:** Bethlehem is about 60 miles north of Philadelphia, by way of Pennsylvania 309 and 378. The Bach Festival is held in the Packer Memorial Church, on the Lehigh University campus. ✳ **Events:** The Bach Festival, for which tickets must be purchased, is regarded as one of the leading classical music events on the American calendar. Guest artists appear with the Bach Choir to perform the composer's greatest works in a celebration that embraces the entire community's musical heritage. Christmas in Bethlehem features candlelight processions and services at the Central Moravian Church, at Main and West Church, which dates from 1806 and is regarded as a masterpiece of federalist-era architecture; nightly caroling, including songs particular to the Moravian church; and special Nativity scenes that are also part of that religious tradition. The celebration is suspended on Christmas Eve and Christmas Day and then resumes for the five nights before New Year's Eve. ✳ **Contact:** For the Bach Festival: The Bach Choir, 423 Heckewelder Dr., Bethlehem, PA 18018, (610) 866-4382. For Christmas in Bethlehem: Bethlehem Tourism Authority, 52 West Broadstreet, Bethlehem, PA 18018, (610) 868-1513; for tickets to the Christmas pageant, (610) 867-2893.

BOALSBURG

◈ Memorial Day Festival: Weekend closest to May 30.

Many communities claim to have originated Memorial Day. In the years immediately after the Civil War, there was an enormous outpouring of national grief, in both the North and South. It was as if the country finally stepped back to regard the horror of what had been done. Honoring the dead became the best way to accomplish a healing, and several places came up with the idea almost simultaneously.

Historians have found twenty-five communities that claim to have been the first to hold the holiday. By proclamation of President Lyndon B. Johnson, the honor officially was given to Waterloo, New York, on the centennial of its first observance in 1866. Waterloo's claim is based on the fact that it was the first that was formally organized on a community-wide basis.

There is also a good deal of sentiment in favor of Columbus, Mississippi. A group of Southern ladies, in decorating the graves of the Confederate dead, also placed flowers on the resting place of Northern soldiers buried in the town. This occurred about a week before the Waterloo observance, and it touched an emotional chord in the country. Poems were written about this tribute and the resulting publicity helped create the sentiment that led to a national observance of the day.

But the first Memorial Day was probably held in this central Pennsylvania town—while the war still had nine months to go. On July 4, 1864, a Boalsburg group decorated the graves of soldiers from the town who had been killed in the conflict. Since all other observances date from after the war, this has to go down as the first Memorial Day (even though it was observed on the date of the other great American patriotic holiday). At any rate, Boalsburg puts on the biggest Memorial Day Festival, with the highest attendance of any Memorial Day event in the country, and it is here that the crowds come in a mood of solemn festivity.

✳ **Location:** Boalsburg is on U.S. 322, about 6 miles east of State College. ✳ **Events:** Parade, Civil War muster, patriotic speeches, Civil War-era crafts. ✳ **Contact:** Boalsburg Heritage Museum, Boalsburg, PA 16827, (814) 466-3035.

❖ While You're There:

Pennsylvania Military Museum honors the state's military units, from the militia organized by Benjamin Franklin to participants in Desert Storm. There are also memorials to those who died in American wars and displays of equipment from several different periods of military history.

HARMONY

 Dankfest: Fourth weekend in August.

The Rappites were another of the perfectionist groups that emerged from the religious turmoil of eighteenth-century Germany. Their leader,

Many items important to a nineteenth-century household are displayed and sold during Dankfest. (Courtesy of Historic Harmony Inc.)

George Rapp, believed in communitarian principles and, after they left Wurtemberg to come to Pennsylvania, he also announced that celibacy would be practiced. Some were displeased. Nonetheless, the Rappites survived for more than a century and, for a while, were a significant economic presence in western Pennsylvania.

Rapp called his organization the Harmony Society. After disposing of all individual property, the group settled here in 1805. They built an industrious community of farms and shops, but stayed for only nine years. Rapp thought prospects looked more promising in the West and moved the group to New Harmony, Indiana, in 1814. That didn't work as well as planned, either, and in 1825 they returned to this area and established themselves in Economy, in what is now the town of Ambridge. The crafts and textiles produced there led to investments in banks and oil. But constant bickering by sect leaders and the problems associated with celibacy eventually tore it apart. The Rappites dissolved in 1906 when the two remaining members decided to leave and the state took title to their holdings.

Mennonites, eventually, took over the property at Harmony, moving in on the well-built structures erected by the Rappite colony. Many of the brick buildings still stand, including a church. The Harmony Museum contains exhibits on the life they made here. About one hundred of the group are buried in the Rappite Cemetery, their graves bearing no names, only numbers, since they believed that with the Resurrection they would arise to new identities.

✳ **Location:** Harmony is on Interstate 79, about 30 miles north of Pittsburgh. ✳ **Events:** Dankfest is a nineteenth-century crafts fair, featuring the sorts of things that would have been turned out by the Rappites at both Harmony and Economy. ✳ **Contact:** Harmony Museum, P.O. Box 524, Harmony, PA 16037, (412) 452-7341.

❖ While You're There:

Old Economy Village, with 17 structures dating from the Rappite era, including the 25-room, brick residence of George Rapp, is in Ambridge. That town is about 30 miles southwest of Harmony by way of Interstate 79 and northbound Pennsylvania 65.

HERSHEY

❖ Chocolate Festival: Presidents' Day weekend.

Probably the best known company town in America, Hershey exists for the best reason possible—to make chocolate. Milton Hershey was a caramel-maker in Lancaster when he saw the possibilities opened by packaging Swiss chocolate in convenient bars. The Tootsie Roll was the first such treat in the United States, making its appearance in Chicago in 1896.

Hershey felt that a market existed for a higher standard of candy and began to turn out the flat candy bars that made his name synonymous with chocolate. Demand was so great that Hershey moved his factory to this planned community in 1903.

It has become a major recreational center, with golf resorts and an amusement park built around a chocolate theme. This celebration, falling conveniently close to Valentine's Day, pays tribute to Hershey's reason for being.

✳ **Location:** Hershey is on U.S. 422, about 15 miles northwest of Pennsylvania Turnpike Exit 19. Festival events are held at the Hotel Hershey and are open to guests of the hotel. ✳ **Events:** Chocolate tasting, displays of various chocolate products, chocolate games, workshops. ✳ **Contact:** Hotel Hershey, P.O. Box 400, Hotel Rd., Hershey, PA 17033, (800) 533-3131.

KUTZTOWN

 ## Kutztown Folk Festival: First week in July.

The Pennsylvania Dutch landed in America in 1682, sought out by William Penn, who heartily approved of their strong religious beliefs and industrious habits. Since Penn wanted his colony to be a haven for religious tolerance, he felt these were the perfect candidates.

Time has proved him correct. The Mennonites, and their even plainer-living branch, the Amish, thrived in the unbiased climate and rich soil of Pennsylvania. After settling first near Germantown, they gradually moved west and north, into the Susquehanna and Schuylkill valleys, and from there fanned out across many of the Midwestern states.

Most of the original colonists were German or Swiss. But in the English-speaking world of that time most people who identified themselves as German, or Deutsch, were simply referred to as Dutch. It was a convention that remained common in this country through the 1930s. Many athletes and gangsters of German ancestry were nicknamed "Dutch." The more clearly defined ethnic identities that came out of World War II changed that.

George Kutz established this town in 1771, and it holds the largest regional observance of Pennsylvania Dutch heritage.

✳ **Location:** Kutztown is on U.S. 222, about 20 miles west of Allentown. Beginning in 1996, the festival will be held at the Schuylkill County Fairground in Summit Station, exit 7 off I-78. ✳ **Events:** Traditional foods and crafts, quilting exhibition, booths offering home-crafted rugs and baskets. Since this is not a religious event, there is also some dancing. ✳ **Contact:** Kutztown Folk Festival, 461 Vine Lane, Kutztown, PA 19530, (610) 683-8707.

Home-crafted quilts continue to be a main attraction of the Kutztown Folk Festival. (Courtesy of Kutztown Folk Festival)

MANHEIM

 Rose Festival: Second Sunday in June.

His neighbors called him "Baron," because of the luxurious life that he favored. But although he owned no real title, Henry William Stiegel was one of colonial Pennsylvania's most colorful characters.

He came from the Rhineland and opened the colony's first glass-making factory in 1762. He was a true craftsman, and the glass he made here is among the most valuable in American history. The rich colors and enameling work were beyond anything done in America at that time. Much of it is now displayed in museums.

Stiegel founded Manheim as a company town and owned all the property within it. He built a mansion in the middle of town and a castle in nearby Schaefferstown. But financial transactions involving iron furnaces turned bad, and there is some evidence that his subordinates at the glass factory plotted against him. In 1774 he was thrown into debtor's prison, losing all his property. Upon his release, he managed to make a living as a teacher in local Lutheran churches. Among them was Zion Lutheran Church, in Manheim. Ironically, Stiegel had donated the property for this church in 1772, asking that one red rose be paid every year as rent. The payment is still made, although the erstwhile baron died in poverty and was buried in an unmarked grave.

✳ **Location:** Manheim is just south of Pennsylvania Turnpike Exit 20, about 10 miles north of Lancaster on Pennsylvania 72. ✳ **Events:** Ceremonial procession to the church for the rose payment to one of Stiegel's descendants. The church that now occupies the site replaced the original in 1891. Traditional crafts and food booths. ✳ **Contact:** Zion Lutheran Church, 2 South Hazel St., Manheim, PA 17545, (717) 665-5880.

PHILADELPHIA

❖ Battle of Germantown Reenactment: First Saturday in October.

As the autumn of 1777 began, the American cause was such a mixture of hope and disappointment that no one could really say how the war was going. Washington's army had been mauled at Brandywine Creek, and on September 26, the British occupied Philadelphia. The Continental Congress had to flee west to York. But the Americans had blockaded the Delaware River, making Lord Howe's hold on the city tenuous. And news from the north indicated that the British had been dealt a crushing defeat at Saratoga.

Washington assembled his troops about twenty miles west of Philadelphia and decided, just as he had at Trenton and Princeton, that he could not afford to hang back. Repeating his tactic of marching secretly at night, he planned a smashing dawn attack, with his entire force aimed at the main body of Howe's troops quartered in Germantown.

This village, which is now part of Philadelphia, lay on the east bank of the Schuylkill, north of the city. Washington's plan was complicated, involving coordination among four different groups. Moreover, the day began in a heavy fog, reducing visibility to almost zero. Initially, the British were stunned by the ferocity of the assault and fell back in disorder. But many of Washington's units became disoriented in the fog. In one tragic mistake, troops under Gen. Adam Stephen opened fire on Gen. Anthony Wayne's forces. The mishap blunted Wayne's successful assault. The British also were able to regroup at the Chew Mansion, behind the

Costumed troops prepare to reenact the Battle of Germantown of October 4, 1777. *(Courtesy of Cliveden of the National Trust)*

line of the American advance, and then attacked from the rear. Washington, eventually, had to withdraw and left the British in control of the city for the entire winter. He had come close to defeating Howe's regulars in battle, however, and the British victory was a closely run thing. Germantown raised colonial spirits just prior to the long ordeal at Valley Forge.

✳ **Location:** Germantown is in the northwestern corner of Philadelphia, with Germantown Avenue its main street. ✳ **Events:** Costumed colonial and British troops re-create the major parts of the battle. ✳ **Contact:** Cliveden, 6401 Germantown Ave., Philadelphia, PA 19144, (215) 848-1777.

❖ While You're There:

The Chew Mansion, Cliveden, built in 1767, still stands on Germantown Avenue as it did on the day of the battle. According to local legend, during the occupation of Philadelphia one of the Chew daughters had a romantic affair with a handsome British officer. He wrote a farewell poem to her when the British evacuated, and then Maj. John Andre went off to meet his fate, hanged as a spy in Benedict Arnold's abortive attempt to betray West Point.

◈ Elfreth's Alley Fete Day: First weekend in June.

The Delaware Expressway came into Philadelphia in the late 1950s, or about 260 years after Elfreth's Alley was laid out in 1690. Preliminary plans for the highway called for it to lop off some of the eastern portion of this street. Freeways do that sort of thing to old neighborhoods all the time. But this street had its defenders and they were fierce. Elfreth's Alley is the oldest continually inhabited residential street in America, and Philadelphia wasn't about to give up any part of it for a freeway.

This thoroughfare, cobblestoned and all of six feet wide, with a drain running down its center, has seen the great men and women of the city. Benjamin Franklin lived there for a time. George Washington may not have slept there, but he visited friends who lived there. Betsy Ross attended school just around the corner and played on its old stones. Philip Seng, the silversmith who made the inkwells from which the Declaration of Independence was signed, was also a resident of Elfreth's Alley.

Jeremiah Elfreth, for whom the street was named, was a prosperous blacksmith who acquired several homes on the street. Eventually, people started calling it by his name and the custom stuck. Tucked away between busier thoroughfares, just a couple of blocks from the riverfront, Elfreth's Alley managed to survive as the best preserved eighteenth-century street in America. People can come here and see what a part of Philadelphia actually looked like when conventions met here to sign the great documents of the nation's history. It is a place to get lost in the past.

✳ **Location:** Elfreth's Alley is between Arch and Race Streets just east of 2nd Street. It is six blocks northeast of Independence Hall. ✳ **Events:** This is the only time of the year that the homes on the street are open to visitors. There is also an art fair, colonial crafts demonstration, and costumed guides explaining the history of the street. ✳ **Contact:** Elfreth Alley Association, 126 Elfreth's Alley, Philadelphia, PA 19106, (215) 574-0560.

✪ While You're There:

The Elfreth's Alley Museum has permanent displays on the street and those who lived there over the centuries. It is located at number 126.

❇ Mummers Parade: New Year's Day.

Some folklorists trace the origin of this Philadelphia tradition to a practice known as bell-snickeling. In the city's German neighborhoods, masked and costumed revelers thronged the streets on New Year's Day to ring bells at passersby and be given cakes and candy if their identity was

Mummers parade through the streets of Philadelphia each New Year's Day in a tradition that can be traced back to the Civil War era. (The Image Works)

not guessed. There are also elements of British Christmas celebrations in the mummers' elaborate costumes and satiric antics.

Most neighborhoods in the city had a mummers group by the Civil War era. Some tried to outdo each other in the feathers and sequins they attached to their getups. Others simply turned their overcoats inside out and let it go at that. Sometimes the competition erupted into full-scale brawls, and there are numerous occasions in the city's history in which police had to be summoned to pull the mummers off each other.

On January 1, 1901, it was decided to assemble all the city mummers and hold a gigantic parade to hail the start of the new century. By that time, the mummers had organized themselves into three groups—comic, fancy, and string bands. It isn't always easy to tell the comic from the fancy, but the strutting bands are known for their rendition of the song that has become the anthem of this parade, "Oh, Dem Golden Slippers." Played on several thousand banjos and glockenspiels at once, it is a melody not easily forgotten by anyone who has ever heard it.

Lingering mummer traditions, such as making up in blackface, got the parade in trouble with civil rights groups in the 1960s. But these practices have been tuned down or abandoned, and the mummers, 30,000 strong, continue to march through the years, from one end of the twentieth century to the other.

✳ **Location:** Down Broad Street through the heart of Philadelphia. More than 1 million spectators brave the January chill, and sometimes bitter cold, to watch the spectacle. ✳ **Events:** Music, elaborate floats, traditional comedy routines and dances. The parade lasts approximately eight hours. ✳ **Contact:** Philadelphia Visitors Center, 16th and JFK Blvd., Philadelphia, PA 19103, (215) 636-1666.

❖ While You're There:

The New Year Shooters and Mummers Museum, filled with displays of the costumes and traditions of the parade, is located at Second Street and Washington Avenue. Marching string bands perform there on Tuesday evenings to give visitors a taste of what they miss on New Year's Day.

P U N X S U T A W N E Y

❄ Groundhog Day: February 2.

It began as Candlemas Day, a church holiday marking the Purification of Mary and falling at winter's midway point. Over the years the celebration got mixed up with pagan fertility practices, in which candlelit processions would wind across the fields to purify them for the coming planting. The rite was also meant to restore the sun's power as the days began to lengthen towards the vernal equinox.

In Germany, badgers were believed to emerge from their holes on this day and look for their shadows to check on the progress of the season. When immigrants to America carried the old tradition with them, the curious animal became a woodchuck or groundhog. The observance was widespread across Pennsylvania. There were elaborate groundhog ceremonials in cities like Allentown, and the town of Quarryville claimed to have begun its ritual in 1907.

But in recent years, Punxsutawney Phil has blown away all competition. The groundhog who lives in this western Pennsylvania town is generally acknowledged by the media to be the top weather forecaster for not only the state but the entire country. His special burrow on Goober's Knob has become a place of midwinter pilgrimages, memorialized in the 1993 film comedy *Groundhog Day*. Locals claim their tradition predates the one in Quarryville by a good twenty years, too.

The town, whose name means "place of gnats," also honors Phil with a life-sized statue in a downtown park.

On Groundhog Day, Punxsutawney Phil—considered the most accurate forecaster of seasonal change—is greeted with much fanfare by local officials. (Wide World Photos)

✳ **Location:** Punxsutawney is on U.S. 119, about 25 miles south of Interstate 80 and about 85 miles northeast of Pittsburgh. ✳ **Events:** Predawn procession to Phil's burrow to await his appearance, parades, entertainment, community dinners. ✳ **Contact:** Punxsutawney Chamber of Commerce, 124 West Mahoning St., Punxsutawney, PA 15767, (814) 938-7700.

UNIONTOWN

◈ **National Pike Festival:** Third weekend in May.

This was the first of the great overland roads to the West. The route that became the National Road was blazed in 1749 after the Ohio Company was created to open the territory beyond the Appalachians. It ran from Cumberland, Maryland, on the Potomac River, to Wheeling, in what was then Virginia, on the Ohio River. It was the route the twenty-two-year-old George Washington followed in 1754 in an attempt to dislodge the French from their fort at Pittsburgh. His skirmish at Fort Necessity along this road was the first engagement of the French and Indian War and his first military success. It was along this track, too, that Gen. Edward

Braddock was buried the following year on the long retreat from his disastrous defeat by the French at the Monongahela River.

After the Revolutionary War, with no impediments remaining towards the settling of Ohio, the Washington-Braddock Road became a major thoroughfare. Wagons plodded along its length to Wheeling and then made the rest of the journey by flatboat. Traffic was so heavy that the federal government authorized construction of a National Road, funded by tolls, in 1806, along the route of the older one. Within twelve years it had been built through Pennsylvania to Wheeling, approximately along the line of the current U.S. 40.

The question of extending the National Road further stimulated one of the major constitutional debates in American history. President James Monroe vetoed the measure on the grounds that he was unsure whether federal powers went so far as to finance internal improvements. The Congressional debate that followed, and the bill that resulted from it in 1825, solidified the growing political strength of the West. It also placed the U.S. government on the path of building roads and canals as part of its powers of regulating interstate commerce.

Uniontown grew up along the National Road and recalls the part it played in its history with this festival.

✳ **Location:** Uniontown is on U.S. 40, about 50 miles south of Pittsburgh.
✳ **Events:** Pioneer wagon train, crafts and food booths, costumed guides at nearby Fort Necessity, Searights Toll Booth, and other historic sites in the vicinity associated with the road. ✳ **Contact:** National Road Heritage Park Inc., 61 East Main, Uniontown, PA 15401; Uniontown Business District Authority, (412) 430-2909.

❖ While You're There:

Fort Necessity National Battlefield preserves the site of Washington's first battle, Braddock's grave, and the restored Mt. Washington Tavern, which served travelers along this road from 1825 to 1855. It is 11 miles east of Uniontown on U.S. 40.

WASHINGTON CROSSING

Reenactment of the Delaware River Crossing:
December 25.

The end of 1776 was one of the most dangerous times in George Washington's military career. Forced to retreat from New York, he tried to keep his forces together in a desperate race across New Jersey, pursued by superior numbers of British and Hessians. Finally reaching the Delaware River, just hours ahead of the enemy, he crossed into Pennsylvania, burning every bridge and boat on the New Jersey shore.

Lord Howe, in command of the British forces, stayed along the river for a week. He finally determined on December 14 that Washington was penned up for the winter, and he returned to his quarters in New York, leaving Hessians to guard the front at Trenton.

But Washington, in one of the war's greatest gambles, had decided to roll the dice. Historians later explained that his move was inevitable. With political pressure mounting for some sort of military success, he could not afford to end the year's campaigning with a series of defeats. He had to keep up the morale of his army and also convince the people, many of whom were still unsure of which side to support, that the British were vulnerable.

On Christmas night, he assembled 2,400 troops at the Delaware, and with a fleet of Durham boats—flat-bottomed and capable of carrying fifteen tons—he crossed back into New Jersey. Men and arms were all on the far side by 4 A.M. and quickly marched the nine miles to Trenton. Caught completely by surprise, the Hessian defenders were routed, with total American casualties numbering four wounded.

Eight days later, Washington pulled off another victory, outwitting Lord Cornwallis, who had been sent down by Howe with 5,500 British regulars, and turning his flank at Princeton. Again the British were severely mauled and forced to retreat to New York.

The many depictions of Washington crossing the Delaware, standing in the stern of the boat as ice floes sweep past in the water, have made this one of the Revolution's most familiar scenes. The victories that followed restored confidence in Washington's leadership abilities and insured that he would remain in command for the duration of the war.

✳ **Location:** Pennsylvania's Washington Crossing State Park is located 3 miles north of I-95 from exit 31, on River Road. ✳ **Events:** Costumed reenactment of the Delaware crossing, beginning in Pennsylvania and ending in New Jersey. ✳ **Contact:** Washington Crossing Historic Park, P.O. Box 103, Washington Crossing, PA 18977, (215) 493-4076.

❖ While You're There:

The Old Barracks Museum, in Trenton, New Jersey, was built by the British in 1759 and is the oldest surviving military housing in the country. This is where the Hessian troops were quartered when they were suddenly attacked in the predawn darkness by Washington's advance guard. It is located on Barrack Street, near West Front Street.

Rhode Island

NEWPORT

❖ Tennis Week and Music Festival: Second week in July.

In colonial times, it was a leading rival of New York City as a port
and commercial center. But after the Revolution had been won, Newport
went into a slow and seemingly irreversible decline. By 1830 it was a
fading shadow of its prosperous past. It was then that a group of planters
from the South and Cuba discovered the place and began purchasing
property along the sea for summer homes.

Its reputation expanded slowly, then suddenly burst into national
prominence in the flush of prosperity that followed the Civil War. Newport became established as the favored summer retreat for socially prominent families from Boston and New York. They vied with each other in
building luxurious mansions (whimsically referred to as "cottages") and
turned Ocean Drive into America's most prestigious summer address.

Among the facilities built at this time was the Casino. This tennis
club was constructed by newspaper publisher James Gordon Bennett in
1880. The following year, the first National Championship matches were
held on its grass courts. The U.S. Open remained here until 1915, when it
moved to what has been its home ever since, New York's West Side
Tennis Club. The Casino is now a shrine to the sport, with the oldest com-
petitive courts in the world. Since the opening of the sport's Hall of Fame
here in 1954, Tennis Week in Newport has become a traditional stop on
both the men's and women's circuit.

Many of the enormous Newport mansions were abandoned during
the 1950s as impractical to maintain. The Preservation Society of Newport
County slowly acquired title to many of the ornate homes and in recent
years has found a way to combine these fabled surroundings with the
sporting events. The Newport Music Festival is held in conjunction with

During simultaneous festivals, Tennis Week matches are played here at the International Tennis Hall of Fame while Music Festival concerts are being held in some of Newport's finest homes. (Courtesy of Michael Baz and the Tennis Hall of Fame)

Tennis Week and features chamber concerts in several of the "cottages." The locations vary from year to year.

✳ **Location:** The Casino is located at 194 Bellevue Avenue in the city itself. The museum here includes historical displays and memorabilia of the sport, especially its associations with Newport. It also has an exhibit on court tennis, the predecessor of the modern game, and demonstrations of how it was played. The mansions in which the Music Festival is held are located along Ocean Drive, south of the city. ✳ **Events:** Tennis matches and concerts. Admission is charged to all events. While tickets to the championship match must be secured far in advance, there is usually no problem getting in for the preliminary rounds. ✳ **Contact:** For Tennis Week: Tennis Hall of Fame, 194 Bellevue Ave., Newport, RI 02840, (401) 849-3990. For Music Festival: Music Festival, P.O. Box 3300, Newport, RI 02840, (401) 846-1133.

❖ While You're There:

The Newport Jazz Festival is the event that brought this place back to national attention in the 1950s, when its status as a summer resort had started to slip. Although not universally popular with longtime residents, the jazz festival introduced the area to young visitors who rediscovered its historic and nautical charms and spurred its development as a major attraction. The concerts are held at Fort Adams State Park on the second weekend of August.

The cottages of Ocean Drive comprise one of the country's great attractions in the field of social history. Among the most notable are: The Breakers, built in 1895 for Cornelius Vanderbilt, a 72-room home noted for lavish use of alabaster, marble, and antique woods. Marble House, modeled after the Grand and Petit Trianons in Paris, was another of the Vanderbilt homes, best known for its gold ballroom and Chinese teahouse. Kingscote, the oldest of the palatial estates, was built in 1839 for George N. Jones of Savannah, featuring Tiffany wall glass and what is regarded as the first use of cork ceilings.

WARWICK

 Gaspee Days: Memorial Day weekend and the week following.

In the spring of 1772, the colonists of Rhode Island and the tax collectors of Great Britain were at an angry standoff. The British accused merchants of smuggling goods to avoid new import taxes levied by Parliament. While smuggling as an occupation was not unknown in the colony, the businessmen resented the high-handed seizures of their ships in Narragansett Bay.

When the schooner *Gaspee* was assigned to aggressively patrol the bay, the situation worsened. On June 9, the *Gaspee* ran aground in pursuit of a suspected smuggler. While the ship lay helpless, it was boarded by a party of raiders, including members of some of Rhode Island's leading families. The ship's commander was shot and the *Gaspee* burned.

In the aftermath of the affair, it was learned that if Parliament had succeeded in fixing guilt for the raid, it would have carried off the accused to London for trial. That revelation so outraged the colonies that they agreed to form Committees of Correspondence, to keep each other informed about threatening activities by the British. It was one of the first actions leading to colonial unity and foreshadowed a growing consensus towards independence.

It was off Warwick that the *Gaspee* ran aground, and the town has celebrated the event annually since 1966.

✳ **Location:** Throughout the towns of Warwick and neighboring Cranston, which are southern suburbs of Providence. The focus is Gaspee Point, site of the ship's destruction. This is north of Warwick, by way of Rhode Island 117 to Hoxsie, then east on Warwick Avenue to the Narragansett Parkway, and north for two miles. ✳ **Events:** Reenactment of the *Gaspee* burning, fife and drum corps parades, concerts, balls, arts and crafts festival, colonial encampment, children's colonial costume contest.

✳ **Contact:** Gaspee Days Committee, P.O. Box 1772, Pilgrim Station, Warwick, RI 02888, (401) 781-1772.

WICKFORD

◈ **International Quahog Festival:** Sunday closest to Columbus Day.

Around Narragansett Bay, quahog is the traditional word for hard-shelled clam. This has proven to be quite confusing for those who do not live around Narragansett Bay.

"I don't know how many people I've talked to who thought we were putting on some kind of pork barbecue here because of that name," says Stu Tucker, who has served as chairman of the International Quahog Festival. "But it's a Narragansett Indian word and that's what we've always called these clams. In fact, it's believed that all the hard-shelled clams along the whole eastern seaboard originated in these waters and were transplanted."

Tucker owns a fishing company and has dedicated a good part of his career to the celebration and the catching of the quahog, which remains an important part of Wickford's sea-based economy.

"I developed recipes for quahog chowder, quahog chili, quahog nuggets ... you name it. But when we started this festival we made a mistake and held it in August. Most of the things we make from quahogs are served hot, and you just don't want to stand around in that August sun eating quahog chili. Once we shifted it to October, we did a lot better."

✳ **Location:** The village of Wickford, located in the town of North Kingstown, is 25 miles south of Providence, by way of Interstate 95 and U.S. 1. The event is held in Wickford Park. ✳ **Events:** Cook-offs featuring baked stuffed quahog, food booths, jazz and blues performers, arts and crafts booths, quahog-shucking contests. ✳ **Contact:** North Kingstown Chamber of Commerce, P.O. Box 454, North Kingstown, RI 02852, (401) 295-5566.

❖ **While You're There:**

Main Street in Wickford is regarded as one of the best-preserved colonial streets in New England. There are 20 homes dating from prior to 1804 along its length and 20 more on the adjoining streets. Old Narragansett Church was built here in 1707.

Vermont

❖ Dairy Festival: First weekend in June.

At the end of the Civil War, Vermont was a place in deep decline. Its population losses per capita were higher than any other Northern state. Its sheep farms were going under because of competition from larger midwestern operations. Young people were leaving the state to find opportunities elsewhere.

It was then that the Jersey arrived. This breed of dairy cow transformed Vermont's economy, making it the nation's top producer of milk and butter for decades. It also acted to preserve Vermont's rural character, propping up the small family farm that was the basis of the state's agriculture.

The dairy herds were formed in the late 1860s. By 1871 Franklin County had established itself as the center of Vermont's dairy industry. Much of New England's milk supply still comes from this area. Vermont's reputation for fine dairy products was solidified with the establishment of Ben and Jerry's Ice Cream in nearby Waterbury in 1978. The roads in this northernmost part of the state are among the most scenic in Vermont, opening out on uninterrupted vistas of rolling farmland and cattle.

✳ **Location:** Enosburg Falls is east of Interstate 89, on Vermont 108, about 50 miles northeast of Burlington. ✳ **Events:** Food booths, country crafts, parade, exhibits of local dairy products, greased pig contest, tractor pull, bathtub races. ✳ **Contact:** Berkson Farms, R.R. 1, Box 850, Enosburg Falls, VT 05450, (802) 933-2522.

◈ **Maple Sugar festival:** In April, dates vary.

To the connoisseur, Vermont's tradition of making maple syrup compares to that of France in making wine. Both call for a mix of science and instinct, a knowledge of nature's timing that cannot be taught but only learned after many seasons in the fields.

When the daytime temperatures reach forty degrees while the nights are still in the twenties, it is generally regarded as the optimum time for opening the taps in the maple trees. The sap is then flowing at its best. The metal device, called a spile, siphons off the sap into buckets. It usually takes forty gallons of sap to produce one gallon of syrup.

The quality of the syrup depends on what happens in the sugarhouse during the boiling process. Most consumers prefer a lighter amber-colored syrup, which is called a shallow boil, and that is the most difficult to time properly. Too light, and the taste is very thin. Too dark, and a touch of caramel creeps in. It takes a master's touch, and most of Vermont's sugarmakers undergo specialized training, sharpening their palates with taste tests while they are blindfolded. The state leads the nation in maple syrup production.

✳ **Location:** St. Albans is off Interstate 89, about 25 miles north of Burlington. ✳ **Events:** Sugarhouse parties, sugar tasting, wood-chopping contests, antiques shows, crafts fair. ✳ **Contact:** St. Albans Chamber of Commerce, P.O. Box 327, St. Albans, VT 05478, (802) 524-2444.

Washington D.C.

◈ Cherry Blossom Festival: First two weeks in April.

The pink and white blossoms that turn the Tidal Basin into one of Washington's most spectacular sights were the inspiration of Jokichi Takamino. In 1907, when Mrs. William Howard Taft, wife of the future president, imported the first eighty Japanese cherry trees to the capital, Takamino was deeply moved. A Japanese citizen living in America, he knew that so few trees could not begin to convey the sensation of joy that the blossoming of these trees brought to his homeland.

So he arranged for 2,000 more trees to be brought here as a gift from the city of Tokyo. The buds were carefully selected at one of the top nurseries in Japan and then grafted onto rootstock at the Imperial Horticulture Station.

Unfortunately, the first shipment arrived infested with insects and had to be destroyed. But in 1909, a total of 3,000 healthy trees arrived and were planted around the Basin. The Yoshino variety on the western edge bloom first, followed about two weeks later by the pink Kwanzan blossoms along the eastern end.

While America's official relationship with Japan has not always been easy, the flowering of Japan's gift has become one of the great sights of Washington.

✳ **Location:** The Tidal Basin is at the southern edge of the Mall, at 17th Street SW. ✳ **Events:** Japanese Lantern Lighting ceremony, parade, nighttime illuminations, historic pageants. ✳ **Contact:** Cherry Blossom Festival, 900 Waters St. SW, Washington, DC 20024, (202) 646-0366.

Southeast

Alabama

1. Blessing of the Shrimp Fleet, Bayou La Batre
2. National Peanut Festival, Dothan
3. W. C. Handy Music Festival, Florence
4. Azalea Trail Festival, Mardi Gras, Mobile
5. Old Cahawba Day, Selma

Arkansas

6. Watermelon Festival, Hope
7. Brickfest, Malvern
8. Lum n' Abner Days, Mena
9. World Championship Duck Calling Contest and Wings over the Prairie Festival, Stuttgart
10. Jonquil Festival, Washington

Florida

11. Florida Citrus Festival, Auburndale
12. Florida Heritage Festival, Bradenton
13. Florida Chautauqua Festival Day, De Funiak Springs
14. Hatsume Fair, Delray Beach
15. Edison Festival of Light, Fort Myers
16. Hemingway Days, Key West
17. Battle of Olustee Festival, Lake City
18. Art Deco Weekend, Miami Beach
19. Spanish Night Watch, St. Augustine
20. Natural Bridge Battle Reenactment, Tallahassee
21. Gasparilla Pirate Invasion, Tampa
22. Epiphany Celebration, Tarpon Springs
23. The Jeanie Auditions, White Springs

Georgia

24. Georgia Peach Festival, Fort Valley
25. Marble Festival, Jasper
26. Fair of 1850, Lumpkin

Kentucky

27. Daniel Boone Festival, Barbourville
28. Kentucky Guild of Artists and Craftsmen Fair, Berea
29. The Patton Museum Fourth of July Demonstration, Fort Knox
30. Kentucky Derby Festival, Strictly Bluegrass Music Festival, Louisville
31. International Bar-B-Q Festival, Owensboro
32. Tobacco Festival and Jesse James Robbery Reenactment, Russellville
33. Shaker Festival, South Union

Louisiana

34. Holiday in Dixie, Bossier City/Shreveport
35. Crawfish Festival, Breaux Bridge
36. International Rice Festival, Crowley
37. Contraband Days, Lake Charles
38. Battle of Pleasant Hill Reenactment, Mansfield
39. Shrimp and Petroleum Festival, Morgan City
40. Cajun Fun Festival, New Iberia
41. Jazz Festival, New Orleans
42. Mardi Gras, New Orleans

Mississippi

43. Delta Blues Festival, Greenville
44. Pilgrimage, Natchez
45. Landing of d'Iberville, Ocean Springs
46. Choctaw Fair, Philadelphia

North Carolina

47. Mountain Dance and Folk Festival, Asheville
48. Macon County Gemboree, Franklin
49. Grandfather Mountain Highland Games, Linville
50. Waldensian Festival, Valdese

South Carolina

51. Iris Festival, Sumter

Tennessee

52. Mule Day, Columbia
53. Dulcimer Harp Fest, Cosby
54. National Storytelling Festival, Jonesborough
55. Beale Street Music Festival, Elvis Week, Memphis
56. International Country Music Fan Fair, Nashville
57. The World's Biggest Fish Fry, Paris
58. Spring Festival, Rugby
59. Tennessee Walking Horse National Celebration, Shelbyville

Virginia

60. George Washington's Birthday Parade, Alexandria
61. Pony Penning Day, Chincoteague
62. Danville Harvest Jubilee, Danville
63. Old Fiddlers Convention, Galax
64. Carter Family Memorial Festival, Gate City
65. August Court Days, Leesburg
66. Battle Reenactment, New Market
67. Apple Blossom Festival, Winchester
68. Yorktown Day, Yorktown

❄ January

6: **Epiphany Celebration,** Tarpon Springs, Florida

Second weekend: **Art Deco Weekend,** Miami Beach, Florida

Last weekend in January to first weekend in February: **Florida Citrus Festival,** Auburndale, Florida

❄ February

Entire month: **Edison Festival of Light,** Fort Myers, Florida

First weekend in February through the end of the month: **Gasparilla Pirate Invasion,** Tampa, Florida

Two weeks before Shrove Tuesday: **Mardi Gras,** New Orleans, Louisiana

Ten days before Shrove Tuesday: **Mardi Gras,** Mobile, Alabama

Weekend closest to February 20: **Battle of Olustee Festival,** Lake City, Florida

Presidents' Day: **George Washington's Birthday Parade,** Alexandria, Virginia

Last weekend: **Hatsume Fair,** Delray Beach, Florida

◆ March

Sunday nearest March 6: **Natural Bridge Battle Reenactment,** Tallahassee, Florida

First weekend to the first weekend in April: **Pilgrimage,** Natchez, Mississippi

Second weekend: **Cajun Fun Festival,** New Iberia, Louisiana

Second weekend: **Jonquil Festival,** Washington, Arkansas

Last two weekends and first week in April: **Azalea Trail Festival,** Mobile, Alabama

Last weekend in March through April: **Heritage Festival,** Bradenton, Florida

◆ April

First weekend in April: **Battle of Pleasant Hill Reenactment,** Mansfield, Louisiana

First weekend (unless it falls on Easter, in which case it is the second weekend): **Mule Day,** Columbia, Tennessee

The two weeks preceding the first Saturday in May: **Kentucky Derby Festival,** Louisville, Kentucky

Third Saturday: **Chautauqua Festival Day,** De Funiak Springs, Florida

Last weekend: **Landing of d'Iberville,** Ocean Springs, Mississippi

Last full weekend: **The World's Biggest Fish Fry,** Paris, Tennessee

Last weekend to first weekend in May: **Jazz Festival,** New Orleans, Louisiana

Dates vary: **Holiday in Dixie,** Bossier City/Shreveport, Louisiana

◆ May

First weekend: **Crawfish Festival,** Breaux Bridge, Louisiana

First full weekend: **Beale Street Music Festival,** Memphis, Tennessee

First two weekends: **Contraband Days,** Lake Charles, Louisiana

Second Saturday: **Old Cahawba Day,** Selma, Alabama

Second Sunday: **Battle Reenactment,** New Market, Virginia

Second full weekend: **International Bar-B-Q Festival,** Owensboro, Kentucky

Second or third weekend: **Spring Festival,** Rugby, Tennessee

Weekend with third Saturday: **Kentucky Guild of Artists and Craftsmen Fair,** Berea, Kentucky

Weekend before Mother's Day: **Apple Blossom Festival,** Winchester, Virginia

Last weekend: **Iris Festival,** Sumter, South Carolina

June

First weekend: **Lum n' Abner Days,** Mena, Arkansas

Second weekend: **Georgia Peach Festival,** Fort Valley, Georgia

Second full weekend: **Dulcimer Harp Fest,** Cosby, Tennessee

Third Saturday: **Spanish Night Watch,** St. Augustine, Florida

Last weekend: **Blessing of the Shrimp Fleet,** Bayou La Batre, Alabama

Last full weekend: **Brickfest,** Malvern, Arkansas

Date varies: **Shaker Festival,** South Union, Kentucky

Dates vary: **International Country Music Fan Fair,** Nashville, Tennessee

July

4: **The Patton Museum Fourth of July Demonstration,** Fort Knox, Kentucky

Week following July 4: **Choctaw Fair,** Philadelphia, Mississippi

Second full weekend: **Grandfather Mountain Highland Games,** Linville, North Carolina

Third week: **Hemingway Days,** Key West, Florida

Fourth week: **Macon County Gemboree,** Franklin, North Carolina

Wednesday before last Thursday: **Pony Penning Day,** Chincoteague, Virginia

August

Begins first Sunday: **W. C. Handy Music Festival,** Florence, Alabama

First weekend: **Mountain Dance and Folk Festival,** Asheville, North Carolina

First weekend: **Carter Family Memorial Festival,** Gate City, Virginia

Second Saturday: **Waldensian Festival,** Valdese, North Carolina

Second weekend: **Old Fiddlers Convention,** Galax, Virginia

Second week: **Elvis Week,** Memphis, Tennessee

Third weekend (Thursday-Sunday): **Watermelon Festival,** Hope, Arkansas

Third weekend: **August Court Days,** Leesburg, Virginia

The ten days leading to the Saturday before Labor Day: **Tennessee Walking Horse National Celebration,** Shelbyville, Tennessee

September

Labor Day weekend: **Shrimp and Petroleum Festival,** Morgan City, Louisiana

Weekend after Labor Day: **Strictly Bluegrass Music Festival,** Louisville, Kentucky

Third Saturday: **Delta Blues Festival,** Greenville, Mississippi

October

First full weekend: **Danville Harvest Jubilee,** Danville, Virginia

First full weekend: **The Jeanie Auditions,** White Springs, Florida

First full weekend: **Marble Festival,** Jasper, Georgia

Weekend with the second Saturday: **Kentucky Guild of Artists and Craftsmen Fair,** Berea, Kentucky

Second full weekend: **National Storytelling Festival,** Jonesborough, Tennessee

Second week: **Daniel Boone Festival,** Barbourville, Kentucky

Second week: **Tobacco Festival and Jesse James Robbery Reenactment,** Russellville, Kentucky

19: **Yorktown Day,** Yorktown, Virginia

Third full weekend: **International Rice Festival,** Crowley, Louisiana

 November

Week preceeding the first weekend:
National Peanut Festival, Dothan, Alabama

First weekend: Fair of 1850, Lumpkin, Georgia

Wednesday through Saturday of Thanksgiving week: World Championship Duck Calling Contest and Wings over the Prairie Festival, Stuttgart, Arkansas

Alabama

BAYOU LA BATRE

❖ Blessing of the Shrimp Fleet: Last weekend in June.

The shrimp boats of Bayou La Batre have been plying the waters of the Gulf of Mexico for the best part of two centuries. The city was founded in 1786 with the bayou as its main thoroughfare. Narrow streets wind down to the water past cottages and yards of flowers. It is a village that draws its sustenance from the sea, the most profitable catch being shrimp.

Many residents trace their roots back to Cajun times and the surrounding area is the most Catholic section of Alabama. So the blessing of the fleet is a much-loved annual tradition, dating back to 1950. Local shrimpers decorate their trawlers and parade around the harbor, then solemnly assemble to receive the blessings that ask for a fruitful year and protection from harm while on the sea.

The village received a tourist boost in 1994 as one of the supposed locales of the year's top movie, *Forrest Gump*. (The scenes set here, however, were actually shot elsewhere.)

✷ **Location:** Bayou La Batre is on Alabama 188, about 35 miles southwest of Mobile by way of Interstate 10. ✷ **Events:** Decorated boat parade, blessing of the fleet, Cajun seafood. ✷ **Contact:** Bayou La Batre Chamber of Commerce, St. Margaret's Church, P.O. Box 365, Bayou La Batre, AL 36509, (334) 824-4088.

DOTHAN

❖ National Peanut Festival: Week preceding the first weekend in November.

Settlers called this southeastern corner of Alabama the wiregrass, and they didn't mean it as a compliment. A bleak land of scrub and pines, it was passed over by farmers who coveted the dark, rich cotton-growing soil of the Black Belt, to the north.

So Dothan was a late-bloomer among Alabama cities. It wasn't incorporated until 1885, as the region concentrated on lumbering and the production of turpentine. For a while, no one could agree on the place's name, either. It was first called Dothen, probably after an individual's last name. But a local minister found a reference in Genesis to a place called Dothan, and residents agreed enthusiastically that a biblical citation was worth the shift of a vowel.

The change seemed to work miracles. Just as the pines gave out and the local economy appeared to be crippled, a few farmers decided to try their luck with the despised wiregrass soil. They found, to their astonishment, that it was surprisingly rich and would support a variety of crops, from melons to sweet potatoes. Chief among them was peanuts, now the agricultural mainstay of the wiregrass. This festival has been held annually since 1938 as a celebration of the nut's place in Dothan history.

✳ **Location:** Dothan is about 100 miles southeast of Montgomery, by way of U.S. 231. ✳ **Events:** Parade, livestock shows, beauty pageant, crafts fair. ✳ **Contact:** National Peanut Festival Offices, 1691 S.E. Ross Clark Circle, Dothan, AL 36301, (334) 793-4323.

FLORENCE

❖ W. C. Handy Music Festival: Begins first Sunday in August.

Before he knew about the Memphis Blues or the St. Louis Blues, W. C. Handy had his own version of the blues in his hometown of Florence. The son and grandson of ministers, he was expected to follow in their path, and when he saved some money and bought a guitar he was told to trade it in for a dictionary.

Florence, Alabama, native W. C. Handy became an important blues composer with hits such as "The St. Louis Blues." (Wide World Photos)

But Handy heard music all around him, not only in the church services, but on the Tennessee River docks and in the fields. It was old music that he took into his memory and never forgot. He was sent off to get a teaching degree but wound up playing the cornet with a brass band in Huntsville. Telling his parents in 1892 that he had landed a job as a musician at Chicago's Columbian Exposition, he failed to inform them that the fair had been delayed for a year. He spent the time wandering the South with a band, instead, and when the year was over he decided not to return home.

He eventually arrived in Memphis and became one of the top composers in America. An astute businessman, he was the first black songwriter to form his own publishing company; the success of "St. Louis Blues" made him a comfortable living for the rest of his long life. Musicologists have traced back several phrases in that song—especially the section that begins "Got the St. Louis Blues, just as blue as I can be"—to traditional chants that Handy would have heard in his father's church. So his early training in Florence never really left him.

Handy's birthplace has been restored and turned into a museum of his life and songs. An attached library has material relating to Handy for the serious researcher.

✳ **Location:** Florence is in the northwestern corner of the state, on U.S. 72, about 45 miles west of Interstate 85. ✳ **Events:** Jazz, blues and gospel concerts, street entertainment and dancing, food booths, parade, athletic events. ✳ **Contact:** W. C. Handy Music Festival Offices, P.O. Box 1827, Florence, AL 35361, (205) 766-7642.

MOBILE

◈ **Azalea Trail Festival:** Last two weeks in March and first week in April.

❋ **Mardi Gras:** The ten days before Shrove Tuesday.

The French left a deep imprint on Mobile. While they stayed only fifty-two years, from the founding of the city in 1711 until its cession to Great Britain, the names of Mobile's streets and squares, the look of its older neighborhoods, and the pace of its life are marked by the city's French beginnings. The French introduced Mardi Gras, the first celebration of its kind in North America. They also imported the first boatload of African slaves. And they brought azaleas, imported from the homeland in 1754.

It may be that the azaleas were their most enduring contribution. Mobile's Azalea Trail Festival, a late-winter tribute to the flowering of these plants, has been a civic tradition since 1930. A thirty-five-mile driving tour through the city is marked out with pink-bordered signs, leading visitors through streets that are aglow with color. The azaleas run from white to deep purple, with all stops on the spectrum in between. Some of the oldest plantings are now thirty feet high and others are dwarf varieties especially imported from Japan. Many private gardens that are closed for the rest of the year open their gates to visitors during this season.

A form of the Mobile Mardi Gras was first celebrated in the year the city was founded. But for 150 years this carnival was held on New Year's Eve, instead of the start of Lent. After its revival in 1869, following a suspension during the Civil War, it was moved to Shrove Tuesday.

Mobile's celebration may predate the one in New Orleans. But that Mardi Gras has become so much the symbol of carnival in America that it is almost impossible to consider any other. Still, in Mobile you will also find the floats and the secret societies, the revelry by night and the music in the street—only on a much smaller, and perhaps more manageable, scale than the Louisiana extravaganza.

✳ **Location:** Both events are citywide observances. ✳ **Events:** The Azalea Trail features house and garden tours, entertainment, concerts, art

Mobile revels in a Mardi Gras of its own. (Courtesy of Alan Whitman)

exhibits. Mardi Gras has 15 parades through the streets of downtown, dress balls, street entertainment. ✳ **Contact:** For Azalea Festival and Mardi Gras: Mobile Chamber of Commerce Visitor Center, 451 Government Blvd., Mobile, AL 36604, (334) 433-6951.

SELMA

◈ Old Cahawba Day: Second Saturday in May.

When Alabama was admitted to the Union in 1819, Cahawba was one of its largest and proudest cities. Strategically located on the Alabama River, near the geographic center of the state, it was a natural choice for Alabama's first capital.

The early organization of the state's government was carried out here, including the grant of a university to Tuscaloosa. The legislature sold land in the surrounding region to finance its operation, and that, too, added to the town's growth. One of the places founded in this manner was Selma, a few miles up the Alabama. By 1821 there was steamboat service to Mobile, connecting Cahawba to the Gulf of Mexico.

But in 1826, the river that brought prosperity to the town took it all away. Floods washed out the heart of Cahawba, and the state government could no longer function in what was left. The capital was moved to Tuscaloosa and, a few years later, the upstart town of Selma took the county seat. Cahawba still hung on as a cotton shipping port through the 1850s, but another flood and the Civil War finished it off. The town was abandoned after the war, and all that was left of it was ruins. The site has been turned into an archeological dig as scientists probe for clues about the life of Alabama's early settlers.

This festival was started in 1979 and tries to recreate the ambience of Cahawba's busiest era, with traditional music, games, and crafts.

✳ **Location:** Cahawba is on a county road, south of Alabama 22, about 15 miles southwest of Selma. ✳ **Events:** Bluegrass concerts, crafts show, barbecue, walking tours, contests, historical reenactment, storytelling, dancing. ✳ **Contact:** Cahawba Park, 9518 Cahawba Rd., Orrville, AL 36767, (334) 872-8058.

Arkansas

 Watermelon Festival: Third weekend in August, Thursday–Sunday.

Watermelon is the treat that is synonymous with summertime down South. The sight of the luscious green globes ripening in roadside patches is enough to touch off a feeding frenzy among Arkansas travelers. As with no other fruit, an entire folklore has grown up around these melons. Tales of young boys carrying off melons bigger than themselves are part of every southern storyteller's repertoire.

In Hope, these are more than just tall tales. When they grow watermelons here, they shoot for the record books. Long before the town became famous as the birthplace of President Bill Clinton, it was celebrated among melon fanciers as the place where the whoppers were grown.

Local tradition ascribes the concentration on big melons to an enterprising salesman who came through in the 1920s. He was pushing a new kind of seed and, to stir up interest among local farmers, he offered prizes for the biggest melons grown. When they started coming in at over 100 pounds, the first watermelon festival was held in 1926. By the end of the 1930s, a Hope farmer had produced a 195-pounder. But even this has been eclipsed by the wonder melons of recent years. The current champ, grown in 1985, checked in at a staggering 260 pounds.

Experts say that the super melons are better for publicity than they are for eating. The standard watermelon, at twenty-five to forty pounds, produces the juicier meat. But the humongous melons are part of the fun at this annual festival.

✳ **Location:** Hope is off Interstate 30, about 30 miles northeast of Texarkana. ✳ **Events:** Street entertainment and dances, seed-spitting

The sweet taste of summer is exalted in Hope's Watermelon Festival. *(Courtesy of Hope-Hempstead County Chamber of Commerce)*

competition, biggest melon weigh-in, games, music, crafts, 5K run, 3-on-3 basketball, tennis contest. ✳ **Contact:** Hope/Hempstead Chamber of Commerce, 108 West Third, Hope, AR 71801, (501) 777-3640.

MALVERN

 Brickfest: Last full weekend in June.

The town bills itself as the "Brick Capital of the World," and the wealth of fine brick structures in its business district indicates that Malvern is a place of its word. The fine clays of southwestern Arkansas have supported the brick industry here since the mid-nineteenth century.

When the first state capitol was built in Little Rock in 1833, the architect's plans specifically called for brick construction. That gave the industry a jump-start in the state, and the Old State House with its time-mellowed bricks is still considered the most splendid public monument in Arkansas. It was there, rather than in front of the present capitol, that Bill

Clinton chose to announce his presidential candidacy and to hold his first post-election press conference.

With the establishment of the Acme Brick Company, Malvern became the center of the industry. The festival celebrates this solid legacy.

✳ **Location:** Malvern is at the U.S. 270 exit of Interstate 30, about 20 miles east of Hot Springs. ✳ **Events:** Brick-tossing competition, best-dressed brick contest, baking competitions, turtle race, dog show, wheelbarrow race, brick car derby, arts and crafts. ✳ **Contact:** Malvern Chamber of Commerce, P.O. Box 266, Malvern, AR 72104, (501) 332-2721.

MENA

 Lum n' Abner Days: First weekend in June.

They went on the air in 1931, two friends from Mena, drawing on their hometown memories to create the Jot-'Em-Down country store and the fanciful world of Lum and Abner. The show remained on radio until 1954. Its low-key, southern style of humor made the program seem so real that thousands of listeners were convinced that there really was a Pine Ridge, Arkansas, where these two storekeepers played an endless game of checkers and greeted their backwoods customers.

Lum was actually Chester Lauck and Abner was Norris Goff. They grew up together in Mena, were fraternity brothers at the University of Arkansas, and returned to their hometown after graduation. Lauck managed an auto finance company, and Goff was a salesman. They also joined the local Lions Club theater group and were picked by the club to go on a statewide radio broadcast to raise money for flood relief.

They cooked up the Lum and Abner personas on the spot and stayed on the air for eight months. Then they were picked up by network radio from Chicago. The show was an immediate national hit, a 15-minute slice of Arkansas life, three nights a week. They were the voices of all the characters who wandered into the store, and they wrote their own scripts, never going for the big laughs but for the constant chuckles. Their Pine Ridge was very much like an early version of Andy Griffith's Mayberry, the fictitious North Carolina town created on television. But Lauck and Goff declined the chance to transfer their characters to television, feeling the visual medium just wouldn't work, and the show went off the air for good.

As a measure of Lum and Abner's popularity, the Arkansas town of Waters changed its name to Pine Ridge, so the place they created actually does show up on state maps today. Their real hometown remembers the pair with this celebration.

✳ **Location:** Mena is at the edge of the Ouachita Mountains, on U.S. 71, about 80 miles south of Fort Smith. The festival is held in the town's Boyd Stadium. ✳ **Events:** Arts fair, children's beauty pageant, quilt show, basketball competition. ✳ **Contact:** Mena Chamber of Commerce, 524 Sherwood, Mena, AR 71953, (501) 394-2912.

❖ While You're There:

The town was named for the last two syllables in the name of Queen Wilhelmina of the Netherlands. Many of the early settlers were of Dutch ancestry. A state park in the Ouachita Mountains is also named for the queen and contains the reconstruction of an inn built in 1896 in an effort to entice her for a visit. She passed up the chance, though. The Talimena scenic drive that leads there is one of the finest in the state.

STUTTGART

◈ World Championship Duck Calling Contest and Wings over the Prairie Festival: Wednesday through Saturday of Thanksgiving week.

While the rest of the country is stuffing itself with turkey, this town has ducks on its mind. Stuttgart is situated on the Mississippi River waterfowl flyway and is surrounded by low-lying rice fields. The combination makes it one of the top duck-hunting areas in the world.

The town is in the middle of the Grand Prairie, the lowlands that lie between the White and Arkansas Rivers. Early settlers insisted on planting the land in cotton, and when the soil was depleted it was used as pasture. Not until 1904 was rice successfully grown in the area. The crop was so well suited to the region that it transformed virtually the entire southeastern quadrant of the state. It is now the country's prime rice-growing area.

After the harvest, the fields are perfect feeding areas for ducks, and through November and December hunters inundate the place. This gathering of duck-callers has been held since 1935 and now is folded into the more extensive Wings over the Prairie Festival. The emphasis of this celebration is on the impact these annual waterfowl migrations have on local history and art.

✳ **Location:** Stuttgart is on U.S. 79, about 55 miles east of Little Rock.
✳ **Events:** Duck-calling competitions, decoy exhibition, Wings over the Prairie arts and crafts show, community dinners. ✳ **Contact:** Stuttgart Chamber of Commerce, P.O. Box 932, 507 South Main, Stuttgart, AR 72160, (501) 673-1602.

WASHINGTON

◈ **Jonquil Festival:** Second weekend in March.

It was once among the most important towns in Arkansas. The great and the restless came through Washington on their way to Texas in the years before the war for independence from Mexico. Davy Crockett and Jim Bowie were visitors, and Sam Houston lived here for a time. It was a U.S. military headquarters during the Mexican War, and when federal troops captured Little Rock in 1863, the government of Arkansas moved here for the rest of the Civil War.

But today Washington dreams of its past. Only a handful of people reside here and most of the area is a state historic park. Many of the buildings associated with these great events still stand: the blacksmith shop where the first Bowie knife supposedly was fashioned (although other states dispute this); the Confederate capitol; the Old Tavern that housed travelers on the Southwest Trail, which opened right after the Louisiana Purchase and was the main overland route from Tennessee to Texas.

Many of the settlers planted jonquils. The spring-blooming flower was a reminder of home and gentler places. Pioneer women often softened the reality of the harsh land they had come to with bright spring flowers. In many of the northern states it was lilacs. When the jonquils bloom in Washington, the town celebrates its history.

✳ **Location:** Washington is on Arkansas 4, about 6 miles north of Interstate 30 at the Hope exit. ✳ **Events:** Traditional music, crafts and artisan demonstrations, antique cars and steam engines, tours of historic buildings. ✳ **Contact:** Old Washington Historic State Park, P.O. Box 98, Washington, AR 71862, (501) 983-2684.

Florida

 Florida Citrus Festival: Last weekend in January to first weekend in February.

The orange groves of Florida have been a symbol of the state since Europeans first arrived. Today that symbol may be Disney World, instead, but the land the amusement complex occupies was once planted solidly in citrus. Much of it, in fact, lies in Orange County.

As early as 1579, Spanish mariner Don Pedro Menendez de Aviles described orange trees growing around St. Augustine (see below). The plant is not native to America, originating in the Far East. But it is thought that Christopher Columbus carried citrus seeds with him on one of his early voyages and introduced them in Haiti. They were planted on the American mainland in 1518, and by the time British plantation owners moved into Florida, in the mid-eighteenth century, they found citrus growing wild all across the peninsula.

The oldest grove in the state dates from the second Spanish occupation, early in the nineteenth century. The Don Phillipe grove, near Clearwater in Pinellas County, was where the Duncan grapefruit was developed. By the later years of the century, the center of the industry had moved into northern Florida. The killing freeze of 1894–95, however, wiped out citrus growth in that part of the state. In the next decade, farmers moved the industry into central Florida, where it has remained ever since.

These groves produce more than 60 percent of the country's citrus supply, although there was another southward shift following the severe freeze of 1985. But U.S. 27, between Leesburg and Avon Park, continues to be the Citrus Highway, passing through tens of thousands of acres of groves. Auburndale, situated right at the center of this belt, is the home of the Florida Citrus Showcase, where this annual festival is held.

✷ **Location:** Auburndale is west of U.S. 27, on U.S. 92, about midway between Orlando and Tampa. ✷ **Events:** Citrus food exhibits, entertainment, crafts fair, carnival rides. ✷ **Contact:** Florida Citrus Showcase, P.O. Box 2008, Auburndale, FL 33823, (813) 967-3175.

BRADENTON

◈ **Florida Heritage Festival:** Last weekend in March through April.

Hernan DeSoto probably landed in Florida near this place, at the mouth of the Manatee River, late in the spring of 1539. He was searching for wealth, power, and a mysterious river that sent fresh water for miles into the Gulf of Mexico. He found only the last, the Mississippi, and died a ruined and broken man on its banks three years after arriving here.

DeSoto was an ambitious adventurer who had fought with Pizarro in the conquest of Peru. But he wanted an expedition of his own to lead, a territory to pillage. That was the way to get ahead in sixteenth-century Spain. So he arranged a financially advantageous marriage, secured concessions in Florida from the king, and set off from Cuba on his great voyage of discovery.

DeSoto landed here only forty-seven years after the first landfall of Christopher Columbus in the Bahamas. Florida already had swallowed up the ambitions of three other Spanish adventurers, among them Ponce de Leon, who first explored the peninsula. But DeSoto had even grander dreams. He proposed to lead his expedition across the unknown lands beyond Florida and find the riches he knew were there.

So he actually wasted scant time in the area that would become Bradenton. Little more than six weeks after his landing, he was on the march, snaking his way through the narrow Indian paths through the swamps. Before his trip was over he had reached the Great Smoky Mountains and Mobile Bay, encountered dozens of Native American nations, and become the first European to see the Mississippi. He pushed on across Arkansas, still searching for the gold that would justify this endless trek and provide him with the honor and wealth he desperately needed to escape ruin. But he died on the banks of the Mississippi in 1542 and was sent to a secret grave in its waters. His expedition finally made it back to Cuba by way of Mexico.

While DeSoto's association with Bradenton is slight, the old conquistador figures as the centerpiece of this historic festival. The place is actually named for an early settler named Braden, whose home was a refuge from Indian attacks.

* **Location:** Bradenton is on the Gulf Coast, about 25 miles south of St. Petersburg by way of the Sunshine Skyway. * **Events:** Nighttime parade, costumed street entertainers, formal ball. * **Contact:** Hernan DeSoto Historical Society, 910 Third Ave. West, Bradenton, FL 34205, (813) 747-1998.

❖ While You're There:

The site of DeSoto's landing is west of the city, on Florida 64 and 564. It is now a National Memorial, containing a replica of his ship, displays that outline his journey, and exhibits of the armor and equipment his force would have used.

DE FUNIAK SPRINGS

◈ Florida Chautauqua Festival Day: Third Saturday in April.

The Chautauqua began on the shores of a New York lake and sent its mixture of culture, religious uplift, and entertainment to every corner of the country for the next fifty years. Next to the circus, the arrival of the Chautauqua meeting, with its troupe of famous lecturers and self-improvement experts, was the biggest thing to hit most American towns all year.

The institution was conceived as a summer training academy for Sunday school teachers in 1874. It won immediate acceptance, and only eleven years later a winter Chautauqua was established here. De Funiak Springs was named for a Louisville and Nashville Railroad official and built around a perfectly circular lake, with a natural spring at its center. It had been something of a college community, with Knox Hill Academy, the only institution of higher learning in northwestern Florida, opening here in 1848. But the coming of the Chautauqua put the town in the academic big leagues.

One early result was the construction of a library to serve the camp attendees. The Walton-De Funiak Library opened in 1887 and remains the state's oldest library in its original building, which measures just sixteen by twenty-four feet. The library houses many rare volumes and also contains a rare armor collection, left to it by the first director of the winter Chautauqua, Wallace Bruce.

The camp was discontinued in 1922 as a changing America lost its interest in education mixed with moral earnestness. But once each year the town tries to rekindle the spark of those meetings.

✱ **Location:** De Funiak Springs is on Interstate 10 at U.S. 331, 75 miles east of Pensacola. ✱ **Events:** Parade, street entertainment, concerts. ✱ **Contact:** Florida Chautauqua Festival, P.O. Box 847, De Funiak Springs, FL 32433.

DELRAY BEACH

❖ Hatsume Fair: Last weekend in February.

Henry Flagler was a rail tycoon who believed in planting prosperous communities wherever he put down tracks. Sometimes he accomplished that simply by persuading millionaires to make their winter homes there. But in 1905, he got the idea of importing a colony of Japanese farmers to work the land in South Florida.

Flagler had read about the industriousness of Japanese immigrants in the West. So he arranged for the Yamato Colony to be established here. While never growing into a sizeable part of the population, the Japanese newcomers did prosper, none more than a pineapple farmer named George Morikami.

A tireless worker and shrewd businessman, Morikami became very wealthy, while continuing to live in a house trailer on his fields. At his death, he bequeathed funds to establish a Japanese Cultural Center here. Different rooms are dedicated to various aspects of Japanese life, and the main building is surrounded by a traditional garden. Morikami Park is the site of this celebration of the Japanese presence in Florida.

✱ **Location:** Delray Beach is 17 miles south of West Palm Beach, along U.S. 1 and Interstate 95. From the Linton Boulevard exit of the freeway, continue to Jog Road, where the Morikami Park is located. ✱ **Events:** Japanese performing arts, crafts, foods, exhibits of miniature gardening techniques and exotic plants. ✱ **Contact:** Morikami Museum, 4000 Morikami Park Rd., Delray Beach, FL 33446, (407) 495-0233.

FORT MYERS

❖ Edison Festival of Light: First three weeks of February.

As Florida was developed in the 1880s and the extent of its semi-tropical vegetation became known, one thoughtful man was intrigued by the possibilities. Thomas A. Edison already was world-famous for his work on the electric light when he arrived in Fort Myers in 1885. His Menlo Park laboratory had been in operation for a decade in New Jersey, and from it had poured ideas that astonished the country.

Always on the lookout for new materials to investigate, Edison decided to establish a winter headquarters here. He came with the thought that the wild bamboo growing profusely in the area might provide a better filament for his light bulbs. He was wrong about that, but the work inspired him to set up a botanical laboratory to try to devise uses for other Florida growths.

Financed by his good friends Henry Ford, who built a home right next door to Edison, and Harvey Firestone, the inventor did extensive research on rubber substitutes. The matter was of grave concern to the automotive and tire magnates, as supplies of the material were located in politically unstable areas. Their fears were justified years later when the start of World War II cut off America from its usual rubber sources. Edison, eventually, planted 600 species of plants to work with in his research garden.

He lived long enough to witness the dedication of the Edison Memorial Bridge here in 1931. Four years after his death, lights were added to the structure after cartoonist Robert Ripley pointed out in his syndicated "Believe It Or Not" feature that the bridge named after the inventor of the electric light was not illuminated at night. Ft. Myers has not slighted its most famous resident since. It celebrates his years here with this festival, one of the most popular in the state, with approximately 450,000 people attending each year.

✳ **Location:** Throughout the city. The Edison Winter House and Gardens are on McGregor Boulevard, from the Colonial Boulevard exit of Interstate 75. ✳ **Events:** Parade of Light, athletic competitions, dances, sail regatta, street and stage entertainment. ✳ **Contact:** Edison Festival of Light organizers, 2210 Bay Street, Fort Meyers, FL 33901, (813) 334-2999.

Hemingway look-alikes celebrate the most famous reveler to frequent the saloons of Key West. (Courtesy of Andy Newman, Florida Keys T.D.C)

KEY WEST

❖ Hemingway Days: Third week in July.

This should more properly be called Hemingway Nights, since those were the hours in which the novelist's reputation here was made. A serious drinker and reveler, Hemingway's name is associated with virtually every Key West saloon that was standing during his residence here, from 1931 to 1940.

It is estimated, though, that something like 70 percent of his literary output was composed here, so maybe some of the tales of celebration are a bit exaggerated. It is known that a good part of *A Farewell to Arms* and most of *For Whom the Bell Tolls* were written in Key West.

Hemingway moved here originally to get away from things. Key West was a world's end sort of place in the 1930s, before the Overseas Highway was built from the mainland. He bought one of the town's finest old homes, built in 1851 and noted as the first in Key West to have running water and a fireplace.

He added a high wall for privacy, a swimming pool, and the cats whose descendants still, allegedly, roam the grounds. Hemingway moved to Havana in 1940 but held title to this house until his death in 1961. It was acquired by a local family and turned into a museum two years later. The entire community, no stranger to the world of arts, recalls its most colorful resident with this celebration.

✳ **Location:** The festival is community-wide. The Hemingway House is located at 907 Whitehead, in the middle of the Historic District. ✳ **Events:** Story-telling competitions, arm-wrestling contests, "Papa" Hemingway look-alike show, Caribbean-style street festival. ✳ **Contact:** Key West Festivals, P.O. Box 4045, Key West, FL 33041, (305) 294-4440; Key West Chamber of Commerce, (305) 294-2587.

LAKE CITY

❖ **Battle of Olustee Festival:** Weekend closest to February 20.

Northern troops captured most of the major ports in Florida, but the interior of the state remained in Confederate hands throughout the Civil War. While lightly populated, the state enthusiastically supported the Southern cause, sending more soldiers to fight for the Confederacy than it had voters.

Florida escaped the worst of the war's carnage. But this battle was the exception, the only one in the state fought with large troop concentrations. Gen. Truman Seymour of the Union forces was sent from Jacksonville against the capital of Tallahassee in February, 1864. He was to tear up railroads and cause as much damage as he could on the way, in the hopes of bringing Florida back to the Union.

But at Ocean Pond, or as it was more commonly called, Olustee, he was intercepted by 5,000 Confederate troops under Irish-born Gen. Joseph Finnegan. A master of entrenchment, Finnegan prepared his position well and forced a Northern retreat. Union soldiers had to fell trees along their escape route to forestall a cavalry pursuit. Total Union casualties in the battle were 709 dead and missing, while the Confederates lost 93 men. The Southern victory is reenacted each winter.

✳ **Location:** Olustee Battlefield is on U.S. 90, about 45 miles west of Jacksonville. ✳ **Events:** Battle reenactment by uniformed participants, art fair, crafts exhibits. ✳ **Contact:** Olustee State Historic Site, Stephen Foster State Cultural Center, P.O. Drawer G, White Springs, FL 32096, (904) 397-2733.

MIAMI BEACH

❖ **Art Deco Weekend:** Second weekend in January.

By an accident of history and taste, Miami Beach rose from the sandbars and mangrove swamps just as the Art Deco movement was at its peak of influence in the United States. Through the late 1920s and 1930s, as the southern end of the Beach was developed, imaginative architects competed with each other in devising the best way to adapt the trendy style to a resort setting.

But the caravan passed on. After World War II, the center of Miami Beach's resort life moved further north. Hotels that looked more like sweeping glass curtains rather than fanciful Deco gems were the rage. The style was out, and soon the Beach's southern portion was out, too. It became an aging community, in terms of both residents and structures. By the 1960s, Miami Beach itself was passe as new development moved up the coast to Ft. Lauderdale and beyond.

Then Deco returned. The nation's tastemakers rediscovered the joys of its streamlined, neon-trimmed buildings, and nowhere was there a greater concentration of them than South Beach. By the 1970s, this area was reinvigorated. Fading Deco hotels were overhauled to emphasize their heritage. Hip young residents moved in and created one of the Miami area's most diverse and attractive communities. Art galleries, restaurants, and coffee bars opened. A defunct resort had been saved by its architecture.

✳ **Location:** The Deco District is usually defined as bordered by the ocean to Lenox Court and 5th Street to 23rd Street. ✳ **Events:** Street entertainment, walking tours, parade of cars, popular music from the Deco period. ✳ **Contact:** Deco District Offices, Art Deco Weekend, P.O. Bin L, Miami Beach, FL 33119, (305) 672-2014.

ST. AUGUSTINE

 Spanish Night Watch: Third Saturday in June.

America's oldest city was ruled by Spain for 235 years, a mark it will not match as a part of the United States until the year 2056. Don Pedro Menendez de Aviles landed here on September 8, 1565, planting a fortified settlement to check French ambitions on this coastline. He named the place after the saint's day on which he first sighted the Florida coast.

Marchers process through the streets of the Spanish Quarter in the United States' oldest city, St. Augustine. (Courtesy of Committee for the Night Watch)

For the next two centuries St. Augustine was the base for Spanish raids against their enemies in Florida, Georgia, and the Carolinas. It was in turn sacked and pillaged by French and British raiders. They were sometimes pirates, like Francis Drake, who took the place in 1586. They were sometimes founders of colonies, like Georgia's James Oglethorpe, who warred ceaselessly with the Spanish presence to his south. Great Britain finally took St. Augustine over in 1762, with the remnant of the Spanish population fleeing to Cuba.

During the American Revolution St. Augustine was a Tory stronghold and a base for raids on American ports in the South. As part of the war's aftermath, Britain returned Florida to Spain and received the Bahamas in exchange. This Spanish twilight lasted thirty-eight years, until Florida's annexation by the United States. This was a policy ardently pursued by its first territorial governor, Andrew Jackson, who had first seen Florida during the War of 1812.

St. Augustine has richly restored the elements of its Hispanic roots. The city's Spanish Quarter, located along St. George Street south of Orange Street, recaptures the ambience of the eighteenth-century town in its narrow streets and tabby-shell houses. There are several festivals held during the course of the year in St. Augustine, but the most colorful, centered around the Spanish Quarter, is this one.

✻ **Location:** Along St. George Street. ✻ **Events:** Candlelit procession through the Spanish Quarter, with costumed entertainers and marchers. Spanish music, crafts. ✻ **Contact:** Night Watch Committee, P.O. Box 3043, St. Augustine, FL 32085, (904) 824-9550.

❖ While You're There:

Castillo de San Marcos is a massive Spanish fortress completed on the harbor in 1695. It is the finest example of a European military structure in North America and was used for years afterwards, by British and Americans, as a prison.

TALLAHASSEE

Natural Bridge Battle Reenactment: Sunday nearest March 6.

It has been called the last victory of the Confederacy, and while the significance of the Battle of Natural Bridge was only symbolic, Florida still feels it is worth a reenactment each year.

As 1865 began, Tallahassee was the last Southern capital east of the Mississippi to remain free of Union occupation. The final act of the Civil War was being played out in Virginia, as the Northern military coils wrapped ever more tightly around besieged Richmond. But Gen. John Newton still felt there was still something to be accomplished that March in Florida. He was based in Key West and believed that the best way to take Tallahassee was by a naval landing at the mouth of the St. Marks River, followed by a surprise overland strike.

It was a fine plan, but it was unworkable. The Union topographic maps of the land between the river mouth and the city were wrong. Much of this country was impenetrable swamp and no seagoing vessels could make it far enough up the river to be of use. Moreover, after the first landing of Northern troops, the weather turned bad and the reinforcements needed for the land attack on Tallahassee couldn't go ashore.

By the time Newton had landed all his troops, the surprise was gone. Southern forces knew they were there. They burned the bridges along the St. Marks and called out a combination of cadets from the West Florida Seminary and the home reserves of the Gadsden County Grays. Newton's attack became hopelessly bogged down in the swamps, and when he did discover the one possible river crossing, at Natural Bridge, the Confederates were massed and waiting for him.

Natural Bridge was not a rock formation but a place where the St. Marks went underground and could be crossed on land. But the well-entrenched Southerners routed Newton when he tried to advance. The Northerners suffered losses of 169 dead or missing soldiers before retreating to their ships, compared to a total of three dead for the South.

"If Georgia had stood up to Sherman the way Florida stood up to Newton, there would have been no March to the Sea," crowed Florida's governor, in a pardonable bit of hyperbole. But Tallahassee was proud of its heroic resistance and scheduled a ball a few weeks later to celebrate the battle. As the dancers gathered, a telegram was read announcing that Lee had surrendered at Appomattox. That ended the party, but the state still celebrates each year by reliving the fight.

✳ **Location:** Natural Bridge is 15 miles southeast of Tallahassee, following Florida 363 to Natural Bridge Road. ✳ **Events:** Costumed participants reenact the key events of this battle. ✳ **Contact:** Natural Bridge Historic Site, Florida State Park Service, 1022 DeSoto Park Dr., Tallahassee, FL 32301, (904) 922-6007.

T A M P A

❄ **Gasparilla Pirate Invasion:** First weekend in February through the end of the month.

Jose Gaspar assuredly left his mark on Florida's Gulf Coast. In a career that presumably extended over more than thirty years, the onetime Spanish naval captain who called himself "Little Gaspar" established a remarkable standard for piracy.

By his own account, a diary retrieved from the government archives in Madrid, Gasparilla sank thirty-six ships in eleven years after going bad in 1784. From his base on an island that is still known as Gasparilla, he raided with impunity across the Straits of Florida. But where historical truth departs from legend, no one can say with any accuracy.

Between the end of the American Revolution and its cession to the United States in 1821, Florida was a Spanish possession. Spain simply had too much territory to police in its American empire to bother much about this obscure corner. So a freebooter such as Gasparilla could have enjoyed a free hand in this area.

But much of the Gasparilla lore came down from a man named Juan Gomez, who claimed to be his brother-in-law. Gomez also claimed to be 117 years old when he died around 1900. He wove tales of Gasparilla capturing a Spanish princess and having her beheaded when she refused his advances. Captiva Island, which is just south of Gasparilla Island, got its name, according to these stories, because that is where the pirate stashed female prisoners. But it was known as Captiva on Spanish maps before his career even began. There are also discrepancies about the date of his death; by some accounts it happened in 1814 and by others not until Florida was under American rule in 1821. Both stories say that Gasparilla, who must have been quite a superannuated buccaneer by then, avoided capture by wrapping an anchor around his body and leaping into the sea.

Such an extended career exceeds the life expectancy of most pirates. It may well be that Gasparilla was a composite of several sea wolves who sailed these waters. Nonetheless, Tampa has adopted the roguish Jose Gaspar as its own. Every February since 1904 it has been fancifully captured by his "pirate" band, made up of some of Tampa's most prominent citizens. This pirate crew is the central part of the month-long festival, a beloved part of the city's life. Even Tampa's professional football team is known as the Buccaneers. Though Gasparilla's career may be a mite exaggerated, he is still a bigger-than-life personality in Tampa.

✳ **Location:** The celebration is citywide. ✳ **Events:** The highlight of the observance begins with the pirate landing along the bayfront. The crew arrives on a three-masted schooner flying the Jolly Roger. After they disembark, there is a parade along Bayshore Boulevard which features floral floats (one of which carries the "kidnapped" mayor) and marching bands. Balls, athletic competitions, and other parades continue for several weeks, with members of the pirate crew in attendance. Then the festival winds up with a street celebration in the old Cuban section of Tampa, Ybor City. ✳ **Contact:** Tampa Convention and Visitors Association, (800) 44-TAMPA.

TARPON SPRINGS

❄ Epiphany Celebration: January 6.

Fishermen from Greece's Dodecanese Islands first began arriving in Florida in 1849 when sponge beds were discovered in Key West. They were located in the shallows and the fishing was done with long hooks. But by the start of the twentieth century, these fields were almost played out. That's when new finds were made at Tarpon Springs.

This little coastal community had enjoyed some international notoriety in the 1880s when the duke of Sutherland deserted his wife in
Britain and took up with an American commoner on a plantation here.
The duke's close relative, Queen Victoria, was not amused and the press
had a fine time with the story.

Some small-scale sponge fishing also went on. But advances made
in deep sea diving equipment were enabling fishermen in the Greek
islands to work previously unharvested waters there. When deep water
beds were found in the Gulf of Mexico by John Cocoris in 1905, a rush of
Greek immigrants arrived with the new technology to take advantage of
the area's resources. The newcomers organized themselves much like
whalers, with voyages that would take several months and crews sharing
in the profits. Tarpon Springs became one of America's most distinctly
Greek communities, and the magnificent St. Nicholas Greek Orthodox
Cathedral was completed in 1943.

Just about then, however, an especially virulent attack of "red tide,"
tiny organisms that periodically invade the Gulf waters, destroyed most of
the sponge beds. The industry was almost wiped out, although it has
recovered to a small extent in recent years. Tarpon Springs retains a
strong Greek identity, though, which reaches a peak during the religious-
cultural celebration of the Epiphany, the Orthodox Christmas.

✳ **Location:** Tarpon Springs is on U.S. 19, about 30 miles north of St.
Petersburg. ✳ **Events:** Processional from the cathedral to the docks and
blessing of the waters. Divers search for a gold cross thrown into the
harbor by the Archbishop. Choir music, costumed children, religious services, civic ball. ✳ **Contact:** St. Nicholas Cathedral, P.O. Box 248,
Tarpon Springs, FL 34688-0248, (813) 937-3540.

❖ While You're There:

Spongeorama is located along the waterfront, on Dodecanese Boulevard. It is a re-creation of the Tarpon Springs of the sponge-fishing
heyday, along with a museum featuring old sponging equipment and a
factory.

WHITE SPRINGS

❖ The Jeanie Auditions: First full weekend in October.

There is absolutely no evidence that Stephen Collins Foster ever
visited Florida or laid eyes on the Suwannee River. Some diehards insist

The musical achievement of Stephen Foster inspires this competition among southern belles to be the next "Jeanie with the Light Brown Hair." (Courtesy of Stephen Foster State Folk Culture Center)

he did make a trip to Ellaville and visited a plantation there before writing the song that begins: "Way down upon the Suwannee River."

But the Pittsburgh-born Foster, who wrote "Old Folks at Home" for a minstrel show in 1851, apparently just liked the sound of the name "Suwannee." What that name means is not quite clear. There is also a Suwannee in Georgia. There it is thought to be of Cherokee origin, but that tribe says it has no clue to the word's possible meaning. They attribute the name to another Native American language group, the Muskogean. Almost no one still holds to the theory that the name is Spanish, San Juanee, meaning the Little St. John River. The river Foster chose eventually became a songwriting shorthand symbol for the South. Dozens of other lyricists, who also never came anywhere near the river, used it for almost a century after Foster and it became identified as a generic symbol of southern life.

Actually, as a musical depiction of plantation days, the Suwannee wasn't a bad choice. This was Florida's cotton and tobacco country in the years before the Civil War, and the traditional pillared plantation house was a familiar sight in this area. White Springs itself housed so many Georgia planters and their families, fleeing the effects of the war, that it was known as "Rebel Refuge." The Stephen Foster State Folk Culture Center here perpetuates his musical contributions to American life and also promotes Florida folk art, crafts, and music.

✳ **Location:** White Springs is just east of Interstate 75, from the south end of the Suwannee River bridge. ✳ **Events:** The Jeanie Auditions are named for Foster's wife, to whom he wrote "I Dream of Jeanie with the Light Brown Hair." There is a vocal competition among female singers from around the state, as well as folk art exhibits and a ball. ✴ **Contact:** Stephen Foster State Culture Center, P.O. Drawer G, White Springs, FL 32096, (904) 397-2733.

Georgia

❖ Georgia Peach festival: Second weekend in June.

Since this is the largest town in a county named Peach, you have a good clue about the top cash crop in this area. Fort Valley is the center of Georgia's peach belt, heartland of the state's best-known agricultural product.

Atlanta's main thoroughfare is named Peachtree, as are several other of the city's streets. But commercial cultivation of peaches didn't begin in the state until the 1870s, when a group of colonists from South Carolina moved to the nearby town of Marshallville. Descendants of a German group that originally had settled near Orangeburg, South Carolina, the newcomers were dedicated to finding a replacement crop for cotton, whose time had passed in this part of the South.

One of them, Lewis Rumph, was a talented horticulturist. He carried on continuous experimentation with Chinese clingstones, pollinating them from native peach varieties. He came up with the Georgia Belle in 1875, named for his sister-in-law. That same season, the 24-year-old Rumph produced his masterpiece, a copper-colored fruit with firm white meat that he named for his wife, Elberta.

The Elberta peach was perfect for shipping, and by 1880 Rumph was serving a national market from his orchards. Peaches from Georgia became so well-known in the next twenty-five years that they provided the nickname for baseball great Ty Cobb, who was born in the state and given the tag "Georgia Peach" by impressed northern sportswriters. It was also the basis for the immortal ragtime song hit, "Everything Is Peaches down in Georgia." The Elberta soon spread to other fields in the area. This is when the area around Fort Valley became so prosperous that it withdrew from Macon County to form a new one, named after the peach.

While its name suggests an early military outpost, Fort Valley was actually the result of a mistake at the Post Office headquarters in Washington. People here wanted to call the place Fox Valley, but it was misread by the bureaucrats and there has been a Fort here, instead, ever since.

✳ **Location:** Fort Valley is on Georgia 96, west of Interstate 75, about 25 miles south of Macon. ✳ **Events:** Parade, food booths with peach products, street entertainment. ✳ **Contact:** Georgia Peach Festival, P.O. Box 2001, Fort Valley, GA 31030, (912) 825-4002.

J A S P E R

❖ Marble Festival: First full weekend in October

You can see it in the Lincoln Memorial and the Corcoran Gallery in Washington. It is the material of the Field Museum of Natural History in Chicago, the Stock Exchange in New York, the state capitol buildings of Utah and Rhode Island.

Georgia marble from the quarries around Jasper is highly prized. The pinkish cast to the stone gives it a warmth and a subtlety of colors in sunlight that is almost unmatched in native stones. It is also durable and nearly free of impurities.

The vein was first worked in 1840, but it was not until after the Civil War, when the Georgia Marble Company was formed, that large-scale quarrying began. The vein is so deep that only a tiny portion of it has been removed. According to the company, there is enough stone there to satisfy the world's demand for marble for the next three millennia.

✳ **Location:** Jasper is located in the hills at the edge of the Chattahoochee National Forest, about 60 miles north of Atlanta by way of Interstate 575. ✳ **Events:** Sculpture competitions, craft shows, marble exhibits, entertainment, tours of the quarries. ✳ **Contact:** Jasper Chamber of Commerce, P.O. Box 327, Jasper, GA 30143, (706) 692-5600.

L U M P K I N

❖ Fair of 1850: First weekend in November.

Col. John West began assembling historic buildings and items from around Georgia in the 1930s. His idea was to recreate an antebellum community, showing what life was like in rural Georgia before the Civil War changed everything.

He found a cotton gin that predated Eli Whitney's, an old farmhouse, a kitchen shed from a plantation, and a cabin. West called the collection the Fair of 1850. It was originally located south of Atlanta, near the town of Jonesboro.

But when suburban sprawl overran the area, it was moved much further south, to Lumpkin, and incorporated into a larger living history complex called Westville. The collection has been augmented with other structures from around Georgia. There is a doctor's office, a blacksmith's shop, a potter's shop, and many others. Crafts people are on the property throughout the year, doing the work they would have performed in the decade before the Civil War.

✱ **Location:** Lumpkin is on U.S. 27, about 35 miles south of Columbus. ✱ **Events:** Re-creation of a country fair of 1850, with crafts, baking, and musical exhibitions recalling that era. ✱ **Contact:** Westville, P.O. Box 1850, Lumpkin, GA 31815, (912) 838-6310.

Kentucky

 Daniel Boone Festival: Second week in October.

He was the archetype of the American pioneer. Always seeking the better place: richer fields, thicker grass. Unable to bear the sight of a neighbor's chimney smoke. Others reached Kentucky before Daniel Boone, and those who came later may have contributed more to the building of the state. But the image of Boone leading the first group of western-bound families through the Cumberland Gap is the image that endures.

He was born in Pennsylvania among Quakers and later lived in North Carolina. But the men who grew to adulthood in the 1760s were a restless generation. Something called them beyond the Appalachians, to land that Britain had placed off-limits. It may have been that very injunction that made Kentucky so irresistible to them.

Boone first came through the Gap in 1769. He remained for two years, hunting and exploring with his brother, Squire, and determining that these were the richest lands he had ever seen. He went back East for his family in 1771, then at the age of thirty-seven returned to Kentucky to stay.

He was not the first white visitor by any means. Nineteen years before Boone arrived in the area, Dr. Thomas Walker, a surveyor for a Virginia land company, built a cabin in a clearing near the site of Barbourville. It was Walker who named the area's major river the Cumberland, in honor of the son of King George II. The name also became attached to the highest mountain range in eastern Kentucky and to the pass through the Appalachians.

Boone's Trace ran north from the Gap for fifty miles. Boone laid it out along a much older trail, the Warriors Road, which connected the

Shawnee and Cherokee lands. And long before them, the buffalo had plowed the track through the hills. Benjamin Logan followed Boone in 1779 and extended the primitive route to Louisville. That trail is what became known as the Wilderness Road, one of the great early highways to the West. After the Revolution, the land-hungry poured across the Gap and onto this road at the rate of 20,000 a year. By 1792, only twenty-one years after Boone first brought his family to a wilderness, there were enough people in Kentucky for it to become a state.

Barbourville grew up along the Wilderness Road, and it recalls the pioneer heritage every fall with this tribute to the spirit of Boone.

✳ **Location:** Barbourville is on U.S. 25E (Boone's Trace), about 31 miles northwest of the Cumberland Gap. ✳ **Events:** Pioneer village, long rifle shoot-out, square dancing, traditional music, pioneer crafts, quilt show, parade. ✳ **Contact:** Daniel Boone Festival, Barbourville Chamber of Commerce, P.O. Box 999, Barbourville, KY 40906, (606) 546-4300.

✥ While You're There:

A replica of the cabin built by Dr. Walker in 1750 stands in a state historic site, 6 miles southwest of Barbourville on Kentucky 459.

BEREA

◈ Kentucky Guild of Artists and Craftsmen Fair:

Weekend with the third Saturday in May and weekend with the second Saturday in October.

Berea College is an institution that started as an experiment in racial integration and developed, instead, into a showcase of Appalachian crafts. The college was the concept of three progressive Kentuckians who felt the best way to fight slavery was to educate blacks and whites together. Cassius Clay, John Fee, and John Rogers endowed the school in 1855, and it became the first college in America to be integrated as a matter of policy.

Although that policy managed to work when Kentucky was a slave state, it couldn't survive Jim Crow. The state legislature made the arrangement illegal in 1904, and the black portion of the college was moved to Louisville. But the part that stayed at Berea developed a new educational mission. It began serving the families of the Cumberland region, the poorest section of Kentucky.

The people of the Cumberland region of Kentucky display the crafts that have become a central part of their community. (Courtesy of Kentucky Guild of Artists and Craftsmen)

Most of the students who enrolled here could not afford to pay for tuition or board. So Berea established the first work-study program in the country, enabling the children of poverty to get an education by holding down a campus job. Among the jobs that developed at Berea were those in its crafts shops. The college found that its students brought rare skills with them, the ability to work in traditional crafts that were being lost in the machine age. Eventually, the entire community became a crafts center, one of the biggest in the South. This festival celebrates Berea's heritage and the work of its current crop of students.

✳ **Location:** Berea is on Interstate 75, about 35 miles south of Lexington. ✳ **Events:** Traditional art, crafts, dances, and singing from the Cumberlands. ✳ **Contact:** Kentucky Guild of Artists and Craftsmen, P.O. Box 291, Berea, KY 40403-0291, (606) 986-3192; Berea Tourist Bureau, (800) 598-5263.

FORT KNOX

❖ The Patton Museum Fourth of July Demonstration: July 4.

This is where the gold is buried, but it is also where the tanks got rolling. Fort Knox was purchased by the government as a World War I training base and named after the first secretary of war, Henry Knox. It is most famous as the home of the U.S. Gold Bullion Depository, a 100-foot-square, bombproof treasure house, built in 1937. "All the gold in Fort Knox" has entered the language as a phrase describing incalculable riches.

But its military importance was established four years earlier when it became the home of the armored cavalry. This is where the capabilities of tank warfare were worked out. The armored museum here honors the general who best realized that, George S. Patton, Jr.

One of the most controversial figures of World War II, Patton, nonetheless, was a brilliant armored tactician. His use of tanks in the North African campaign, and then across France and Germany in 1944 and 1945, is still studied as a model of mobility and concentrated power. Many of his personal memorabilia are displayed here, as is the car in which he was killed shortly after the end of the war. There are also exhibits on America's other wars, including the devastating use of armor in the Persian Gulf campaign of 1991.

✳ **Location:** Fort Knox is on U.S. 31W, about 35 miles southwest of Louisville. The Patton Museum is housed in Building 4554. ✳ **Events:** World War II Battle reenactment using authentic equipment and uniformed troops. ✳ **Contact:** Patton Museum, P.O. Box 208, Fort Knox, KY 40121, (502) 624-3812.

LOUISVILLE

◆ Kentucky Derby Festival: The two weeks preceding the first Saturday in May.

❀ Strictly Bluegrass Music Festival: Weekend after Labor Day.

Bluegrass means two things in Kentucky. It is, first of all, the lush pastureland where thoroughbreds grow to greatness. And it is the traditional music of the hills, played in a style that is unmistakably Kentucky-grown. Both the racing and the musical traditions are celebrated in Louisville.

The men who settled Kentucky were horse-fanciers, mostly from Virginia and North Carolina. They saw immediately that the meadows of the central part of the state were a horseman's paradise. Not only the grass itself (which is blue only in May when it blossoms) but the nutrients in the soil make the area ideal for raising horses. One of the first suggestions made by Daniel Boone to the territorial legislature was a government effort to improve the breed.

Thoroughbreds, which were first produced in England around 1750, were introduced in America before the Revolutionary War. By the Civil War, Kentucky was nationally famous for the quality of its stock. It suffered for the reputation as its barns were raided endlessly by both sides in the conflict. But the postwar recovery did have one unanticipated benefit. Kentuckians went to England to study breeding methods in order to replenish their own stock. While in the country, they attended the Epsom Derby, the greatest horse race in the world. Feeling that Kentucky should have an event to match, they organized the first Kentucky Derby, held in Louisville, in 1875.

The race was regarded as little more than a regional event for its first twenty-five years. But when a master publicist, Matt Winn, took over management of Churchill Downs, it soon became a national phenomenon. Winn encouraged New York sportswriters to attend, and even paid their travel expenses, while showering them with thick Kentucky nostalgia and juleps. The stories they produced gave the Derby an aura, and the horses that entered its winner's circle went on to national prominence.

But Winn's big payoff came in 1915 when Regret, a filly owned by millionaire New York sportsman Harry Payne Whitney, came home a winner. Whitney's joy was unbounded and he called it "the greatest race in the world." From then on, the country pretty much agreed and Derby Day in Louisville grew into a media extravaganza. The weeks leading up to the big race have become a Kentucky original, with celebrations going on throughout the city. The race is now the first event in horseracing's Triple Crown, followed by the Preakness and Belmont Stakes races.

The music that became known as bluegrass is of a more recent origin. In 1938, the same year that Eddie Arcaro had his first Derby winner with Lawrin, a Kentucky musician, Bill Monroe, decided to go on the road with his own band. He was after a certain sound, traditional but new. Monroe did not like the changes coming over the music, and he especially disapproved of the expanded role for guitars. Formerly a rhythm instrument, guitars were now carrying the melody. That wasn't right to Monroe's ear, especially since he was a mandolin player. So he brought the mandolin, banjo, and fiddle out front to play lead, and relegated the guitars to handling the beat.

The style was called bluegrass, but the sound took decades to break through to a mass audience. Only connoisseurs of "real" country music took to it at first. But by the 1960s an entire new generation of bluegrass musicians had emerged, all influenced by Monroe, and the style became accepted as the true sound of country music. Monroe's trademark "Blue Moon of Kentucky" is its anthem, and each year Louisville celebrates it with the biggest musical gathering of its kind.

✳ **Location:** The Derby Festival is citywide. The Bluegrass Festival is held in Iroquois Park, which can be found by taking I-264 to exit 9 and following the road south for 2 miles. ✳ **Events:** For the Derby there is "the world's largest fireworks show," a parade, a steamboat race on the Ohio River, a balloon race, concerts, entertainment, and the running of the Derby at Churchill Downs. The Bluegrass Festival features free concerts and dancing along the river, as well as arts and crafts. ✳ **Contact:** Kentucky Derby Festival, 137 W. Muhammad Ali Blvd., Louisville, KY 40202, (800) 928-FEST. Strictly Bluegrass Festival, 1907 Neville Dr., Louisville, KY 40216, (502) 488-9107 or (502) 447-8657.

OWENSBORO

◊ **International Bar-B-Q Festival:** Second full weekend in May.

There are many schools of thought about barbecue. In North Carolina, they'll tell you anything other than pork is preposterous. In Texas, however, they claim that beef is the only bona fide barbecue there is.

Western Kentucky, however, is a little different. This is the center of the mutton belt, perhaps the last place in America where sheep are regarded as a prime delicacy. Moreover, Owensboro is also the home of burgoo. This is a traditional Kentucky dish, a stew virtually unknown in other parts of the country. Originally, say the experts, it was made with squirrel meat. But that is no longer done. Now the primary ingredients are chicken, beef, and mutton, along with corn, lima beans, potatoes, tomatoes, and a medley of spices to suit each individual cook.

This festival is one of the few times mutton and burgoo are the major culinary attractions. They may not be to every taste, but they are a part of Owensboro's heritage.

✳ **Location:** Owensboro is the largest city in western Kentucky, about 45 miles southeast of Evansville, Indiana. ✳ **Events:** Cooking competitions, pie-eating contest, old-time fiddling, crafts fair, dancing, keg toss.

Mutton is the meat of choice during the International Bar-B-Q Festival in Owensboro. (Courtesy of Dan Dry & Assoc./International Bar-B-Q Festival)

✻ **Contact:** International Bar-B-Q Festival, P.O. Box 434, Owensboro, KY 42302, (502) 926-6938.

RUSSELLVILLE

◈ Tobacco Festival and Jesse James Robbery Reenactment: Second week in October.

This town, with its surrounding tobacco plantations, was a center of secessionist sentiment during the Civil War. Confederate sympathizers met here in 1861, declared Kentucky out of the Union, and approved the move of the capital to Bowling Green. No one paid any attention to them, though, and Kentucky remained in the United States, albeit deeply divided, for the war's duration.

Maybe it was these Southern sympathies that drew a group of former rebels to Russellville on May 20, 1868. Disguised as cattle buyers, the strangers entered the Long and Norton Bank and tried to pass a counterfeit bill. When the teller objected, Cole Younger pulled a gun on him, and when the teller tried to run, Jesse James creased his scalp with a bullet. After wounding another man, the bandits galloped off, with half the town blazing away and chasing after them. But the trail was lost, and so were the bank's funds.

This was the easternmost bank robbery pulled by the notorious James Gang. The former Confederate raiders previously had confined their activities to the Missouri area. But this job, which netted them $9,000, also brought them to the attention of the Pinkerton Detective Agency. Hired by a syndicate of bankers, the Pinkertons pursued the gang relentlessly for the rest of their careers. They even managed to catch one participant in the Russellville holdup, George Shepherd, who was imprisoned for two years. But the others escaped. Realizing that they might have gone too far, though, they waited eighteen months before resuming their criminal careers.

Northfield, Minnesota (see entry), also celebrates a James Gang robbery, one that ended with the capture of most of its members. They got away in Russellville, but the town felt it gave a good account of itself in the fight and is willing to celebrate.

✳ **Location:** Russellville is on U.S. 68, about 25 miles west of Bowling Green. ✳ **Events:** Bank robbery reenactment, tobacco displays, antiques show, old-time bicycle rides, entertainment, parade. ✳ **Contact:** Russellville Chamber of Commerce, 116 South Main St., Russellville, KY 42276, (502) 726-2206.

SOUTH UNION

 ### Shaker Festival: In June, date varies.

Their official title was the United Society of Believers in Christ's Second Coming. But their religious dances, during which bodily appendages were shaken vigorously, made the greatest impression on outsiders and earned them their most durable name, Shakers. They believed that bodily agitation led to the gift of prophecy.

The Shakers originated in France but enjoyed their greatest growth in England after 1758. A Manchester woman, Mother Ann Lee, converted then and promptly declared herself God the Mother. She also declared that sex would henceforth be unnecessary because the world would soon be coming to an end and further propagation was a waste of time.

A broom-making demonstration draws the interest of visitors to the Shaker Festival. *(Courtesy of Shaker Museum at South Union)*

Her message appealed to some of the more radical elements among the Quakers and Baptists, despite pronouncements that declared: "A consummated marriage is a covenant with a death and an agreement with hell." Mother Ann moved to America with her followers in 1774 and settled in upstate New York. After her death in 1784, the Shakers decided to move into several colonies separate from the rest of the world.

South Union was formed in 1807 and it endured for 115 years, despite the group's belief in celibacy and the requirement to constantly recruit new members. When the last nine Shakers here returned to New York, the property was sold at auction. As in other Shaker communities, the South Union group was industrious and artful. It owned 6,000 acres in the vicinity, planted orchards, and is credited with introducing crop rotation to Kentucky.

The Shaker Museum, housed in the colony's Centre House, built in 1824, contains exhibits of typical crafts and the life of the colony here.

* **Location:** South Union is on U.S. 68, about 10 miles west of Bowling Green * **Events:** Traditional Shaker meals and music, crafts demonstrations, tours of the colony. * **Contact:** Shaker Museum., P.O. Box 30, South Union, KY 42283, (502) 542-4167.

Louisiana

BOSSIER CITY AND SHREVEPORT

◈ Holiday in Dixie: In April, dates vary.

On April 11, 1803, the American minister to France, Robert Livingston, met with officials in Paris, expecting to discuss an offer by the United States to buy landing rights in New Orleans. The economy of the West depended on continuation of those rights. They had been suspended during the transfer of the area from Spain to France and that was a major concern to President Thomas Jefferson. Instead, to the utter astonishment of Livingston, the French government wanted to sell the entire Louisiana Territory. He had been authorized to spend $10 million on the port and now the French were offering territory that would double the size of the United States for $15 million.

Livingston did not quibble, and a treaty was signed on April 30. "This is the noblest work of our whole lives," he said on the occasion. The boundaries of this territory, however, were left purposely vague. "You must take it as we received it," shrugged the French ministers. But, eventually, the map's blank spaces were filled in. The Louisiana Purchase transformed the United States overnight from one of several countries claiming the western lands into the master of a continent.

The Purchase was popular throughout the nation, giving America a proud empire. It led directly to Jefferson's overwhelming election to a second term. When Lewis and Clark returned from their voyage of exploration to these new lands in 1806, it fired the nation's imagination like few events in its history. This festival, which was first celebrated in 1949, is a celebration of the Purchase. Although Shreveport didn't even exist when it was signed, the access the Purchase gave the United States to the Red

River led directly to the founding of this town, and a few hundred others all across the West.

✻ **Location:** The festival goes on across Shreveport and in neighboring Bossier City. ✻ **Events:** Parades, street dancing, art exhibits, balls, air show. ✻ **Contact:** Holiday in Dixie Office, P.O. Box 44067, Shreveport, LA 71134-4067, (318) 865-5555.

BREAUX BRIDGE

 Crawfish Festival: First weekend in May.

Agricole Breaux put up a toll-free bridge across Bayou Teche in the 1870s and a grateful populace decided to name their town after him. But it is in the waters under the bridge that the greatest treat in Cajun country is found.

The crawfish is the signature dish of Louisiana. Regarded as a rather disgusting creature in the rest of the country, the mud-crawling crawfish is transformed by the wizardry of Cajun cuisine. The state's Office of Tourism even uses it as a visual symbol for the entire Cajun area. A bucket of hardshells, a bottle of Tabasco sauce from Avery Island, some crusty white bread, and a beer and everything is right with the world in Louisiana.

Crawfish can get a bit messy because when they are boiled in the shells, only the tail is eaten. The rest is disposed of. The tasty little crustaceans are found throughout the state but it is in the parishes of south central Louisiana that they reach their highest degree of refinement. Beaux Bridge is located almost at the geographic heart of crawfish country.

Louisianans also fancy the soft-shelled variety. These are taken when a natural molting process occurs every thirty to forty days in the life cycle. Since the crawfish doesn't eat for a few days before molting, it is also a cleaner way of enjoying them. The growing popularity of Cajun cooking in the 1980s has turned crawfish into a national delicacy and brought visitors pouring in for this festival.

✻ **Location:** Breaux Bridge is just south of Interstate 10, about 12 miles east of Lafayette. ✻ **Events:** Crawfish dinners, Cajun music, dancing, crafts. ✻ **Contact:** Crawfish Festival Association, P.O. Box 25, Beaux Bridge, LA 70517, (318) 332-6655.

CROWLEY

❖ **International Rice Festival:** Third full weekend in October.

Pat Crowley was a section foreman on the Southern Pacific Railroad as it extended its tracks west from Lafayette in the 1880s. Residents of this area persuaded Crowley that if he could contrive to send the tracks on a very slight jog through the middle of their town they would name the place for him. He did and the town kept its promise.

It is estimated that one-quarter of all the rice grown in the United States comes from fields within fifty miles of this seat of Acadia Parish. The Cajun farmers had to be convinced to try this crop, though. While the low-lying, watery prairies of this part of Louisiana are ideal for growing rice, the farmers laid out their farms along the streams, instead. When they were persuaded to switch to rice, which involves flooding the fields for about three months, the local economy took off.

Crowley today is a town in which almost every aspect of life is related to rice. There are several mills in the town itself and an experimental station on the western outskirts. Both of them may be visited with advance arrangements through the local chamber of commerce.

✳ **Location:** Crowley is off Interstate 10, about 25 miles west of Lafayette. ✳ **Events:** Parades, traditional music, street dancing, entertainment. ✳ **Contact:** International Rice Festival, P.O. Box 1900, Crowley, LA 70527, (318) 783-3067.

LAKE CHARLES

◆ **Contraband Days:** First two weekends in May.

In all of Louisiana's swashbuckling history there is no one who cut a figure quite like Jean Lafitte. A pirate and patriot, he preyed on ships along the Gulf Coast from Galveston to the bayou country. But when the British offered him a fortune to fight with them in the planned attack on New Orleans in 1815, Lafitte informed the American authorities. The Americans, however, marched on Lafitte's hideaway and, when he refused to fire on them, they destroyed it. Undeterred, Lafitte asked Gen. Andrew Jackson to be allowed to fight by his side in the defense of the city, in return for a pardon for him and his men. Jackson assented and by all accounts the pirates fought valiantly. Then they kept their bargain and sailed off to Texas to do their plundering there.

Lafitte has been in his grave since around 1825, although that is only a guess because the exact date and circumstances of his demise remain a mystery. But there is hardly a place in Louisiana that isn't touched by his legend. In the French Quarter of New Orleans, there is a shop in which he supposedly worked in disguise in order to gather information and sell his booty. In Destrehan, on the Mississippi, he haunts an old plantation. In his old hangouts near Barataria Bay (the word is Spanish and means deception, referring to the mistaken belief of many sailors that it was the mouth of the Mississippi), the Jean Lafitte National Historical Park has been established by the federal government.

Lake Charles claims Lafitte for its own in this festival. The town founder's real name was Carlos Salia, a man of Spanish ancestry who came from New Orleans. But when he came to the bayous he changed his name to Charles Sallier, and that gave both the town and its lake their name in 1803. Sallier allegedly knew Lafitte well, and when the pirate was being pursued in this area he sank a schooner near Sallier's house, after first removing the treasure and burying it in the area. The treasure has never been found, but the adjacent bayou was known for many years as Contraband.

✳ **Location:** This is a citywide celebration. ✳ **Events:** Sail and power-boat races, parades, carnival, street dances, food booths, arm wrestling contest, concerts, bike tour, 5-mile run. ✳ **Contact:** Contraband Days, P.O. Box 679, Lake Charles, LA 70602, (318) 436-5508.

MANSFIELD

 Battle of Pleasant Hill Reenactment: First weekend in April.

The Red River campaign of 1864 was planned as a quick strike to put down the last Confederate resistance in Louisiana. But it accomplished nothing and ruined the career of the Union general who turned it into a near farce.

President Lincoln himself had approved the idea of reattaching Louisiana to the Union before moving on to the final campaigns in the East. Unfortunately, Gen. Nathaniel P. Banks had other priorities. He was busy planning the ceremonies marking the return of civil government to New Orleans. As he explained to an impatient Gen. William Sherman, this celebration would include a performance by the massed bands of his army, with church bells ringing and cannons being fired by electricity.

Sherman felt such celebrations were entirely inappropriate with the war still raging and urged Banks to get going, so he could be back in time for the forthcoming assault on Mobile. But Banks got started weeks later than planned and then once past Alexandria became overly cautious, although outnumbering Confederate forces two-to-one.

His opponent, Gen. Richard Taylor, skillfully withdrew until he came to a place that could be defended to advantage. At Sabine Cross-roads, he turned on Banks and took the offensive, forcing the Northern troops to retreat. They regrouped at Pleasant Hill on April 9 and Taylor went at them again. While suffering greater casualties, the Confederates knocked the will to fight out of Banks, who began retreating to the east. Taylor wanted to go after him, but was restrained because it was felt the defense of Shreveport was his most important priority.

The battle was the last major engagement fought on Louisiana soil, and Shreveport remained in Confederate hands for the rest of the war. Banks returned to New Orleans too late to assist at Mobile. There were reports that he was most intent during the campaign in obtaining cotton stores to send to the mills in his home state of Massachusetts. A disgusted Adm. David Porter, who had to proceed to Mobile without Banks's support, said the campaign was "discreditable to a boy nine years of age." When asked what it had been supposed to accomplish, Porter replied: "I never understood."

Nonetheless, Louisiana commemorates the Southern victory with this annual battle reenactment.

✳ **Location:** Pleasant Hill is east from Mansfield on Louisiana 175, about 35 miles south of Shreveport. ✳ **Events:** Parade, beauty pageant, Confederate ball, battle reenactment. ✳ **Contact:** Mansfield Chamber of Commerce, P.O. Box 591, Mansfield, LA 71052, (318) 872-1310.

MORGAN CITY

 ## Shrimp and Petroleum Festival: Labor Day weekend.

This is a town that clings to its traditions, even when the economic realities of the twentieth century changed them completely. Morgan City sits on the Atchafalaya River, a mile and a half wide here on its way to the Gulf of Mexico. It is, in fact, the closest Louisiana port of any size to the open sea waters.

The blessing of the fleet in Morgan City includes both the shrimp boats and the petroleum vessels. (Courtesy of Karla F. Byron, Portrait Gallery)

As a result, Morgan City, named for a railroad president, has always drawn its livelihood from the Gulf. For many years, that was as a major fishing port and seafood processing center. Jumbo shrimp and oysters were its staples, and there was also a major muskrat fur industry based in the nearby bayous.

But everything changed in 1947. That's when Louisiana's first big offshore oil deposits came in. Morgan City suddenly became an oil boomtown. It remains the state's top petroleum port and oil dwarfs everything else in economic importance. But what sounds like a more likely festival theme to attract visitors—gloppy oil or sizzling shrimp? Morgan City pairs up this unlikely combination in an annual celebration of past and present.

✳ **Location:** Morgan City is on U.S. 90, about 65 miles southeast of Lafayette. ✳ **Events:** Coronation of the festival queen and her court, street and water parade, fireworks, crafts fair, blessing of the shrimp and oil fleet, music, antique show, cajun culinary carnival, shrimp cookoff. ✳ **Contact:** Shrimp and Petroleum Festival, P.O. Box 103, Morgan City, LA 70381, (504) 385-0703.

NEW IBERIA

◈ **Cajun Fun Festival:** Second weekend in March.

The name of the town is Latin for Spain. But make no mistake. In New Iberia, you are in French-speaking Cajun country. But when the Cajuns first arrived in this area from Canada in 1779 they were joined briefly by a group of Spanish colonists. The Spaniards got to name the place and called it Nueva Iberia, which was later Anglicized. Other than that, New Iberia has remained deeply Cajun throughout the years and is the site of a top celebration of that unique culture.

Cajun is short for Acadian. These were the French Catholics who were expelled from Nova Scotia when the British captured that colony during the French and Indian War. In the years following 1760, some of them slipped into what is now Maine. But many others were left homeless with nowhere to go.

Louisiana at that time was undergoing an unpopular transfer from French to Spanish rule. So local residents were sympathetic to the plight of their countrymen. The Acadians were encouraged to settle on the lightly-settled lowlands west of New Orleans.

There they have remained for two centuries, developing a style of cooking, an original music, a lilt of speech that only now is becoming widely appreciated throughout the United States. This festival features all of that.

✳ **Location:** New Iberia is on U.S. 90, about 25 miles southwest of Lafayette. The festival is held on the grounds of New Iberia Catholic High School. ✳ **Events:** Cajun food, dancing, music, crafts. ✳ **Contact:** New Iberia Catholic High School, 1301 DeLasalle Dr., New Iberia, LA 70560, (318) 364-5116.

NEW ORLEANS

 Jazz Festival: Last weekend in April to first weekend in May.

Jazz has many homes. Kansas City, Chicago, New York, San Francisco—each claims its own distinctive style of this musical form. But jazz has only one birthplace and that, indisputably, is New Orleans.

Some musical scholars trace its origins back to slave gatherings in the city's Congo Square, where rhythmic dances were a local attraction before the Civil War. Others find its roots in Storyville, the former red-light district, where black musicians performed before a mainly white clientele. There were the "spasm" bands on the city streets, borrowing a musical phrase from the blues, another from the church, another from some old French or Spanish tune that was familiar to anyone from New Orleans.

Sometime around 1900 this new music started rolling out of the city's black neighborhoods. It was first known as jass, which was the slang term for the sex act. Legendary figures such as Bunk Johnson and Jelly Roll Morton and King Oliver were playing it, in the nightclubs and on the riverboats. Then in 1917 two local groups—The New Orleans Rhythm Kings and the Original Dixieland Jass Band—signed recording contracts and the music suddenly spilled out to the rest of the world.

Calling for a high degree of improvisational skill within a structured framework, jazz demanded discipline and creativity, genius in a mold. It changed from Dixie to swing to bop and swept the world as America's most distinct sound. But it almost died in the city that invented it. By the late 1950s, traditional jazz musicians could not get work here and the music they had played in their youth was seldom heard. But the establishment of Preservation Hall in the French Quarter returned the music to its roots. Old-timers everyone had forgotten suddenly found themselves revered as guardians of a precious legacy, which has now been passed on to another generation's stewardship.

Every variety of jazz is heard in this festival, from the home-grown original to some of the latest sounds from deep space. But it all came first from the streets of this city.

✳ **Location:** Many concerts are held at the Fair Grounds Racetrack, on Gentilly Boulevard, but the music goes on citywide. ✳ **Events:** Performances of every kind of jazz on 10 stages at the Fair Grounds; concerts are also held on riverboats and in nightclubs. New Orleans-style food and crafts in booths at the Fair Grounds. ✳ **Contact:** Jazz Festival Office, P.O. Box 53407, New Orleans, LA 70153-3407, (504) 522-4786.

❖ **Mardi Gras:** The two weeks before Shrove Tuesday.

Mardi Gras already was established for a century in Mobile (see Alabama) when a group of high-spirited youths from New Orleans returned home from a stay in France in 1820, determined to organize a pre-Lenten celebration in their town. That was the seed that erupted into America's most spectacular festival—the one that draws the biggest crowds, induces the wildest behavior, possesses the most colorful history, and summons up the most vivid example of carnival abandon on the continent. Not even Super Bowl tickets are as hard to come by as admittance to one of the masked balls of a major Mardi Gras krewe. A krewe is an organization, whose membership is secret, that exists to participate in Mardi Gras. Even staid businessmen join the crowds on the curbs to holler "Hey, mister, throw me somethin'" as the bead-tossing riders on their splendidly adorned floats roll through the narrow streets of the Vieux Carre.

The oldest of the Mardi Gras organizations, the Mystic Krewe of Comus, dates back to 1857. But not until after the Civil War, in 1872, did the celebration assume anything like its present form. According to the story, that was the season that a Russian grand duke came to town, in

One of the most spectacular festivals in the country, the traditions surrounding Mardi Gras in New Orleans date back to the 1800s. (Archive Photos, Inc.)

romantic pursuit of actress Lydia Thompson. He had seen her perform her best-known song, "If Ever I Cease to Love," in New York and was smitten to his aristocratic fingertips.

New Orleans has always enjoyed a good love story, and the entire city was taken by this romantic tale. That year's Mardi Gras was shaped to the love affair. A new character, Rex, Lord of Misrule, was introduced, meant to represent the nobleman. Miss Thompson's song was played throughout the festival, as all the krewes combined for the first time to plan a joint celebration.

There are no more dukes, grand or otherwise, in Russia, and the beautiful Miss Thompson is now only a faded photograph in an old book. But Rex still rules in New Orleans, the music of the love song still echoes in its streets, and the revelry of Mardi Gras parades down the years to lift hearts at carnival time.

✳ **Location:** The events are citywide and spill over into the suburbs, too. The parades of Rex and Comus, held on Mardi Gras Day, are the climactic celebrations. ✳ **Events:** Parades, balls, street entertainment, dancing, costumed events—you name it and it's probably here. ✳ **Contact:** New Orleans Visitor's Bureau, 1520 Sugar Bowl Dr., New Orleans, LA 70112, (504) 566-5068.

GREENVILLE

◈ Delta Blues Festival: Third Saturday in September.

Greenville may not be ground zero of the Mississippi Delta blues country. That distinction usually goes to Clarksdale, a town a few miles to the north. But Greenville is close enough. It is the largest city in the Delta region and a place that has known some hard times of its own.

The Greenville that exists today is entirely different from the city's first two incarnations. River and war destroyed them both. The first Greenville, founded in 1828, was flooded out and the second was burned out by Union Army shelling in 1863.

Greenville then moved back closer to its original location and grew into the biggest cotton-shipping port in Mississippi. But it couldn't keep the Mississippi River away from its door. Massive flooding in 1927 put the place under water for more than two months. Rather than relocate again, though, Greenville got rid of the river. By building a new system of levees, the town formed Lake Ferguson and forced the river channel into a course several miles further west. So while Greenville is still a major river port, it is no longer, strictly speaking, on the river.

Musicologists say that one of the birthplaces of the blues were the cotton docks in towns like Greenville. Gangs of laborers sang to get through the strain and tedium of loading the heavy bales. The blues returns to the place of its nativity with this celebration at the end of summer.

✳ **Location:** Greenville is about 120 miles northwest of Jackson. ✳ **Events:** Concerts, cookouts. ✳ **Contact:** MACE/Delta Arts, 119 South Theobald, Greenville, MS 38701, (601) 335-3523.

NATCHEZ

 Pilgrimage: There are two annual Pilgrimages, but the better-known one runs from the first weekend in March to the first weekend in April.

Many towns throughout the country sponsor tours of their historic homes. Some of them even use the same term to describe them—pilgrimage. But it is in Natchez where the term is most apt. For those who see the antebellum South as a flowering fantasy of chivalry and graciousness, this is the place where that dream comes alive.

The town was built by the French in 1716 and named for a nearby Indian tribe that the settlers had exterminated. After it became a part of the United States, in 1798, the cotton culture was quickly established in the surrounding country. The cotton gin was just coming in to magnify the economic potential of that crop. Men who were willing to take their chances in cotton on this frontier realized fabulous rewards. The land was cheap and rich, the crops were bountiful, and the labor was enslaved.

Natchez was also the starting point for the Natchez Trace, the overland route to Nashville. The road was used before the coming of the steamboats, when a trip upriver was a tedious and slow journey. The flatboatmen would all stop in Natchez before starting the trip back north, and the town grew fat on the trade. It was as a cotton port, however, that Natchez knew its greatest prosperity.

From the 1820s through the 1850s, magnificent homes rose in the city. Built mainly by plantation owners, their pillared facades, sheltering oaks, and gardens gave Natchez an appearance unmatched along the Mississippi. Despite an attachment to slavery, many of the planters were well educated. They took an active interest in domestic architecture as an expression of their own deepest beliefs. It was one of those rare eras in which money came into the hands of men with a cultivated sense of beauty.

The place was lightly touched by the Civil War compared to the massive destruction visited on other river ports in the state. So Natchez emerged with its past intact. Not only intact, but fiercely protected. Organizations like the Natchez Garden Club took an active interest in the preservation and restoration of the city's landmark homes long before the value of the past was understood and celebrated elsewhere. Around 500 buildings from the antebellum era still stand in central Natchez. The spring Pilgrimage, when the gardens of Natchez are in full bloom and the Mississippi sun is still mild, is when this past opens its doors to the present.

✳ **Location:** Natchez is about 90 miles north of Baton Rouge, Louisiana. ✳ **Events:** Tours of historic homes and gardens, entertainment. ✳ **Contact:** Natchez Pilgrimage, P.O. Box 347, Natchez, MS 39121, (800) 647-6742.

OCEAN SPRINGS

◈ **Landing of d'Iberville:** Last weekend in April.

Hernan DeSoto may have been the first European to see the Mississippi River (see Bradenton, Florida). Not until a century after his death along its banks in 1542, though, was the great river truly explored. That task was left to the French who approached it from Quebec across the Great Lakes. Robert Cavelier, Sieur de la Salle, reached the river's mouth in 1682 and claimed the entire valley for France.

Sixteen years later, it was decided by Louis XIV that the crown should make a more permanent stake in this vast area. So Pierre Le Moyne, Sieur d'Iberville, was commissioned to plant a colony somewhere near the mouth of the Mississippi. He sailed from the port of Brest in October 1698, with about 200 colonists aboard. Six months later he arrived at Biloxi Bay and landed on its east side. The colony founded here was the first European settlement in the lower Mississippi Valley and the seat of government over a territory that ranged from the Ohio River to the Yellowstone.

Fort de Maurepas lasted just three years. It was decided that Mobile Bay was the more strategic location for the colony, so in 1702 d'Iberville moved there. A few years later, most of the remaining settlers moved across the bay to what is now Biloxi. The site of the original colony hung on as a fishing village. But in the 1880s the place was developed as a resort, taking advantage of the natural springs and fine Gulf beaches. A number of buildings put up in the 1880s and 1890s, including a church designed by Louis Sullivan, still stand in Ocean Springs. It is also something of an artists' colony, and the nearby Shearwater Pottery is noted for the distinct glaze placed on its products.

✳ **Location:** Across the U.S. 90 bridge from Biloxi. ✳ **Events:** Reenactment of the landing on the bayfront, arts festival, entertainment. ✳ **Contact:** Ocean Springs Chamber of Commerce, P.O. Box 187, Ocean Springs, MS 39566, (601) 875-4424.

PHILADELPHIA

◈ **Choctaw Fair:** Week following the 4th of July.

The Choctaw, who occupied most of central Mississippi at the coming of the Europeans, were an industrious people with farsighted leadership. They allied themselves with the Americans from the time of their arrival, refusing invitations to join other southern tribes and assist Britain during the War of 1812. Their leader, Pushmataha, visited Washington in 1824 to remind Congress of Choctaw loyalty.

But when planters wanted their lands, none of it did any good. A minority of the tribe was forced to sign the Treaty of Dancing Rabbit Creek in 1830 and, like the Indians in neighboring states, the Choctaw were removed to Oklahoma. Mississippi, however, permitted a few thousand of them to remain. But that was not a great favor. They lost title to their lands and were reduced to sharecropping. They also were on the wrong side of the state's rigorous Jim Crow laws.

In 1918 a reservation was established here for the Choctaw remnant, and in 1945 a tribal council was organized for self-government. Four years later, it put on the first Choctaw Fair. Since then it has become one of the top Native American events in the region. The Choctaw also are a major local employer, operating several tribal industries.

✳ **Location:** Philadelphia is about 35 miles north of Interstate 20, by way of Mississippi 15. The Choctaw Fair is held in the Pearl River Community, immediately east of town. ✳ **Events:** Traditional tribal ceremonies and dances, Native American foods, stickball games, crafts fair. ✳ **Contact:** Tribal Offices, P.O. Box 6010, Philadelphia, MS 39350, (601) 656-5251.

North Carolina

❖ ☀ Mountain Dance and Folk Festival: First weekend in August.

Back in 1927 it was still called hillbilly music. It went virtually unheard in the North, where cultural opinions were set. A few university folklorists roamed the southern highlands collecting material, but for the most part the traditional songs and dances of this region were regarded as unworthy of serious attention.

This was the setting in which Bascom Lamar Lunsford introduced his first festival celebrating this form of music in Asheville. Lunsford was a first-rate musician and collector of traditional songs. He called himself the "Minstrel of the Appalachians" and invited clog dancers and square dancers and balladeers from the hills down to this city to perform in a style that traced its lineage to British folk art of centuries before. His aim was not to popularize, but to expose more people to folk traditions in their purest forms.

The festival now is regarded as the finest of its kind in America and was instrumental in winning a larger and more serious audience for this sort of music.

✷ **Location:** The festival is held at the Thomas Wolfe Auditorium, in the Asheville Civic Center. ✷ **Events:** Concerts of traditional music and dance, crafts fair. ✷ **Contact:** Asheville Chamber of Commerce, 151 Haywood St., Asheville, NC 28801, (704) 258-6101.

FRANKLIN

◆ Macon County Gemboree: Fourth week in July.

Before 1849 North Carolina was one of the top gold-producing states in the country. A seventeen-pound nugget was found here in 1799, and precious metals have been found in more than 400 locations around the state. But the mines were small-scale, and after the rich strikes in California serious gold-seekers headed elsewhere.

But in the hills of Macon County, at the edge of the Great Smoky Mountains in the state's southwestern corner, the treasure remains. This is one of the richest gemstone areas in the East. There are several ruby mines in the vicinity, and quantities of sapphire also have been found here. A few mining conglomerates, including one that supplied Tiffany's, once worked the area. But they have gone and left the field to the independent adventurer.

Many of the mines welcome visitors who pay a fee, are handed a pail, and wished well. Sometimes the rockhounds even come up with some glitter in the nearby streams. Gem fever reaches its height during this annual celebration, in which participants are encouraged to make their fortunes while being festive.

✳ **Location:** Franklin is at the junction of U.S. 23, 64 and 441, about 70 miles southwest of Asheville. ✳ **Events:** Gem-hunting expeditions, exhibits of local gemstones, field trips to likely new discovery sites, community dinners. ✳ **Contact:** Franklin Chamber of Commerce, 180 Porter St., Franklin, NC 28734, (800) 524-7829 or (704) 524-3161.

❖ While You're There:

The Franklin Gem and Mineral Museum contains year-round displays of wealth taken from the local rocks and streams. Fittingly enough, it is housed in what used to be the city jail.

LINVILLE

◆ Grandfather Mountain Highland Games: Second full weekend in July.

To the Scottish Highland clans of the eighteenth century, North Carolina was a refuge. They had suffered a disastrous defeat on the

Traditional Scottish pageantry is just one facet of the Grandfather Mountain Highland Games of Linville, North Carolina. (Courtesy of Grandfather Mountain)

moors of Culloden in 1746. The forces of Bonnie Prince Charlie, last of the Stuart pretenders to the English throne, had been routed by British troops and a terrible vengeance taken afterwards on those who had supported him.

Groups of Highlanders had begun settling the Cape Fear Valley in 1729. The future city of Fayetteville was one of their largest settlements, and when their clansmen had to flee the wrath of England at home they had a welcome waiting for them in this colony. Among those who came was Flora MacDonald, a heroine among the Scots. She had helped the prince escape the pursuing British by disguising him as a servant girl and taking him to the Isle of Skye, from where he could get away to France. She was later arrested, but her courage was also admired in London and public sympathy won her a release.

She and her husband, Allan MacDonald, joined the migration to North Carolina in 1774, where they promptly picked the wrong side in the revolutionary ferment. They were loyal Tories and identified the colonies' Whigs, who were for independence, with their enemies in Britain. When Britain tried to separate the South from the rest of the colonies early in 1776, Allan MacDonald led a troop of Highlanders in support of Lord Cornwallis. They were beaten at Moores Creek by local militia. MacDonald was arrested and his property was confiscated. The valiant Flora accompanied him back to Britain in 1779.

But the highland influence remains strong in North Carolina. This gathering of the clans is the best established of all such Scottish celebrations in America and attracts members of more than a hundred ancestral organizations.

✳ **Location:** Linville is just off the Blue Ridge Parkway on U.S. 221, about 65 miles northeast of Asheville. ✳ **Events:** Traditional Scottish sports, highland dancing, pipe and drum concerts, clan pageantry and ceremonies. ✳ **Contact:** Grandfather Mountain Highland Games Office, P.O. Box 1095, Linville, NC 28646, (704) 733-1333.

VALDESE

 ## Waldensian Festival: Second Saturday in August.

Among the groups who sought freedom in North Carolina was a band of Italian, French-speaking Protestants from the Alps who called themselves the Waldensians. They followed the teachings of a twelfth-century religious reformer, Peter Waldo, and believed in a vaguely communitarian style of life.

The group was persecuted for reasons of religion and ethnicity for centuries, but prospered during brief periods of tolerance. Seeking a permanent respite from the uncomfortable cultural gap they occupied in Italy, a colony of fifty Waldensians arrived here in 1893. They bought a 3,000-acre tract, built a town, and started cultivating vineyards on the adjacent hillsides.

Two brothers who were sent off to study industrial development returned to Valdese in 1901, bringing them with the technical ability to establish a textile factory. That established a solid base of prosperity. While the town has abandoned its early communal principles, Valdese still recalls its past with this summer celebration.

✳ **Location:** Valdese is off Interstate 40, about 15 miles west of Hickory. ✳ **Events:** The festival comes as the climax of the month-long presentation of the historical drama *From This Day Forward,* which retells the story of the Waldensians. On the festival day there are traditional games, crafts, foods, and dances. ✳ **Contact:** Historic Valdese Foundation, P.O. Box 655, Valdese, NC 28690, (704) 879-2129.

South Carolina

◈ Iris Festival: Last weekend in May.

This celebration commemorates a mistake. A local gardening enthusiast, Hamilton C. Bland, grew frustrated when some iris bulbs he had purchased refused to grow in his yard. He decided to give up and tossed the bulbs into a bog near his property.

The following season the Japanese iris Bland had thrown away unexpectedly bloomed in the waters. Sumter had a history of appreciation for horticulture. At one time, it was the only place in South Carolina to employ a full-time landscape architect, and many of its early residents owned plantations in the surrounding countryside. So the irises were greeted with enthusiasm.

One of Bland's neighbors donated some land so the small lake could be expanded in 1938. The area is now known as Swan Lake Gardens and is stocked with twenty-five varieties of iris and seven species of swans, including the Australian black. The festival which commemorates the annual renewal of Bland's error was first held in 1940 and has been saluted as one of the outstanding floral shows in the South.

✳ **Location:** Sumter is on U.S. 76, about 45 miles east of Columbia. ✳ **Events:** Floral displays, community dinners, parade, shag-dancing competition, crafts show, entertainment. ✳ **Contact:** Sumter Chamber of Commerce, (803) 775-1231; Convention and Visitor's Bureau, P.O. Box 1229, Sumter, SC 29151.

Tennessee

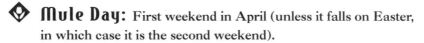 **Mule Day:** First weekend in April (unless it falls on Easter, in which case it is the second weekend).

Some people do not like mules. Mules admittedly do not have the best of reputations. They are symbols of stubbornness, purveyors of the unreasoning kick. There are those who call them stupid. But mule-fanciers patiently explain that is only because these people do not know them. In reality, mules are not only highly intelligent but sweet-tempered, durable and brave. Or so they say. To hear their advocates tell it, the only thing a mule lacks is the power to procreate. They are the offspring of male donkeys and female horses and are born sterile.

"America never lost a war in which it used mules," a military historian once declared, in deploring the phaseout of the animals from active duty. They were so vital during World War I that Germans were sometimes instructed to shoot the mules before the soldiers. They were airlifted into Afghanistan in the 1980s to help Muslim rebels in their war against the Soviet Union. The Tennessee variety was much stronger than the local breed and better able to carry loads over mountain passes.

One may argue that American agriculture was built on the backs of mules, the all-purpose farm animal. The twenty-mule teams of the western mines were legendary, especially in the punishing climate of Death Valley. The peak year in U.S. mule production was 1926 when 6 million colts were born. As farms became increasingly mechanized, the mule population has dwindled.

Tennessee prides itself on the mules it raises, and this city carries on an enduring admiration for the animal. Columbia holds the biggest mule market in the world, and the parade of the animals through the middle of town during this celebration, held annually since 1934, is regarded as reverentially as a royal procession. It is one of Tennessee's great traditions.

The hard-working mule is honored during the world's largest mule market, held in Columbia each spring. (Courtesy of Mule Day Office)

✳ **Contact:** Columbia is on U.S. 31, about 40 miles southwest of Nashville. ✳ **Events:** Mule parade and auction, mule pulls, flea market, liars' competition, square dancing, crafts fair, Western mule show, clogging contest, talent show. ✳ **Contact:** Mule Day Office, P.O. Box 66, Columbia, TN 38402-0066, (615) 381-9557.

❖ While You're There:

Columbia was also the home of the eleventh president, James K. Polk. The family home is in town and contains many items relating to his term in the White House, from 1845–48.

COSBY

❖ Dulcimer Harp Fest: Second full weekend in June.

Those who play the dulcimer say that it produces the sweetest of musical sounds, a delicate and soft timbre unlike any other stringed instrument. The poet Samuel Taylor Coleridge heard one being played in a dream, and the sound inspired him to write one of his greatest works, *Kublai Khan*.

In the United States, the trapezoidal-shaped instrument, which is played by striking felt hammers on metal strings, is associated with the Appalachian states. But almost every culture in the Northern Hemisphere, from China to Iran to Britain, has some version of the dulcimer in its music. Some students of the instrument believe the Crusaders brought it back from Asia Minor, while others contend it was the Arabs who brought it with them when they entered Europe through Spain.

Because it uses the diatonic scale (no sharps or flats), dulcimers are among the easiest instruments to play. "It can take a year just to get the fingering on a violin straight," said one dulcimer player. "But if you can tap out a tune on the white keys of a piano, you can play a dulcimer. Besides, even if you strike notes at random, it still sounds haunting."

The players who turn up at Cosby play more than just random notes. The setting of this celebration, at the foot of the Great Smokies, enhances the traditional sounds they make.

✳ **Location:** Cosby is on U.S. 321, near the northeastern corner of Great Smoky Mountains National Park, 19 miles east of Gatlinburg. ✳ **Events:** Concerts, crafts, storytelling, workshops, dancing, watermelon seed spitting contest. ✳ **Contact:** Dulcimer Harp Festival, P.O. Box 8, Cosby, TN 37722, (615) 487-5543.

JONESBOROUGH

 National Storytelling Festival: First full weekend in October.

The Ballad of Davy Crockett told us that he was "born on a mountaintop in Tennessee." But that wasn't quite the case. When Crockett was born in 1786, this was the state of Franklin, and Jonesborough was its capital.

The so-called Lost State of Franklin was formed in 1784. North Carolina decided it wasn't worth the cost to defend its territories west of the Appalachians and ceded the entire area to Congress. The residents of the region were quite provoked with their ex-state. Rather than wait for Congress to figure out what to do, they called a convention, adopted a constitution, and declared themselves as the fourteenth state.

Congress was nonplussed, not knowing what to do next. Moreover, North Carolina changed its mind and decided it wanted this territory back. So the state sent officials here to set up their own government. The two sets of leaders clashed repeatedly and chaos was general in Franklin.

In 1788, however, the claim of statehood was withdrawn. Instead, Franklin's leaders accepted Congress's offer to be incorporated in a new territory that, eventually, became Tennessee. Within eight years, it was admitted to the Union. But it lost Franklin's claim of being the fourteenth state. Vermont and Kentucky already had joined before it was Tennessee's turn.

Andrew Jackson came to Jonesborough as a young man to practice law in Franklin. It is also regarded as the oldest town in the state, established in 1779. With this historical legacy to draw from, Jonesborough is the perfect locale for a national gathering of storytellers, who use folk material and fairy tales from around the world to hold their listeners rapt.

✱ **Location:** Jonesborough is on U.S. 11E, about 7 miles west of Johnson City. ✱ **Events:** Storytelling performances, with an emphasis on regional history and folklore. ✱ **Contact:** National Storytelling Association, P.O. Box 309, Jonesborough, TN 37659, (800) 525-4514.

MEMPHIS

◈ **Beale Street Music Festival:** First full weekend in May.

◈ **Elvis Week:** Second week in August.

The two men came from other places to find immortality in Memphis. Alabama-born W. C. Handy became the Father of the Blues. And Elvis Presley, of Mississippi, was the King. Together they shaped the musical legacy of this city, and the entire country.

Handy arrived with his cornet in the first years of the twentieth century and came directly to Beale Street. This mile-long thoroughfare that runs east from the Mississippi River was already the center of African-American life in Memphis. It was at its peak then, jammed with night clubs and restaurants, music pouring out of every door, honest men and pickpockets on every corner.

Out of this rhythm and clatter, Handy wrote "Memphis Blues" in 1905. It was first a political campaign song, then a popular tune. Musical historians regard it as the first jazz composition, containing pauses in the musical line that were to be filled in with improvisational phrases. A few years later came the "Beale Street Blues."

Although Handy called both of these compositions blues, he was really breaking out of that form, pulling it in an entirely new direction. His jazz-tinged blues became the bedrock sound of Memphis, the Delta gone slightly uptown. Beale Street declined after the 1920s, but in recent years it has undergone restoration. Not only physically, but in an emotional sense, too, Memphis is trying to recapture the ambience of the street in its great days. The effort succeeds best during the annual Music Festival.

Presley shopped for much of his early wardrobe along Beale Street, just as he shopped for his musical style among the blues musicians of Memphis. The owner of the city's Sun Records, Sam Phillips, often said that "If I can find me a white boy who sings like a Negro, I'll make a million dollars." He wasn't the one who cashed in, but when Phillips heard a demo record of Presley singing "That's All Right Momma," he knew he'd found his man.

Since Presley's death in 1977, the singer has become one of Memphis's largest industries. The outpouring of nostalgia for the man and for the era he represents shows no sign of abating, indeed, it seems to increase with each passing year. Pilgrimages to his Graceland mansion are an international phenomenon, and Elvis imitators are as much a part of the American scene as Mickey Mouse. The whole brew comes to a head during the anniversary week of his death, when Memphis turns itself over to a tribute to rock and roll's once and future King.

✳ **Location:** Beale Street is at the southern edge of downtown. The Elvis tribute is citywide, but much of it is centered around Graceland, south of the Brooks Road exit of Interstate 55, on Elvis Presley Boulevard, in the southern part of the city. ✳ **Events:** Music is the big attraction in both celebrations, with blues on Beale Street and rock around Elvis. The Beale Street celebration also features barbecue cookoffs and is wrapped into the larger Memphis in May Festival, which includes several concerts and ethnic events. ✳ **Contact:** For Beale Street: Memphis in May Festival Office, 245 Wagner Place, Ste. 220, Memphis, TN 38103-3815, (901) 525-4611. For Elvis Week: Graceland, P.O. Box 16508, Memphis, TN 38186, (901) 332-3322.

NASHVILLE

 International Country Music Fan Fair: In June, dates vary.

It went on the air in 1925 under the name of "WSM Barn Dance." But George Hay, its founder, was amused by the fact that on the schedule it followed a program of grand opera. So he took to calling his show the Grand Ole Opry.

To call it an institution is to understate the case. The Opry became the symbol of Nashville and turned it into Music City USA, the center not only of country music but the busiest recording and musical advertising community in the country. The odd part is that it almost went off the air in the early 1960s, losing most of its network, because country music was regarded as passe. But it was merely on the verge of its greatest period of sustained popularity, a time when, as the song says, "I Was Country When Country Wasn't Cool."

Nashville is full of stories about dirt-poor kids who hit town with nothing more than a guitar, a voice, and a dream. You can see their mansions all across the countryside. The city rivals Hollywood as the place where stars are made. But within country music there is a greater sense of loyalty than in any other branch of show business. Performers are regarded as friends, and the biggest stars usually do not forget the people who put them where they are. There is a sense of accessibility and gratitude here that is almost totally lacking in most show business venues.

The city returns the favor with this celebration, a chance for fans to meet their favorites in performances and autograph sessions.

✳ **Location:** This is a citywide event, with concerts in several locations.
✳ **Events:** Entertainment, celebrity autographs and softball games, barbecue competitions. ✳ **Contact:** International Country Music Fan Fair Festival Offices, 2804 Opryland Dr., Nashville, TN 37214, (615) 889-7503; Nashville Chamber of Commerce, (615) 259-4700.

PARIS

◈ **The World's Biggest Fish Fry:** Last full week in April.

Southerners have labored long and hard to explain the joys of catfish to the rest of the nation. "There is an old saying in the South," a Louisiana congressman once said, "that if there is anything better than catfish, the good Lord kept it for himself." "It's nothin' like shrimp, nothin' like lobster," said a Texas connoisseur. "I just don't know how to tell you."

While catfish sometimes appears on menus in the North, it is still primarily a regional delicacy. With the start of systematic catfish farming in the early 1970s, there are claims the taste of the fish has improved. The fish no longer has to be a scavenger and so its flesh, supposedly, is sweeter. Prepared in the time-honored fashion of frying in cornmeal, the fish is more popular than ever. Some purists, however, swear that they like the natural variety, even though its taste is "fishier."

Paris is near Kentucky Lake, which was formed by damming one of the great catfish streams, the Tennessee River. The lake supplies the bulk of the food for this fish fry, in which catfish is the star attraction.

✳ **Location:** Paris is on U.S. 79, about 32 miles north of the Interstate 40 exit for U.S. 641. The Fish Fry is held at the county fairgrounds.

✳ **Events:** Parades, rodeo, catfish race, crafts show, food booths, antique car show, parade. ✳ **Contact:** Paris Chamber of Commerce, 2508 East Wood St., Paris, TN 38242, (901) 642-3431.

R U G B Y

 Spring Festival: Second or third weekend in May.

One of the great best-sellers of the Victorian Era was *Tom Brown's School Days*. It was a description of life at England's famous Rugby School, which provided the model moral and educational upbringing for a young gentleman. Under its famed headmaster, Thomas Arnold, it molded the Victorian self-image.

The author of that book, Thomas Hughes, felt that a school on the lines of Rugby should be established in America. Using royalties from *Tom Brown*, Hughes, a social reformer, built his new Rugby in the east Tennessee hills in 1877. It was intended to train young American working-class men and younger members of British families who were excluded from an inheritance. Hughes felt they should be educated, but able to work with their hands and "be able to meet princes ... without embarrasement or self-assertion."

Although a 7,000-volume library, an Episcopal church, and several stately homes were built in the colony, it failed in seven years because of financial mismanagement. Hughes returned to England, cheerily convinced that "good seed was sown." The Rugby experiment remains a curious footnote to Tennessee history, and in this celebration its noble goals are remembered.

✳ **Location:** Rugby is on Tennessee 52, about 75 miles northwest of Knoxville. ✳ **Events:** Crafts, British Isles and Appalachian music and dance, historic buildings open, storytelling. ✳ **Contact:** Historic Rugby, P.O. Box 8, Rugby, TN 37733, (423) 628-2441.

S H E L B Y V I L L E

 Tennessee Walking Horse National Celebration: Ten days leading to the Saturday before Labor Day.

As rhapsodic as Tennessee gets about its mules (see Columbia, above), the state attains a near-euphoric state over its walking horse.

Strong, intelligent, gentle, stylish, the Tennessee walking horse is all things to all riders and has become one of America's most popular breeds of saddle horse.

The walker was developed for work on large plantations, where a slow and steady gait was required by the overseers for long days in the saddle. The horse has three distinct gaits, from its characteristic dignified slow walk to its canter, which has been likened to the movement of a rocking chair. The Tennessee walking horse has bloodlines descending from thoroughbreds and mixed with standardbreds, Morgans, and pacers. The result is a deep-chested animal with a short back that runs about 1,200 pounds.

The farms of middle Tennessee have become the home of this horse, with forty-four walking horse stables within a short drive of downtown Shelbyville. The championship show trials here bring the holiday crowds in to admire their favorites.

✳ **Location:** Shelbyville is on U.S. 231, about 55 miles south of Nashville. ✳ **Events:** Horse show, trade fair, barn decorating contest, community dinners, dog show. ✳ **Contact:** Tennessee Walking Horse Festival Offices, P.O. Box 1010, Shelbyville, TN 37160, (615) 684-5915.

Virginia

ALEXANDRIA

❖ George Washington's Birthday Parade:
Presidents' Day.

From the time when as a young surveyor's assistant he helped lay out the place in town lots, George Washington had an intimate relationship with Alexandria. Members of his family were among the first property owners here in 1748. The first troops Washington led were raised locally and drilled in the middle of town before embarking to the western frontier. He raced horses at the Jockey Club, built a house in town, entertained in Gadsby's Tavern. His estate at Mt. Vernon was only nine miles from Alexandria. This, to a large degree, was Washington's hometown.

When the town elected delegates to the Virginia convention of 1774 to oppose the closing of the port of Boston, Washington was the presiding officer. When its first Masonic lodge was chartered in 1788, Washington was named its first Worshipful Grand Master, just months prior to becoming the first president.

And for fifty-seven years, Alexandria was actually a part of the city named for Washington. Virginia donated it to the District of Columbia, before residents petitioned to be returned to the state in 1846. So it is altogether fitting that the country's biggest Washington's Birthday celebration is held here, on streets he would have little problem recognizing if he returned to walk them today.

✳ **Location:** Alexandria is directly across the Potomac from Washington, D.C., and connected to it by subway. ✳ **Events:** Parade, colonial drum and bugle musters, art show. ✳ **Contact:** Alexandria Convention and Visitors Bureau, 221 King St., Alexandria, VA 22314, (703) 838-4200.

Alexandria boasts the country's largest birthday parade for George Washington. (Courtesy of Alexandria Convention & Visitors Bureau)

❖ While You're There:

Gadsby's Tavern, with many historical associations with Washington and other Virginia leaders of the colonial era, is now a museum, at 134 North Royal Street.

CHINCOTEAGUE

❖ Pony Penning Day: Wednesday before the last Thursday in July.

No one really knows how the ponies first came to these barrier islands on Virginia's Atlantic Coast. Romantics say that they swam ashore

Assateague ponies make their annual swim from their island habitat to the shores of Chincoteague. (Courtesy of Chincoteague Chamber of Commerce)

from a shipwrecked Spanish galleon or that they were left by pirates when they roamed this shore in the early eighteenth century.

A more likely explanation is that they are descended from horses that strayed or were turned loose by early colonists. Over generations of a diet limited to marsh grass, they diminished in size until they are little taller than Shetland ponies, averaging 50 to 54 inches in height.

Most of the horses are found on neighboring Assateague Island, which is primarily a National Seashore. On Penning Day, the Assateague ponies are guided across a narrow channel to swim to Chincoteague at low tide. There they are branded and some of the foals sold at auction. The rest swim back to Assateague where they roam wild for another year.

Penning Day is a tradition that probably dates back to colonial times, when local farmers came to the islands to obtain workhorses. The ponies were celebrated in a series of children's books in the 1940s, including *Misty of Chincoteague* and *King of the Wind*, which brought them to national attention.

✳ **Location:** Chincoteague is about 75 miles north of the Chesapeake Bay Bridge-Tunnel, east of U.S. 13. ✳ **Events:** Pony swim, penning and auction, carnival, stage entertainment, community dinners. ✳ **Contact:** Chincoteague Chamber of Commerce, P.O. Box 258, Chincoteague, VA 23336, (804) 336-6161.

❖ While You're There:

The Chincoteague Miniature Pony Farm allows visitors to see the little horses close up and to get a look at the original Misty, who now is mounted.

DANVILLE

 Danville Harvest Jubilee: First full weekend in October.

This town is in the midst of the nation's bright leaf tobacco belt. While it also has a thriving textiles industry, it is tobacco that gives Danville its character. Most of the tobacco used in American cigarettes is grown within a 100-mile radius of Danville, and the town grew up in the 1790s around tobacco inspection warehouses.

It was a difficult proposition to get the tobacco from the fields to the market. It meant either a trek to Richmond, rolling hogsheads of tobacco over unpredictable roads, or selling cheap at home and letting the buyers pay the expense of transport. A canal along the Roanoake River gave Danville access to the Atlantic in the 1820s. But it was the organization of the auction system that put the industry on a profitable basis.

Buyers came to Danville in the late summer, starting in the 1850s, and bought loose leaf by the pile. The rapid, hypnotic chant of the auctioneers became the trademark of these meetings, so readily identifiable that for years the American Tobacco Company used the calls as the basis for its radio commercials. There are now nine of these auction houses in Danville covering 1.5 million square feet. The veteran callers who do the selling there have become a tourist attraction in their own right, an authentic sound of Americana.

✳ **Location:** Danville is on the North Carolina border, about 70 miles southeast of Roanoake. ✳ **Events:** Auctioneering contest, crafts shows, entertainment, exhibits, clogging contest. ✳ **Contact:** Danville Parks and Recreation, P.O. Box 3300, Danville, VA 24543, (804) 799-5200.

GALAX

 Old Fiddlers Convention: Second weekend in August.

While Galax celebrates an old musical tradition, the town itself is a rather youthful place. It wasn't settled until 1904 when a spur of the Norfolk and Western Railway came through to carry timber out of the surrounding hills.

Galax was named after an evergreen leaf which grows in the Blue Ridge and is used as a decorative bloom. Later the town developed a textile industry base. But it is the town's music that made it famous. The farming areas in these remote highland valleys had to make their own entertainment, and for generations crack fiddle-players were prized by their hometowns as local treasures.

Musicians from around the region make their way to the Old Fiddlers Convention to reembrace an old musical tradition. (Courtesy of Old Fiddlers Convention)

When Galax organized its first Moose Lodge in 1935, the group decided to put on a fund-raiser based on this old-time music. Even then there was a fear that it was dying out under the impact of radio. But the first Old Fiddlers meet drew a huge response, overflowing the auditorium that had been set aside for it. The performances had to be moved to the town park, where they have been held ever since. The celebration is now one of the top musical attractions in the South and draws traditional bands from across the region.

✳ **Location:** Galax is in the southwestern corner of the state, about 80 miles southwest of Roanoake. ✳ **Events:** Concerts, traditional dances, food booths. ✳ **Contact:** Old Fiddlers Convention, P.O. Box 655, Galax, VA 24333, (703) 236-8541.

GATE CITY

✧ Carter Family Memorial Festival: First weekend in August.

Late in the 1920s, Victor Record Company executives figured that there might be some money to be made in the field of country music.

Small labels had already recorded some local groups, but Victor was think-ing in terms of a regional market. Of course, in those long ago days, before there was a Grand Ole Opry or other radio shows to send traditional music across the airwaves, no one had any idea that there any kind of market for it outside the South.

Victor scout Ralph Peer discovered the Carter family in southwest-ern Virginia. A. P. Carter ran a grocery store to make a living, but he col-lected traditional mountain songs and was a composer, too. He also had a powerful bass voice. With his wife, Sara, and sister-in-law, Maybelle, he formed the Carter Family. Peer first recorded them in 1927, and for the next fifteen years they were a major influence in the development of country music. Sara Carter's haunting lead vocals, described as "mournful and as beautiful as the Appalachians from which [they] came," transfixed listeners who heard her perform "Wildwood Flower" and "Bring Back My Blue-Eyed Boy." Maybelle Carter's guitar style was copied by several other country musicians.

The original Carter Family continued performing until A. P. Carter's death in 1960. Other family members came in and out of the group, including Maybelle's daughter, June Carter, who married Johnny Cash and became a major performer in her own right.

The Carter Family Museum is now housed in the onetime grocery store and a music shed was built adjacent to it in 1976. Each August, the family commemorates the first Victor recording with a celebration of tradi-tional music (only acoustical instruments allowed) and mountain culture.

✳ **Location:** The Carter Family Museum is located outside of Gate City at Maces Spring, an unincorporated crossroads, on County Road 614, about 25 miles west of Bristol, by way of U.S. 58, 421. ✳ **Events:** Con-certs, Appalachian crafts displays, clog dancing. ✳ **Contact:** Carter Family Museum, (703) 386-9480.

LEESBURG

 August Court Days: Third weekend in August.

History has brushed this old town lightly. Great events have occurred on its margins. It is just beyond the suburban orbit of metropoli-tan Washington. A Civil War engagement was fought just outside of town, at Balls Bluff. But the center of Leesburg itself looks very much the same as it did in the first days of Virginia's statehood.

That is the basis of this celebration. It is a re-creation of the circuit court meeting of 1790. The year was chosen because in that era the

Colonial dances are only a part of the festivities surrounding Leesburg's recreation of a circuit court meeting in 1790. (Courtesy of J. Patterson)

meeting was one of the most important civic and social events on the calendar. George Washington, from not too far down the road, is in the second year of his presidency, up in New York City. The Lee family, for whom the town was named, are living on their local property holdings.

The courthouse itself has changed. The original colonial structure was torn down in the 1890s and replaced by a red-brick building. But it is true to the spirit of colonial times, and many other streets in the heart of Leesburg have been restored to reflect their appearance in the eighteenth century. This celebration is history that comes remarkably close to time travel.

✳ **Location:** Leesburg is on Virgina 7, about 40 miles west of Washington, D.C. ✳ **Events:** Street fair with costumed performers, crafts and musical entertainment of the eighteenth century, Revolutionary War encampment. ✳ **Contact:** Loudoan County Visitor and Conference Bureau, 108 D South St. E, Leesburg, VA 22075, (703) 777-0519.

NEW MARKET

◈ **Battle Reenactment:** Second Sunday in May.

The Civil War, it has been written, began in gallantry and ended in trenches. By the spring of 1864, most of the gallantry had been knocked out of the conflict. The North was finally bringing its massive advantages in population and industrial output into the field and had a general, U. S. Grant, who knew how to use them. To Grant, it had become a matter of simply hammering the Confederate forces again and again, taking the casualties in the effort to destroy Robert E. Lee's ability to wage offensive war.

The Battle of New Market was a sideshow to the main struggle for Richmond. But it contained one of the last moments of gallantry in the war and one of its finest moments, the charge of the cadets from the Virginia Military Institute.

The military school had furnished many of the South's top officers, including Stonewall Jackson. The student-soldiers had been called up previously but never used in battle. But now Gen. John C. Breckenbridge recognized that he was outnumbered and needed to call up any able body he could.

Gen. Fritz Sigel had been sent by Grant to break up rail communications through the Shenandoah Valley at Staunton. Sigel had not performed well in the war. A rift had developed in his command between German-speaking officers and native-born Americans. Moreover, Sigel had given no evidence of being able to coordinate troop movements over a wide front. One historian described him as "not only incompetent, but a fool." Nonetheless, Sigel approached New Market with a clear advantage in numbers.

Breckenridge seized the offensive early in the day and forced Sigel back. But a gap developed in his line. "Put the boys in," he said, "and may God forgive me for the order." Confederate veterans, who had taunted the youngsters by humming nursery rhymes, watched in awe as the cadets, most of them teenagers, advanced into the teeth of the Northern assault. "As brave and chivalrous a command as ever fired a gun," wrote one officer. "It surpassed anything I ever witnessed during the war."

The cadets captured a Northern gun and the legend grew that they had turned the tide of the battle. Historians debate that, but the battle was fought so closely that every unit was important, and it can be said that without them the battle may have been lost. Ten of the boys were killed and forty-seven wounded.

When Grant heard the news he is supposed to have said with some satisfaction, "They now must rob the cradle and the grave to fight." But

The Battle of New Market was distinguished by the gallant charge of the cadets of the Virginia Military Institute. (Courtesy of New Market Battlefield Historical Park)

Sigel lost his command four days after the battle and the Virginia Military Institute had won the most inspiring prizes of its long history.

✳ **Location:** New Market is on Interstate 81 at U.S. 211, about 50 miles south of Winchester. ✳ **Events:** Costumed re-creation of the battle and the charge of the cadets. ✳ **Contact:** New Market Battlefield Park, P.O. Box 1864, New Market, VA 22844, (703) 740-3101.

WINCHESTER

◈ Apple Blossom Festival: Weekend before Mother's Day.

Dozens of places around America hold festivals in honor of the apple. From the midwestern groves left by Johnny Appleseed to the great farms of the Pacific Northwest, this is the characteristic national fruit. It is no casual image when something is described as "American as apple pie."

Winchester, however, may have the best claim for being the apple capital. According to some accounts, the first systematic cultivation of the fruit here was carried out by local landowner George Washington. He had first seen the area as a teenaged surveyor and later made the town his headquarters during the French and Indian War. After purchasing land here, he required his tenants to plant the trees.

The area around Winchester now harvests 3.5 million bushels annually. Gigantic refrigerated storage facilities and processing plants, among the largest in the world, are located in Winchester, and the town, at the northern end of the Shenandoah Valley, is surrounded by orchards. Civil War battles raged all across the area, and Winchester changed hands seventy-two times during the fighting. During those years it was also the headquarters of Stonewall Jackson.

But when the apple blossoms appear, this is one of the most tranquil corners of the South. The Apple Blossom Festival is the best known of its kind in the country.

✳ **Location:** Winchester is in the northwestern edge of the state, 75 miles west of Washington, D.C., at the intersection of Interstate 81 and U.S. 50.
✳ **Events:** Coronation of apple queen, parades, concerts, food booths, marching band competitions, entertainment. ✳ **Contact:** Apple Blossom Festival, 135 North Cameron, Winchester, VA 22601, (703) 662-3863.

YORKTOWN

 Yorktown Day: October 19.

Six and one half years and one day after it had begun, the American Revolution ended here. The long road from Lexington and Concord led to this Virginia peninsula, just a few miles from Britain's first colony in America, at Jamestown.

There are historians who claim that Britain actually had lost the war in 1778 when France entered it. The French had shown their ability to work with the Americans in the cooperative campaign to take Newport, Rhode Island, that summer. As the theater of the war then spread to Europe, the British no longer could focus their military efforts on North America. It became just a matter of time before the final triumph.

The Old Guard Fife and Drum Corps perform on the Yorktown battlefield. (Courtesy of National Park Service, Colonial National Historical Park)

The British, however, decided that they could still win with a shift in grand strategy. It had always been the hope of Parliament that enough Loyalists could be found in the northern states to disrupt any concerted colonial efforts. That had not happened, but Parliament was convinced that Loyalists were more numerous in the South. So it switched the British military efforts to that region.

Through 1779–80, the fighting swirled across the Carolinas. But Cornwallis was dealt a series of stinging defeats by frontier militias who refused to fight in formation and devastated the top British battalions with their long rifles. The British had captured the seaports, but the interior belonged to the colonials. There was no uprising in favor of the Crown, but instead unremitting hostility.

Lord Cornwallis abandoned the southern plan and marched north into Virginia, right into a French and American trap. While Cornwallis fortified Yorktown, George Washington feinted at New York City and then marched the main body of his army south. The French naval units, under the Comte de Grasse, followed by sea. A British fleet sailing to relieve Cornwallis was forced to turn back and Cornwallis was left to the mercy of the land forces. On October 9, the siege of Yorktown began. After enduring a week of shelling, and with no hope of reinforcements reaching him, Cornwallis was left with no alternative but surrender.

It would be another two years before a peace treaty was signed, and scattered engagements would still be fought. But the war truly ended here, with the British band playing "The World Turned Upside Down" and a new nation about to be born.

✻ **Location:** Yorktown is on U.S. 17, about 15 miles east of Williamsburg. ✻ **Events:** Costumed reenactment of Cornwallis's surrender, military parade, patriotic music and entertainment. ✻ **Contact:** Yorktown Day Association, P.O. Box 210, Yorktown, VA 23690, (804) 898-3400.

Great Lakes &
Ohio Valley

Illinois

1. Broom Corn Festival, Arcola
2. Julmarknad and Lucia Nights, Bishop Hill
3. International Horseradish Festival, Collinsville
4. Tutty Baker Days, Freeport
5. Abraham Lincoln National Railsplitting Festival, Lincoln
6. Old Canal Days, Lockport
7. City of Joseph, Grape Festival, Nauvoo
8. Summer Rendezvous, Prairie du Rocher
9. Grand Levee at the Statehouse, Vandalia

Indiana

10. Auburn-Cord-Duesenberg Festival, Auburn
11. Johnny Appleseed Festival, Fort Wayne
12. James Whitcomb Riley Festival, Greenfield
13. Forks of the Wabash Pioneer Festival, Huntington
14. The 500 Festival, Indianapolis
15. Circus City Festival, Peru
16. Covered Bridge Festival, Rockville
17. Popcorn Festival, Valparaiso
18. Spirit of Vincennes, Vincennes

Michigan

19. Cereal City Festival, Battle Creek
20. Magic Get Together, Colon
21. International Freedom Festival, Detroit
22. Bavarian Festival, Frankenmuth
23. Tulip Time Festival, Holland
24. Colonial Fort Michilimackinac Pageant, Mackinaw City
25. National Cherry Festival, Traverse City

Minnesota

26. Wild Rice Festival, Deer River
27. Tall Timber Days, Grand Rapids
28. Fiesta Days, Montevideo
29. Midsummer Scandinavian Festival, Mora
30. Fasching, New Ulm
31. Defeat of Jesse James, Northfield
32. St. Paul Winter Carnival, St. Paul

Ohio

33. National Cambridge Glass Show, Cambridge
34. Dayton International Air Show, Dayton
35. Tri-State Pottery Festival, East Liverpool
36. Annie Oakley Days, Greenville
37. Return of the Buzzards, Hinckley
38. Zane's Trace Commemoration, Zanesville

West Virginia

39. Apple Butter Festival, Berkeley Springs
40. Mountain State Forest Festival, Elkins
41. Election Day, 1860, Harpers Ferry
42. West Virginia Oil and Gas Festival, Sistersville
43. Stonewall Jackson Heritage Jubilee, Weston
44. King Coal Festival, Williamson

Wisconsin

45. FyrBal Fest, Ephraim
46. Cheese Days, Monroe
47. Swiss Volksfest, New Glarus
48. Hodag Festival, Rhinelander

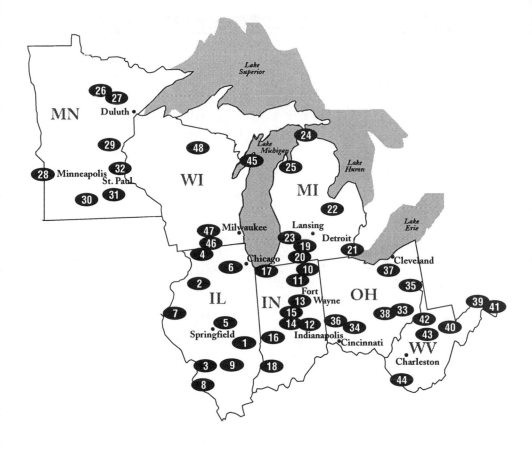

❄ January

Last weekend of January and first week of February: **St. Paul Winter Carnival,** St. Paul, Minnesota

❄ February

Weekend before Ash Wednesday: **Fasching,** New Ulm, Minnesota

◆ March

Third Sunday: **Return of the Buzzards,** Hinckley, Ohio

◆ May

First weekend: **International Horseradish Festival,** Collinsville, Illinois

First full week: **Tulip Time Festival,** Holland, Michigan

Three weeks preceding Memorial Day weekend: **The 500 Festival,** Indianapolis, Indiana

Memorial Day weekend: **Colonial Fort Michilimackinac Pageant,** Mackinaw City, Michigan

Memorial Day weekend: **Spirit of Vincennes,** Vincennes, Indiana

◈ June

First weekend: **Summer Rendezvous,** Prairie du Rocher, Illinois

Second Saturday: **Cereal City Festival,** Battle Creek, Michigan

Second weekend: **Fiesta Days,** Montevideo, Minnesota

Second week: **Bavarian Festival,** Frankenmuth, Michigan

Father's Day weekend: **Grand Levee at the Statehouse,** Vandalia, Illinois

Third weekend: **Old Canal Days,** Lockport, Illinois

Third weekend: **Tri-State Pottery Festival,** East Liverpool, Ohio

Third weekend: **Zane's Trace Commemoration,** Zanesville, Ohio

Weekend closest to 21st: **FyrBal Fest,** Ephraim, Wisconsin

23: **Midsummer Scandinavian Festival,** Mora, Minnesota

Last full weekend: **National Cambridge Glass Show,** Cambridge, Ohio

Last week to July 4: **International Freedom Festival,** Detroit, Michigan

◈ July

Weekend after July 4: **Wild Rice Festival,** Deer River, Minnesota

First full week: **National Cherry Festival,** Traverse City, Michigan

Second full weekend: **Hodag Festival,** Rhinelander, Wisconsin

Third weekend: **Dayton International Air Show,** Dayton, Ohio

Third week: **Circus City Festival,** Peru, Indiana

Last full weekend: **Annie Oakley Days,** Greenville, Ohio

◈ August

First Sunday: **Swiss Volksfest,** New Glarus, Wisconsin

First weekend: **City of Joseph,** Nauvoo, Illinois

First weekend: **Magic Get Together,** Colon, Michigan

First weekend: **Tall Timber Days,** Grand Rapids, Minnesota

First weekend: **Tutty Baker Days,** Freeport, Illinois

September

Labor Day weekend: **Auburn-Cord-Duesenberg Festival,** Auburn, Indiana

Labor Day weekend: **Grape Festival,** Nauvoo, Illinois

Labor Day weekend: **Stonewall Jackson Heritage Jubilee,** Weston, West Virginia

Saturday after Labor Day: **Popcorn Festival,** Valparaiso, Indiana

Weekend after Labor Day: **Defeat of Jesse James,** Northfield, Minnesota

Second weekend: **Broom Corn Festival,** Arcola, Illinois

Second week: **West Virginia Oil and Gas Festival,** Sistersville, West Virginia

Second weekend after Labor Day: **Abraham Lincoln National Rail-Splitting Festival,** Lincoln, Illinois

The week preceding the third Saturday: **King Coal Festival,** Williamson, West Virginia

Third weekend: **Johnny Appleseed Festival,** Fort Wayne, Indiana

Third weekend (even-numbered years only): **Cheese Days,** Monroe, Wisconsin

Fourth full weekend: **Forks of the Wabash Pioneer Festival,** Huntington, Indiana

 October

First weekend: **James Whitcomb Riley Festival,** Greenfield, Indiana

First weekend that includes a Thursday: **Mountain State Forest Festival,** Elkins, West Virginia

Columbus Day weekend: **Apple Butter Festival,** Berkeley Springs, West Virginia

Begins the second Friday, lasting ten days: **Covered Bridge Festival,** Rockville, Indiana

Second weekend: **Election Day, 1860,** Harpers Ferry, West Virginia

November

First two weekends after Thanksgiving: **Julmarknad and Lucia Nights,** Bishop Hill, Illinois

Illinois

ARCOLA

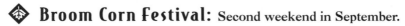

◈ Broom Corn Festival: Second weekend in September.

The first American to grow broom corn was probably Levi Dickinson. He experimented with the plant in 1798 on his Massachusetts farm, knowing that its thicker tassels would make a better broom than the birch splint variety New Englanders had borrowed from Native Americans. With Dickinson's corn, the Northeast dominated the early broom industry.

But a stronger strain was developed on the Illinois prairies in the mid-nineteenth century. Arcola was the center of this new broom corn belt, and by 1900 it was estimated that 95 percent of the national crop was grown in its vicinity. Red sheds along the railroad tracks, where the broom was laid out for shipping, were a signature of Arcola.

Rising labor costs made the crop more expensive to harvest and area farmers dropped it. Most broom corn is now grown in Mexico. Nevertheless, a few of the old broom factories are still in operation in Arcola, and with the start of autumn the town turns out to celebrate the crop that brought it prosperity.

✳ **Location:** On Interstate 57, about 35 miles south of Champaign. ✳ **Events:** Broom-making demonstrations, downtown parade, crafts show. ✳ **Contact:** Arcola Chamber of Commerce, P.O. Box 274, Arcola, IL 61910, (217) 268-4530.

❖ While You're There:

Rockome Gardens features gardens and rockwork in a setting that recalls the Amish settlers in the area. West on Illinois 2.

Residents of central Illinois' Arcola pay tribute to the broom corn crop. *(Courtesy of Arcola Chamber of Commerce)*

BISHOP HILL

❄ Julmarknad and Lucia Nights: First two weekends after Thanksgiving.

Religious and political dissent swept across Europe in the 1840s and resulted in one of the great waves of immigration in American history. These newcomers from central and northern Europe were drawn by a dream of a more liberal community where they could practice new ideas without interference by the state.

Among them were the Janssonists. They followed the teachings of Swedish preacher Erik Jansson, who broke with the established Lutheran church and insisted that only the Bible should be used in worship services. Much of his teaching followed Marxist lines, but it had a strong religious foundation. He burned hymnals and catechisms and was arrested repeatedly by Swedish authorities. In 1846, he and his adherents decided to leave Sweden and practice religious freedom "among the heathen" in Illinois.

Things did not go well at the Bishop Hill (named for Jansson's birthplace of Biskopskulla) settlement. Religious and economic dissension tore it apart, and the communistic system favored by Jansson proved unworkable. Jansson ran the place in an authoritarian manner and was murdered by a disenchanted follower in 1850. By 1861, the communal living system he set up had been dissolved and the remaining population had converted to other religions. The Janssonist experiment was history.

The area retained a strong Swedish identity, however, and the surviving structures of Bishop Hill are now a state historic site. Traditional Swedish observances are celebrated throughout the year, most memorably around the Christmas season. A Yule market and candlelit caroling are features of the observance.

✱ **Location:** Bishop Hill is north of U.S. 34, about 25 miles northeast of Galesburg. ✱ **Events:** Costumed Swedish folk characters, traditional foods and baked goods, Swedish crafts markets, holiday singers in the church and on the streets. ✱ **Contact:** Bishop Hill State Historic Site, P.O. Box 104, Bishop Hill, IL 61419, (309) 927-3345.

❖ While You're There:

Sixteen of the Bishop Hill buildings have been restored and can be visited. There is also a museum, featuring the work of primitivist painter Olof Krans.

COLLINSVILLE

◈ International Horseradish Festival: First weekend in May.

This is not an event for the most delicate of palates or sensitive of noses. The pungent tuber which we call horseradish was imported to southern Illinois by German immigrants in the mid-nineteenth century. It was so popular in their homeland that the condiment was referred to by the French as "German mustard."

The original English translation was something more like "coarse radish," because of the bristly exterior of the plant. Over the years, common usage turned it into "horse." Since the early 1900s, the origin of the term has been further confused by its use as a strong expression of disbelief that substitutes for a cruder word (which also begins with "horse").

Demand for horseradish shoots up in early spring when it is one of the staples of the traditional seder meal during the Jewish observance of Passover. It is eaten on matzoh as a symbol of the bitterness of slavery in Egypt.

About 60 percent of the national crop is grown in the Collinsville area, which bills itself as the "Horseradish Capital of America." The primary support of the local agricultural economy, horseradish has been celebrated in this festival since 1988.

✳ **Location:** Collinsville is on Interstate 55, about 13 miles east of St. Louis, Missouri. The festival is held in Woodland Park. ✳ **Events:** Cooking contests, root-tossing competition, horseradish-eating contest, 5K run. ✳ **Contact:** Collinsville Chamber of Commerce, 221 West Main, Collinsville, IL 62234, (618) 344-2884.

FREEPORT

❖ Tutty Baker Days: First weekend in August.

William Baker was a cheery soul who settled in this area in 1835. Baker, who was nicknamed "Tutty," was so delighted to have the company of travelers along the wagon road that is now U.S. 20 that he frequently served them meals without requiring payment.

This was not a popular policy with Mrs. Baker. "If you keep sharing your meals with all comers," she supposedly told him, "this is going to turn into a free port." The nautical term, which refers to a town where a ship could unload without paying a tariff, became attached to this landlocked community.

A farming center and industrial town of about 25,000 people, Freeport remembers its hospitable past with this celebration named for its founder.

✳ **Location:** Freeport is on U.S. 20, about 30 miles west of Rockford. The festival is held downtown, on Main, Chicago, and Stephenson Streets. ✳ **Events:** Entertainment, juried arts and crafts, carnival. ✳ **Contact:** Freeport Chamber of Commerce, 26 South Galena, Freeport, IL 61032, (815) 233-1350.

LINCOLN

Abraham Lincoln National Rail-Splitting Festival: Second weekend after Labor Day.

As the Chicago and Mississippi Railroad edged its way into central Illinois, a major conflict was touched off over the route. The seat of Logan

County, Mt. Pulaski, anticipated that the railroad would come through that area. But a group of land speculators bought a town site to the northwest, called on the state legislature to hold a special election to move the county seat, and offered a right-of-way to the railroad. Their attorney in all this maneuvering was a former politician who was practicing law in Springfield—Abraham Lincoln.

They decided to name the new town after him, despite his warning that "I never knew anything named Lincoln to amount to much." So in 1853, seven years before his election as president and hardly known outside of Illinois, Lincoln had the first of many communities named for him.

He returned often, arguing many cases in the local courthouse, which must have been a daunting experience for the opposing attorney. That courthouse was moved to Greenfield Village, near Detroit, Michigan, in the 1930s. Ironically, the courthouse in Mt. Pulaski, the town from which Lincoln helped remove the county seat, still stands and is one of two surviving buildings in which the future president actually practiced law.

* **Location:** Off Interstate 55, about 30 miles north of Springfield. Held at the Logan County Fairgrounds. * **Events:** Junior and senior rail-splitting competition, flea market, frontier displays. * **Contact:** Logan Rail-Splitting Association, P.O. Box 352, Lincoln, IL 62656, (217) 732-7146.

❖ While You're There:

The surviving Lincoln-era courthouse in the area is located in Mt. Pulaski, 11 miles southeast on Illinois 121. A replica of the original Lincoln Courthouse is at 914 Fifth Street, in Lincoln. There is a small museum devoted to Lincoln at the McKistry Memorial Library, on the campus of Lincoln College.

LOCKPORT

❖ Old Canal Days: Third weekend in June.

The Chicago Portage was among the most important passages in early America. Used for generations by Native Americans, the portage between Lake Michigan and the Des Plaines River was discovered by French explorers in the 1670s. Louis Jolliet, the first European to use this connection between the Great Lakes and Mississippi River, immediately saw the advantages of a canal. Upon further examination, however, it turned out that the ditch would have to extend one hundred miles to

A Civil War encampment along the I & M Canal is a feature of Old Canal Days, a celebration of the importance of the canal to the area's history. (Courtesy of Lockport Old Canal Days Festival)

ensure a steady supply of navigable water. That was beyond the technology of the age.

But 160 years later, in 1836, the Illinois and Michigan (I & M) Canal was begun, making Chicago the transportation hub of the Midwest. The town of Lockport, built along the old Chicago Portage trail, was its headquarters. The administrative offices of the canal company and four locks were erected within the community. Work on the canal went on until 1848. This canal was closed after about 30 years of use.

The Chicago Sanitary and Ship Canal, opened in 1900 for the dual purposes explained in its name, was built along the same route as the I & M Canal. The path of the older waterway has been converted to recreational purposes, with bike and hiking paths along its side. Lockport, now a Chicago suburb, remains one of the best-preserved canal towns in America. Several of its buildings, dating from canal construction days in the 1830s, serve as a backdrop for this celebration.

* **Location:** Lockport is about 5 miles north of Exit 133 off Interstate 80, just east of Joliet. * **Events:** Downtown parade, carriage and wagon rides, pioneer crafts exhibits, carnival. * **Contact:** Lockport Old Canal Days, P.O. Box 31, Lockport, IL 60441, (815) 838-4744.

❖ While You're There:

The I & M Canal Museum is at 803 South State Street and contains exhibits on the history of the waterway. It is housed in the Canal Commissioner's Office, built in 1837.

NAUVOO

◈ **City of Joseph:** First weekend in August.

✦ **Nauvoo Grape Festival:** Labor Day weekend.

Nauvoo is best recalled in American history for its role in the west-ward migration of the Mormons. It was here that prophet Joseph Smith established his church in 1839. After enduring seven years of mounting hostility from their neighbors, culminating in the murder of Smith by a mob in nearby Carthage, the Latter-Day Saints began their trek to Utah under the leadership of Brigham Young in 1846.

But Nauvoo did not disappear when they departed. Three years after the Mormons left, a group of French settlers moved into the abandoned town. They called themselves the Icarians and, like the Janssonists who settled in nearby Bishop Hill (see above), they practiced a religious-based communism. Their leader was Etienne Cabet, who advocated the sort of benevolent despotism that seemed to develop in most of these utopian colonies. He rebuilt Nauvoo and even tried to complete the temple that the Mormons had left unfinished, but the structure was destroyed in a storm, its walls collapsing in the wind.

Cabet believed the community could support itself by cultivating grapes for wine. But discontent crept into the settlement, and in 1856 Cabet was defeated for its presidency. He tried to organize a strike against the winners and wound up being locked out of the community hall. So he departed with his followers to St. Louis and the colony folded a few months later.

German settlers moved into Nauvoo and their descendants continue to work the vineyards planted by the Icarians. Both aspects of this town's past are celebrated. City of Joseph is a retelling of the Mormon experience here, while the Nauvoo Grape Festival celebrates the heritage of the Icarians.

✳ **Location:** On a bluff above the Mississippi River, Nauvoo is about 30 miles north of Keokuk, Iowa, and can be reached by way of Illinois 96. City of Joseph is held in the streets of the Nauvoo Restoration, which is operated by the Church of the Latter-Day Saints. The Grape Festival is in Nauvoo State Park, just south of the town. ✳ **Events:** City of Joseph is a free outdoor drama, with music and dancing, depicting Nauvoo's history during the seven-year habitation by the Mormons. The Grape Festival features a 5-mile run, parades, a carnival, and the traditional wedding ceremony of the cheese and wine (a French custom dating from medieval times). ✳ **Contact:** For City of Joseph: Nauvoo Visitors Center, P.O. Box 215, Nauvoo, IL 62354, (217) 453-2237. For Nauvoo

Grape Festival: Grape Festival Association, P.O. Box 431, Nauvoo, IL 62354, (217) 453-2528.

❖ While You're There:

'The Joseph Smith Historic Center preserves many of the buildings associated with the Mormon Church leadership, including Smith's home, store, and grave. Nearby are the homes of Young and several other figures in the church's early history. The Nauvoo Historic Society Rhineberger Museum, in the state park, has displays on all the groups that made this town their home.

PRAIRIE DU ROCHER

❖ Summer Rendezvous: First weekend in June.

This village, now a tiny settlement clustered against the river bluffs, is the oldest European town in Illinois. It was part of a famed swindle, the Mississippi Bubble, manipulated by financier John Law. Law, a Scot living in France, managed to obtain a charter for settlement of the Louisiana Territory and indulged in a wild round of speculative land purchases involving some of the leading figures in the French court. When the scheme collapsed in 1722, the French banking system almost went down with it.

But Prairie du Rocher, the one settlement established by Law's company, survived. Well into this century, it maintained French traditions that had disappeared in most other parts of the world. One of them, La Guiannee, a New Year's morning celebration in which costumed singers go from house to house and serenade the inhabitants with wishes for a good year, still is practiced. But it is a private community observance, not a public celebration.

In nearby Fort de Chartres, however, there is a re-creation of French frontier life in the early eighteenth century. The fort, intended as protection for the town, was rebuilt in 1756 with stone ramparts 18 feet high over four acres of ground. From this garrison, French soldiers were dispatched to many of the battlegrounds of the French and Indian War, including the massacre of British forces under Gen. Edward Braddock in Pennsylvania in 1755. Never taken in battle, the fort was surrendered to Britain by the treaty that ended the war in 1763, although it was two more years before the new owners actually arrived to take over. They held it only until 1772, when the rising river level forced its abandonment and destruction. The Rendezvous provides a glimpse of America's eighteenth-century French frontier and the way of life that supported Prairie du Rocher.

The site was acquired by the state of Illinois in 1915. With the Mississippi running in a new channel, the fort was rebuilt on the same spot.

✳ **Location:** Prairie du Rocher is about 45 miles south of St. Louis, Missouri, by way of Illinois 3. Fort de Chartres is northwest of the town. ✳ **Events:** Traders and settlers, dressed as they would have appeared in the 1740s, hold an annual rendezvous, with crafts, demonstrations of frontier skills, and military flag ceremonies twice a day. ✳ **Contact:** Fort du Rocher State Historic Site, 1350 State Route 155, Prairie du Rocher, IL 62277, (618) 284-7230.

VANDALIA

 Grand Levee at the Statehouse: Father's Day weekend.

In the early days of statehood, the Illinois legislature, meeting in the capital of Kaskaskia, encountered a severe money crunch. Its solution was to move the state capital and sell land at the proposed town site to speculators. That is how the seat of government wound up in Vandalia in 1819.

In those years the population of the state was concentrated on its southern borders, along the Ohio and Mississippi valleys. Chicago was barely a collection of cabins on a lake, and, in fact, its first charter was issued at Vandalia. But as numbers and political influence swung to other parts of Illinois, a group of legislators, led by Abraham Lincoln, lobbied to have the capital moved to Springfield. They were called the "Long Nine" because they were all six-footers. In fact, one persistent legend says that Lincoln used his height to ease out of an upper-story window during a vote on the switch, to avoid having a quorum present.

Vandalia tried its best to hold on to the government. It even built a handsome new statehouse in 1836 in the Greek Revival style. But it was to no avail. In 1839, just twenty years after it arrived, the state government left and the new statehouse became merely a county courthouse. It now has been restored to its appearance of the 1830s, when Lincoln, Stephen A. Douglas, and other frontier statesmen debated the issues of the day in its chambers.

Vandalia Statehouse, the state capitol of Illinois from 1819 to 1839. (Courtesy of Illinois Historic
Preservation Agency)

✳ **Location:** Vandalia is on Interstate 70, about 75 miles east of St. Louis,
Missouri, and 75 miles southeast of Springfield. ✳ **Events:** Candlelit
tours of the statehouse, crafts and music of the 1830s, food booths on the
statehouse lawn. ✳ **Contact:** Vandalia Statehouse, 315 West Gallatin,
Vandalia, IL 62471, (618) 283-1161.

Indiana

 Auburn-Cord-Duesenberg Festival: Labor Day weekend.

For a few short years in the 1920s and 1930s, the most beautiful cars ever made in America were manufactured in this northeastern Indiana town by the Auburn Company. E. L. Cord had joined the organization as a salesman. Driven by a vision of what a great car should be, he rose to chief executive in 1926 at the age of thirty-one.

He wanted high performance and rejected the boxy look that was the industry standard. Influenced by the Art Deco movement, he designed cars with low, sweeping lines that looked as if they had been arrested in mid-flight. He acquired the Indianapolis-based Duesenberg Company, which was producing the kind of car he wanted. Then he set about to build the ultimate driving machine, which he called the Cord.

These cars still are regarded as the epitome of style and perfor-mance. Unfortunately, Cord's timing was off. He introduced them in the middle of the Depression, when a price tag of $2,700 was beyond the reach of all but a handful of Americans. The company folded in 1937, but left behind a rich automotive legacy.

Owners of these classic automobiles return to the home base each summer to show them off and to trade.

✳ **Location:** Auburn is on Interstate 69, about 25 miles north of Fort Wayne. ✳ **Events:** Classic car parade, automotive art show, crafts show, car auction, antique sale. ✳ **Contact:** Auburn-Cord-Duesenberg Office, P.O. Box 271, Auburn, IN 46706, (219) 925-3600.

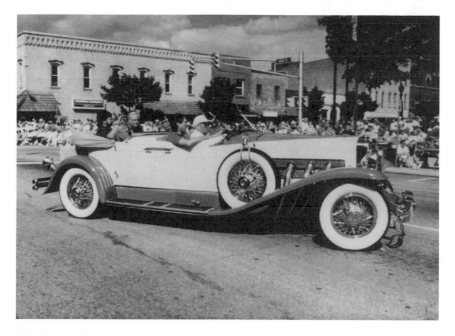

The Parade of Classics includes some of the Cords and Duesenbergs once produced here in Auburn. *(Courtesy of Auburn-Cord-Duesenberg Festival)*

❖ While You're There:

The Auburn-Cord-Duesenberg Museum, located in the former showroom of the hometown dealership, has the world's largest collection of these cars.

FORT WAYNE

❖ Johnny Appleseed Festival: Third weekend in September.

Many people think Johnny Appleseed was a myth. This strange barefoot man with a tin pot on his head and a flour sack for a coat, spreading his little seeds all across the Midwest—it doesn't seem he could have been real.

But John Andrews actually did walk the fields of the Midwest, when this part of the country was still a raw frontier and an unarmed man faced danger at every hand. Born in Massachusetts in 1774, Andrews experienced a religious conversion as a young man, shortly after being kicked in the head by a horse. He became a Swedenborgian and decided to give up all possessions in order to go out to the wilderness and preach. He explained that he had a vision of apple orchards, a religious symbol in his mind, filling this land. So he would call on isolated farmhouses, leaving some religious tracts and planting his seeds, getting a meal and a bed for the night, and then go on his way. By the 1820s he was known as Johnny Appleseed.

The Native Americans revered him as a holy man and welcomed him at a time when tensions still ran high with white settlers. It is estimated by regional historians that he tramped across a territory of about 100,000 square miles. There are still orchards in the Midwest, from Ohio to Missouri, which are credited to the hand of Johnny Appleseed. Memorials to him exist in several locations. But it is at the place where he was buried in 1845 that the largest festival dedicated to his memory and spirit has been celebrated since 1974.

✳ **Location:** The festival is celebrated in the city's Johnny Appleseed Park, on Parnell Avenue near the War Memorial Coliseum. ✳ **Events:** Pioneer village and "Living History Hill," in which characters portray life on the Indiana frontier of Johnny Appleseed's time. Crafts, folk music, art show. ✳ **Contact:** Fort Wayne Parks and Recreation, 705 East State St., Fort Wayne, IN 46803, (219) 427-6000.

❖ While You're There:

Historic Fort Wayne is a reconstruction of the American outpost that was a focus of the Indian campaigns and the War of 1812.

GREENFIELD

◈ James Whitcomb Riley Festival: First weekend in October.

In the early years of the twentieth century, Indiana occupied a special place in American culture. It was the repository of small-town wisdom and virtue. Rural Hoosiers were all folksy philosophers, and the gentle joys of country life, which even then were passing from the American scene, were still preserved here.

Much of that reputation can be traced to the work of James Whitcomb Riley. Writing first in Chicago newspapers and then in his own

James Whitcomb Riley captured the simple delights of country life in his poetry. (Courtesy of James Whitcomb Riley Festival Association, Inc.)

books of poetry, Riley touched a deep strain of sentiment. At a time when an historic demographic shift from farms to cities was under way, his poems recalled precious scenes of a small-town childhood. His readers could also recall golden autumn mornings "when the frost is on the pun'kin and the fodder's in the shock." They knew little girls like "Little Orphan Annie" who made them shiver with the warning: "The goblins will get ye, if ye don't watch out." And they remembered the joys of "The Ole' Swimmin' Hole." Or, at least, they wished they remembered.

Most of Riley's works stemmed from his boyhood days in Greenfield. He spent the first twenty years of his life here, but also toured the state playing the banjo with medicine shows and a troupe of actors, acquiring an understanding of Hoosier dialect and life. His poems began appearing in the 1870s, and within a decade he was a national figure, appearing on sold-out reading tours. Though frequently writing in the voice of a child, he was a lifelong bachelor and had no children of his own.

After his death in 1916, the home in which he grew up was acquired by a local group and turned into a memorial to the Hoosier poet.

✷ **Location:** Greenfield is on U.S. 40, about 20 miles east of downtown Indianapolis. ✷ **Events:** A downtown parade, crafts shows, home arts and photography competitions, flea market, food booths. ✷ **Contact:** James Whitcomb Riley Festival Association, P.O. Box 554, Greenfield, IN 46140; Greenfield Chamber of Commerce, (317) 462-4188.

HUNTINGTON

 ### Forks of the Wabash Pioneer Festival: Fourth full weekend in September.

At the place where the Wabash River divides to form the Little Wabash was one of the most important Native American settlements in the Midwest. The Forks controlled access to a heavily-used portage route from the Great Lakes to the Mississippi, along the Maumee and Wabash Rivers. The Miami nation, in the days of its great military leader, Little Turtle, controlled the area. Later, it was the place favored for the signing of treaties in which Little Turtle's successors gave away their rights to these lands.

The home of Richardville and his son-in-law, Francis La Fontaine, last chiefs of the Indiana branch of the Miami, still stands here. La Fontaine was forced to sign the 1840 treaty that ended the last Indian claim to the land. The tribe was then transported to Kansas. But La Fontaine, who had been named chief as a teenager, could not bear to be away from the land where he had grown up. He tried to make his way back to The Forks and the house his father-in-law had built there in 1833, but died before he could complete the journey. The legend is that he was given poison by his people, who felt he was deserting them.

On the grounds where so much of Indiana's history was determined, this festival re-creates the appearance of The Forks during the 1830s. Pioneers and Indians meet again as they did in the last years before Native American community life was extinguished in Indiana.

✷ **Location:** The Forks is 2 miles west of Huntington, about 25 miles west of Fort Wayne on U.S. 24. ✷ **Events:** Pioneer village, entertainment, banjo and old-time fiddling contests, craft booths. ✷ **Contact:** Forks of the Wabash Pioneer Festival Committee, P.O. Box 187, Huntington, IN 46750, (219) 356-3916.

The pioneer spirit is celebrated in this reenactment of military life at the Forks of the Wabash in Indiana. (Courtesy of Forks of the Wabash Pioneer Festival)

INDIANAPOLIS

 The 500 Festival: Three weeks preceding Memorial Day weekend.

For eleven months of the year, Indianapolis is a rather sedate Midwestern community, with a variety of cultural and business pursuits. But in May it becomes Indy, and all the city can think of then is cars and those who drive them fast.

People who know absolutely nothing about auto racing know the Indianapolis 500, the premier closed-track event in the world. It has given its name to an entire class of racing cars, and its winner goes on to international fame and wealth.

The Indianapolis 500 began as a way for automakers to test their products. (Archive Photos, Inc.)

The Indy 500 began modestly and comparatively slowly in 1911 as a way for automotive manufacturers to test new engines and equipment. In those years, Indiana rivaled Detroit as a center of the emerging automotive industry, so it was a natural location for the race. Ray Harroun won the inaugural event with a speed of just under seventy-five miles an hour. The pace has picked up since then, by a factor of about two and a half.

More than that, the Indy 500 has become an American institution. About a quarter of a million people attend the actual race and many more come to Indianapolis for parties and cultural events, or just to be part of a scene that accelerates in intensity as race day nears. This is where America's passion for high speeds and fast cars reaches its culmination.

✳ **Location:** The 500 Festival goes on all across the city. The Speedway is located 7 miles west of downtown, at 4790 West 16th Street, in the suburb of Speedway. ✳ **Events:** Parade, Queen's Pageant and Ball, Mechanics' Recognition Day, Mayor's Breakfast, Children's Day, Mini-Marathon Run. The Checkerfest, which includes seventy concerts and cultural events, is held at Union Station, the restored rail terminal downtown. Many events during the 500 Festival are free and open to the public, but for some tickets must be obtained. As in most top festivals, tickets are difficult to come by unless you have an inside connection or plan far in advance. A year ahead is not too long. ✳ **Contact:** Indy Festivals Inc., 201 South Capitol, Ste. 201, Indianapolis, IN 46225, (800) 638-4296.

PERU

 Circus City Festival: Third week in July.

The circus came to town in 1883 and never really left. Ben Wallace, who owned the local livery stable, acquired a bankrupt traveling show. According to one inventory, it consisted of a camel, two monkeys, a one-eyed lion, some dogs and horses, and a band wagon. But Wallace and his partners managed to build it into the second largest circus in America, right after Barnum and Bailey. It toured America for half a century, and Peru was its home base.

The company, which became known as the Hagenback-Wallace Circus, began wintering on a tract of land across the Wabash River in 1891. Soon those facilities were being used by several other circuses, among them Sells-Floto and Howes Great London. Railroad connections to Peru were good, and the vast barns built by Wallace made it convenient to store livestock there. Many of the performers also bought homes in Peru for the off-season and when their traveling days were done settled into town as retirees.

Wallace sold out after suffering financial losses in the flood of 1913, which inundated the winter quarters. The American Circus Corporation, a syndicate formed by the new owners, continued to run five traveling shows from Peru. But the operation was sold to John Ringling in 1929, and just before World War II he moved the winter quarters permanently to Florida.

Peru, however, never quite got the smell of sawdust out of its nostrils. In 1958, a group of local businessmen formed Circus City Festival, Inc., to revive the heritage. Assisted by big top retirees, local teenagers were trained to put on a circus of their own. The idea was a smash and it was decided to make it an annual event. Children were recruited in grade school to train in circus specialties, and the local performance, held each summer, quickly developed a professional gloss. By 1968 it had moved into its own arena in a converted lumber company warehouse. This building is now the Circus City Museum, at the corner of Broadway and West Seventh, with displays of circus memorabilia, as well as a permanent big top.

✳ **Location:** Peru is at the junction of U.S. 24 and U.S. 31, about 65 miles west of Fort Wayne and 70 miles north of Indianapolis. ✳ **Events:** Circus performances, downtown parades, rides, carnival. ✳ **Contact:** Circus City Festival, Inc., 154 North Broadway, Peru, IN 46970, (317) 472-3918.

✧ While You're There:

The big barn at the old winter quarters still stands and was declared a National Historic Site in 1988. It is being transformed into the Circus

The Circus City Festival features actual circus acts performed by local youths. (Courtesy of Circus City Festival Inc.)

Hall of Fame, with planned exhibits of circus life and live performances. Auxiliary buildings that were torn down are being reconstructed according to original plans, so that the quarters will once again appear as they did when the Greatest Show on Earth made Peru its home.

ROCKVILLE

 ### Covered Bridge Festival: Begins the second Friday in October, lasting 10 days.

In the American mind, covered bridges are associated most closely with New England. In all probability, they did originate there. In that part of the country, familiarity with the principles of shipbuilding would have been invaluable in the construction of these bridges. But Indiana's Parke County has the most intensive concentration of covered bridges in the country, a total of thirty-two.

The "kissing bridges" of romantic lore actually served a more utilitarian function. The covered top, which protected the planking on the

Tours of the thirty-two bridges of Parke County take place during the Covered Bridge Festival. (Courtesy of Allan Miller)

road from the wear of rain and snow, evolved from basic solutions to bridge-building problems. It was discovered that trusses raised perpendicular to the roadway strengthened the bridge. But the trusses were subject to wind pressure in winter storms and the roadway became uneven, so transverse braces were added. Once they were in place, it was a simple matter to add the roofing, much like raising a miniature barn. By the eighteenth century, the bridges were a familiar part of the roadway in the Northeast and Pennsylvania. As settlers from these states moved west, they brought the bridge style with them.

Just east of Rockville is Billie Creek Village, a community assembled from historic structures brought here from all over the county. Three of the county's covered bridges are located here—Leatherwood Station, Beeson, and Billie Creek, which is the oldest, dating from 1895. All three are of the Burr arch type. This laminated wooden arch was developed by

Pennsylvania architect Theodore Burr, who used it in 1815 to build the country's longest covered bridge, extending 360 feet across the Susquehanna River.

Two of the county's most picturesque bridges are southeast of Rockville, in the towns of Mansfield and Bridgeton. Mansfield is an old mill town, and the gristmill here, dating from the 1820s, is a National Historic Landmark. Just a few yards away is the 247-foot-long bridge across Big Raccoon Creek, built in 1867. Adjacent buildings in the village have been turned into shops.

Even more spectacular, and a bit more remote, is Bridgeton. From Mansfield, continue south on Indiana 59 to westbound county road 720S, and follow the signs. Bridgeton has been declared a National Historic District, and the double-span bridge there is perched atop a dam and gristmill. Both the Mansfield and Bridgeton bridges were designed by Indiana architect Joseph J. Daniels.

✳ **Location:** Rockville is on U.S. 36, about 60 miles west of Indianapolis, at the intersection with U.S. 41. ✳ **Events:** Tours of bridges, live entertainment, wagon-pulling competition, costumed historical characters, crafts, weavers, antiques. There is a hog roast in Montezuma and local Hoosier food specialties, including "buried" roast beef, are sold at stands throughout the county. ✳ **Contact:** Parke County Inc., P.O. Box 165, Rockville, IN 47872, (317) 569-5226.

VALPARAISO

◈ Popcorn Festival: Saturday after Labor Day.

Popcorn is a treat at least as old as America, and probably much, much older. It is believed that Native Americans brought it to the table as their contribution to the first Thanksgiving feast. But evidence of popcorn has been found in cave dwellings in New Mexico that go back some 5,600 years.

Nowhere is popcorn taken as seriously, though, as in northwestern Indiana. While the crop is grown throughout the Midwest, the area around Valparaiso was the birthplace of gourmet popcorn, developed by local farmer Orville Redenbacher in the 1950s.

"I always had this theory that people would pay more for good popcorn," he explained in a 1978 interview. "I was told it wouldn't work. Popcorn was sold for a price. That is, the lower the price the more the vendor would sell." His popcorn was turned down as impractical by every major

A float made of popcorn carries Orville Redenbacher and other popcorn enthusiasts. (Courtesy of Valparaiso Popcorn Festival Inc.)

company. So in 1971 he put it on the market himself and it zoomed to number one in the field. The famous treat is grown on 17,000 acres of Indiana land, most of it around Valparaiso. The town knows what side its kernels are buttered on and in this annual celebration pops its lid off.

✳ **Location:** Valparaiso is on U.S. 30, about 20 miles south of Gary. ✳ **Events:** Parade, stage shows, arts and crafts, hot air balloon rides, airplane show, food booths. ✳ **Contact:** Popcorn Festival, P.O. Box 189, Valparaiso, IN 46384, (219) 464-8332.

VINCENNES

◈ **Spirit of Vincennes:** Memorial Day weekend.

This outpost on the Wabash was the site of the battle that brought the West under American control during the Revolutionary War. George Rogers Clark, a twenty-five-year-old Virginian, saw the war as a great chance to evict the British from all the land north of the Ohio River. This vast expanse would later become the Northwest Territory. Since Virginia still had title to most of the region, Clark obtained approval of its legislature to raise a military expedition against British bases in the area.

He quickly captured Fort Kaskaskia on the Mississippi in 1778 and then moved overland to take Vincennes. He was eagerly assisted in the campaign by the French inhabitants of the area. The French had settled this country in the early eighteenth century and were happy to rid themselves of British rule. But when the British sent a force that succeeded in recapturing the fort at Vincennes, Clark returned to Ft. Kaskaskia from where he would embark on one of the great military achievements of the war. In the depth of winter, with the surrounding prairie frozen or flooded, he returned to Vincennes with a force of 170 men and surprised its shocked defenders. On February 25, 1779, the fort surrendered and American control of the area was secured.

February is a rotten time for a festival in Indiana, so Vincennes chooses to celebrate Clark's victory in May. A national memorial to Clark and his men was completed here in 1936 and is the focus of the festival, which has been celebrated since 1977.

✳ **Location:** Vincennes is on U.S. 41, about 50 miles north of Evansville.
✳ **Events:** Battle reenactment, period crafts and music, traditional foods, a re-creation of a late eighteenth-century frontier community. ✳ **Contact:** Spirit of Vincennes, 1320 Upper 11 St., Vincennes, IN 47591, (812) 882-6440.

❖ While You're There:

Vincennes is a richly historic place with many mementoes of its days as a French community and a territorial capital. The Old Cathedral dates to 1826 and is a vivid reminder of French cultural influence. Grouseland, the residence of territorial governor and future president William Henry Harrison, is also in the town. It was from here that he planned the campaign against the Indian alliance led by Tecumseh. His victory at Tippecanoe in 1811 made him a national hero and led to his election as president in 1840.

Michigan

 ## Cereal City Festival: Second Saturday in June.

The Seventh-Day Adventists grew up in New England in the 1840s. They were an offshoot of the millenarian movement of the times, sects predicting the imminent end of the world. Many of the faithful even climbed mountains on a designated day to await the end while closer to heaven. When life went on, the followers of these teachings decided, instead, to emphasize better living habits on earth. Temperance and a meatless diet were part of the plan.

The Adventists were the most successful of these groups and found a large body of converts in Michigan. Eventually, the church moved its headquarters to Battle Creek and many of its adherents relocated in the area. Among them was the Kellogg family. Dr. John H. Kellogg was a brilliant physician, who combined accepted medical practice with his vegetarian beliefs. He became director of the Battle Creek Sanitarium, run by the Adventists, and by 1894 was serving many of the cereal products he had devised to the guests. The tastiest was cornflakes.

A satisfied patient at Kellogg's table was C. W. Post. Seeing the promotional possibilities of these products, Post made some variations and brought them on the market himself. Post Toasties and Grape-Nut Flakes and a coffee substitute called Postum were soon pouring from his new Battle Creek plant. Dr. Kellogg's brother, Will, decided that consumers would prefer the original. So Kellogg's Cornflakes went into national production, along with a noisier cereal called Rice Krispies.

By 1900, Post and the Kelloggs had revolutionized the American breakfast. The introduction of their products coincided with the mass movement from farms to cities. Commuting factory workers no longer had time for a massive meat-and-eggs country breakfast. These fast and nutritional breakfast foods answered a demographic need, as well as a dietary one.

More than 60,000 people sit down to the world's largest breakfast table each year in Battle Creek.

(Courtesy of Battle Creek Cereal

Festival Offices)

Post was acquired by General Foods and while its home office is no longer in Battle Creek there are still production facilities here. Ralston also makes cereal in town. Kellogg's remains a major influence in the city's life, and a statue of its corporate symbol, Tony the Tiger, on the factory grounds is a local landmark.

✳ **Location:** Battle Creek is on Interstate 94, about 20 miles east of Kalamazoo. ✳ **Events:** The world's largest breakfast table is extended for half a mile through downtown and 40,000 visitors are served bowls of cereal, along with doughnuts, milk, and coffee. Costumed figures representing breakfast food advertising symbols walk around the streets. Other activities are a strawberry festival, raft race, beauty pageant, and two parades. ✳ **Contact:** Mass Mutual, 15 Capital NE, Ste. 225, Battle Creek, MI 49017, (616) 962-2240.

❖ While You're There:

The name Kellogg appears throughout the community, as the family's philanthropic foundation has endowed the city with many of its cultural facilities. Among them is the Leila Arboretum, an excellent display garden named for the mother of the Kellogg brothers. It is at West Michigan at 20th Street.

COLON

 Magic Get Together: First weekend in August.

It started when Harry Blackstone bought a summer cottage on a nearby lake in 1927. He was then one of the best-known magicians in the world, touring constantly on the vaudeville circuit. Other magical pals came to visit, including an Australian named Percy Abbott. He already had made the decision to retire from the stage and go into the business of making paraphernalia for magicians. The obscure town of Colon looked ideal for his purposes.

Obscurity was a big part of its charm. Abbott did not want crowds; secrecy was what he was selling. Once a trick is explained, it is no longer a trick. His Abbott's Magic Company became the leading manufacturer of magic wands, flowering handkerchiefs, decks of deceptive cards, and all the other props that are not quite what they seem. "They have to be pretty, functional and sturdy," an Abbott's executive once explained. "But only the magician has any business knowing how they work."

Since 1938, Abbott's has sponsored an annual convention for magicians. They pour into the little town and turn its streets into the world's largest magic show. The best in the world perform each evening in the high school auditorium. There is a fee for shows and lectures, but much of the magic is free and impromptu. No videotaping is permitted.

✳ **Location:** Colon is about 15 miles west of Interstate 69, by way of Michigan 86 from Coldwater. ✳ **Events:** Junior and adult magic competitions, stage shows and lectures, street performances. ✳ **Contact:** Abbott Magic Company, 124 St. Joseph, Colon, MI 49040, (616) 432-3235.

DETROIT

 International Freedom Festival: Last week of June to July 4.

This border between the United States and Canada was not always peaceful. It was a battleground during the War of 1812, with invading armies moving back and forth across the frontier. Detroit fell to British forces from Canada in the first months of the war without firing a shot. Its

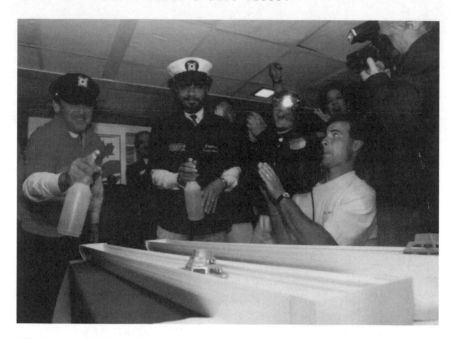

Windsor mayor Michael Hurst and Detroit mayor Dennis Archer battle to win a toy boat race in celebration of their peaceful border. (Courtesy of Joe Cracchiola, Detroit Edison Photography)

aging commander, Gen. Isaac Hull, was terrified by threats of an Indian massacre if resistance did not end. A vengeful American army arrived the following year and pursued the British and their Indian allies halfway across Ontario before defeating them at the Battle of the Thames and killing the great Native American leader, Tecumseh.

For decades afterwards, memories of those campaigns haunted this border. Forts were built and manned on both sides of the frontier, and at times of international tension rumors of war swept across the Detroit River. But the peace always held. The border along the Great Lakes, unchanged since it was set by the Rush-Bagot Agreement of 1817, is now celebrated as the longest unfortified frontier in the world.

Detroit and its sister community of Windsor, Ontario, observe this peaceful proximity each summer in a festival scheduled to coincide with two patriotic holidays—Canada Day and the Fourth of July. Windsor, like Detroit, is an automaking city, but there are subtle differences in the pace of life and cultural influences that make it a distinctly separate place. Detroiters cross the river for Windsor's gambling casino, tranquil streets, and wealth of Asian restaurants, while Canadians come the other way for professional sports and theater. The border can be crossed either by bridge or tunnel with minimal formalities. All that is needed is proof of citizenship. For adults, a voter registration card will suffice.

✳ **Location:** All across Detroit and Windsor. ✳ **Events:** Entertainment, concerts, and craft and food booths are concentrated in the riverfront parks of both cities. In Detroit, it is Hart Plaza at the foot of Woodward Avenue. In Windsor, it is Dieppe Park, at the foot of Ouelette Avenue. Both command outstanding views of the opposite skyline and the traffic on the Detroit River, busiest inland waterway in America. The culminating event of the festival is the fireworks display, one of the largest in the world. Dates are subject to change, but the display is usually held on the Thursday night prior to July 1. An estimated 4 million people attend the show, and downtown streets are usually closed to car traffic hours before the fireworks begin. You must arrive early and stake out a vantage point, or—long in advance—reserve a hotel room facing the river. ✳ **Contact:** Parade Company, 9600 Mt. Elliott, Detroit, MI 48211, (313) 923-7400.

FRANKENMUTH

◈ **Bavarian Festival:** Second week in June.

The Franconians landed in Michigan's Cass River Valley in 1845, determined to bring the Lutheran faith to the Chippewa. While the Chippewa had their own ideas about religion, the immigrants from Bavaria settled in contentedly on the rich farmland and built a thriving town. One member of the community opened a restaurant in 1888 that specialized in traditional Bavarian dishes. But for the most part Frankenmuth, which means "courage of the Franks," remained an out-of-the-way rural community.

But in the late 1940s, things changed in a hurry. Urban residents looking for places to drive in their brand new postwar cars discovered this little town with its German, family-style chicken dinners and old world ambience. Having tasted the joys of tourism, Frankenmuth went all-out. It redid the central business district, altering the look from central Michigan to south German. Word of the local brewery that turned out a beer with character also spread around the state. By the 1950s, Frankenmuth had transformed itself into a major weekend destination.

The Bavarian Festival follows through on the theme. While many German towns in America prefer holding a traditional Oktoberfest, Frankenmuth goes its own way—figuring a stein of cold beer tastes better in the heat of June than the chill of autumn. Otherwise, the festivals are very much the same.

✳ **Location:** Frankenmuth is about 25 miles north of Flint, by way of Interstate 75 and Michigan 83. ✳ **Events:** Name entertainment, Bavarian music, beer and dance gardens, traditional German foods (especially chicken and wurst), parades, the world's largest Chicken Dance. A special wurst dinner is by advance ticket only. ✳ **Contact:** Bavarian Festival Office, 637 South Main, Frankenmuth, MI 48734, (517) 652-8155.

HOLLAND

◈ **Tulip Time Festival:** First full week in May.

By the 1920s, this western Michigan community seemed in danger of squandering the rich Dutch heritage of its founders. Holland was settled by a group of religious dissenters from the Netherlands, led by Rev. Albertus Van Raalte. Their original destination in 1846 was Wisconsin. But by the time they arrived in Michigan, winter had ended the navigation season on the Great Lakes. Gov. Lewis Cass heard about their plight and helped the stranded group find land in his state. They settled in western Michigan near Black Lake. "With many there was a faith in God and a consciousness of a noble purpose," wrote Van Raalte.

But with the end of persecution and amid increasing prosperity, that purpose waned. Holland was turning into just another place on the Michigan map. That's when high school biology teacher Lida Rogus had a brainstorm. What more visible symbol of Holland's unique ethnic background than the colors of the Dutch national flower, the tulip. The plant's origin in the Netherlands has been traced back to 1591, about thirty-five years after it first appeared in Europe as an import from Turkey. Miss Rogus suggested the tulip be brought to the New World's Holland as a symbol of its bond with the Old.

Her idea was greeted enthusiastically, and the Dutch government helped the town obtain 250,000 bulbs. They were planted in time for the 1927 flowering and the first Tulip Time was under way. It has grown into one of the largest historic and ethnic festivals in America, with tens of thousands coming here every year to see the magnificent floral displays, the traditional Dutch dances, and the colorful spectacle of brigades of local volunteers scrubbing down the main streets.

✳ **Location:** Holland is at the intersection of Interstate 196 and U.S. 31, about 25 miles west of Grand Rapids. ✳ **Events:** Klompen dancing, scrubbing of the streets, parades, name entertainment, traditional music, Dutch markets, floral displays. ✳ **Contact:** Tulip Time Inc., 171 Lincoln Ave., Holland, MI 48423, (616) 396-4221; Holland Chamber of Commerce, (616) 392-2389.

An artisan demonstrates the traditional Dutch method of carving wooden shoes at Holland's annual celebration of its heritage. (Courtesy of Tulip Time Inc.)

❖ While You're There:

Windmill Island is a park just off downtown. It is built around an eighteenth-century mill imported from the Netherlands with the special permission of the Dutch government. Usually, windmills are not allowed to be taken from the country and are protected as a cultural treasure. There is also a miniature Dutch town and acres of tulip displays.

MACKINAW CITY

◈ Colonial Fort Michilimackinac Pageant: Memorial Day weekend.

The British garrison on the Straits of Mackinac had no reason to worry. They had taken over the former French fort here several months before, as

Participants costumed as Native Americans and British soldiers reenact the 1763 surprise attack on Fort Michilimackinac. (Courtesy of the Mackinaw Area Tourist Bureau)

part of the agreement that ended the French and Indian War. Now the long northern winter was over and there was a promise of spring in the air.

Some of the local Native American tribes, Chippewa and Ottawa, had been unhappy with the departure of the French. But that was all in the past, and a group of Indians was playing lacrosse just outside the fort. The soldiers walked out to watch, unarmed, never wondering why so many of the women were wearing heavy blankets on such a warm day.

The British had no idea that the western frontier was in flames. Many of the tribes had united under a forceful Ottawa leader named Pontiac, and in the spring of 1763, acting in perfect coordination, they had attacked every British fort on the Great Lakes. Only Detroit held out, and it was surrounded. But Fort Michilimackinac knew none of this.

Suddenly, the lacrosse players hurled the ball towards the fort and raced to where the women were seated. The blankets were flung aside. Beneath them were hatchets and knives. The Indians turned on the unsuspecting soldiers and began cutting them down where they stood. Only a handful escaped the massacre and managed to be hidden by horrified French traders.

Pontiac's Rebellion failed, however, as Detroit held out and reinforcements arrived from the East. It had been the last real chance the tribes had to, at the least, delay the European settlement of their lands in the Great Lakes. The events here are recalled each spring at the restored old fort, which is located right below the abutment of the Mackinac Bridge.

✳ **Location:** Mackinaw City is on the southern edge of the Straits of Mackinac, on Interstate 75. ✳ **Events:** Reenactment of the lacrosse contest and the massacre at the fort. Guides in period dress take the role of actual participants and explain their roles in the life of the eighteenth-century fort.

✳ **Contact:** Mackinaw City Chamber of Commerce, 706 South Huron, Mackinaw City, MI 49701, (616) 436-5574.

❖ While You're There:

Archeologists have discovered at nearby Mill Creek what they believe to be an industrial complex operated by the fort in the 1780s. The lumber that was used to build Fort Mackinac, on Mackinac Island, was milled there. It is now a state historic park, just south of Mackinaw City. The island itself, a top scenic and historic attraction, is a 20-minute boat ride from the Mackinaw City docks.

TRAVERSE CITY

❖ National Cherry Festival: First full week in July.

The big trees were gone. The lumber camps were moving out to the north and west. It seemed that the economy of Traverse City was about to be wiped out, that it would join the list of other lumbering towns that had fallen into decline and, finally, oblivion.

It was at this time, in the 1890s, that local farmer B. J. Morgan began experimenting with growing red tart cherries. The moderating influence of Grand Traverse Bay on the local climate had been understood since the earliest French settlements. There is evidence of apple plantings here in the eighteenth century. Morgan suspected that cherries would thrive under the growing conditions.

He was right. By the turn of the century, Traverse City was the top cherry-producing area in the country. It was certainly the most intensively planted—by necessity. Just a few miles inland, the harsh northern winters would not support the crop. Much of the Old Mission Peninsula, the slender finger of land that divides the bay into its two branches, was turned into orchards as was the narrow band of farmland on the eastern and western margins of the bay. In recent years, the biggest threat to the cherry orchards has been tourism rather than weather. Traverse City is now a major resort area and much farmland has been lost to condominiums and golf courses. But the town still celebrates the fruit that rescued it once.

✳ **Location:** Traverse City is about 50 miles west of Interstate 75, by way of Michigan 72. ✳ **Events:** Three parades, band competitions, entertainment in the city's waterfront parks, pageant and coronation of the Cherry Queen, cherry pit spitting contest, cherries served in a variety of combinations. ✳ **Contact:** National Cherry Festival, 108 West Grandview Parkway, Traverse City, MI 49684, (616) 947-4230.

Minnesota

DEER RIVER

◈ Wild Rice Festival: Weekend after July 4.

It was Minnesota's manna. The wild rice that grew in the state's swampland sustained the Native Americans who lived here. The culture of the Menominee people, whose name means "people of the beneficent seed," was built around the annual harvest. This had to be done in canoes. The harvester carried two long sticks, one to pull the stalk close and the other to beat the kernels loose.

When white pioneers learned the secret of its cultivation, they too turned to it as a staple. In recent years, the crop has been successfully grown in controlled paddies and cultivated by machine. But it is expensive and regarded as a delicacy by most cooks.

Wild rice, which is actually an aquatic grass, still forms one of the bases of the Chippewa economy on their seven reservations scattered across Minnesota. Deer River is located right at the edge of the Leech Lake Reservation in marsh country where cultivation has gone on for generations.

✸ **Location:** Deer River is about 95 miles west of Duluth on U.S. 2. ✸ **Events:** Parade, carnival, church dinners featuring wild rice dishes, chain-saw carving competition, Indian gathering. ✸ **Contact:** Deer River Clerk's Office, 208 Second St., SE, P.O. Box 70, Deer River, MN 56636, (218) 246-8195.

GRAND RAPIDS

❖ **Tall Timber Days:** First weekend in August.

The lumbering industry arrived in Minnesota with a crash in the 1890s. With the stands of white pine played out in Michigan and Wisconsin, the crews continued their march westward, bringing both colorful folklore and destructive cutting practices here.

Allied with agricultural interests at the time of the state's greatest population expansion, the lumbermen made the political case that they were actually performing a vital function—clearing the land for cultivation. Early conservationists who tried to slow them were shouted down as being against progress. The cutting was so frantic and so careless that by some estimates more acres of woodland were lost to fires than to saws.

Nonetheless, historians say that Minnesota's first great accumulation of capital was made possible by lumber. It was the basis of the Weyerhaeuser fortune, a company that is still active in the field. It also gave lumberman John S. Pillsbury the funds to establish the milling industry that transformed the economy of Minneapolis.

Grand Rapids, at the head of the navigable waters of the Mississippi River, became a prime lumbering camp. Much of the wounded land now has healed in the surrounding Chippewa National Forest. The fun and the color of logging days are recalled in this festival, one of the top lumbering-era celebrations in America.

✳ **Location:** Grand Rapids is about 80 miles west of Duluth on U.S. 2. ✳ **Events:** Lumberjack demonstrations, including logrolling, pole climbing, log sawing and axe throwing. There are also chainsaw sculpture competitions and a northern crafts fair. ✳ **Contact:** Tall Timber Days Festival Office, P.O. Box 134, Grand Rapids, MN 55744, (218) 326-5618.

❖ **While You're There:**

The Forest History Center is a reconstruction of a Minnesota logging camp of about 1900. Costumed guides play the roles of actual residents and explain the practices of the lumbering industry, then and now.

MONTEVIDEO

◈ Fiesta Days: Second weekend in June.

The valley of the Minnesota River is about as unlikely a place in the United States as you can imagine for an Hispanic celebration. Yet this Minnesota fiesta has strengthened the bonds between a little town and a country thousands of miles away.

It was customary among nineteenth-century land promoters to name frontier towns after foreign capitals. It was an expression of hope, and also an advertising come-on, enabling their rude collection of huts to bask in the glow of a world-famous city. So there is a plenitude of Cantons and Berlins and Londons on the American map. Not many promoters chose the capital of Uruguay. But the settlers here thought Montevideo was a good fit. Surrounded by hills, "view from the mountain" was a nice description of their community.

In 1948, Uruguay donated a statue of its national hero, Jose Artigas, to the people of Minnesota; it stands today in downtown Montevideo. Since then, this fiesta has been held to celebrate the bonds between this town and the South American country.

✳ **Location:** Montevideo is at the intersection of U.S. 59 and U.S. 212, about 125 miles west of Minneapolis. ✳ **Events:** Street dancing, Hispanic and midwestern crafts, traditional foods and music from both Uruguay and Minnesota. ✳ **Contact:** Montevideo Chamber of Commerce, 110 North First St., Ste. 2, Montevideo, MN 56265, (612) 269-5527.

MORA

◈ Midsummer Scandinavian Festival: June 23.

Minnesota's reputation is that of the most Scandinavian of states. It was a stronghold of immigration from Norway, Sweden, and—to a lesser degree—Denmark in the late nineteenth century. The numbers of foreign-born from these countries, about 200,000, dwarfed any others in the 1900 census. The ties remain strong in both directions. A major Swedish film epic, *The Immigrants*, about the settlement of Minnesota, was made in the 1970s. When Sweden switched from driving on the right side of the road to the left in the mid-1960s, it was regarded as a big enough story in Minneapolis that a local columnist was sent over to cover it.

Many of the newcomers had decided to leave home for political reasons and carried with them an affinity for liberal populism. The state government was dominated for generations by officials with Scandinavian names, adding to Minnesota's national image. According to historian William Lass, however, the groups retained very strong individual identities. "They tended to settle not as Scandinavian communities," he wrote, "but as Norwegian or Swedish towns. It affected the ethnic composition of the state."

Internal movement to the cities broke down some of these ethnic divisions on the map of Minnesota. But the state still treasures the heritage of each particular homeland. Mora lies between the Mississippi and St. Croix Rivers, regarded as the center of Swedish settlement. It is, in fact, named for a sister community in Sweden. While the annual midsummer festival is designed to embrace all the cultures of Scandinavia, Mora gives the celebration its own distinct Swedish spin.

✴ **Location:** Mora is about 70 miles north of Minneapolis on Minnesota 65. ✴ **Events:** Traditional midsummer observances, with costumed dancers, foods and crafts, maypole dancing. ✴ **Contact:** Mora Chamber of Commerce, 20 North Union, Mora, MN 55051, (800) 291-5792.

NEW ULM

 Fasching: Weekend before Ash Wednesday.

The Lenten customs of the Latin countries made the trip to the United States in pretty good shape. Mardi Gras and Carnival are familiar, and in some cases gigantic, American festivals.

The German Catholic celebration of Fasching is less well known. In cities like Munich and Cologne, it is celebrated with the same sense of joy, with masked balls and street dances and parades. The settlers who came to New Ulm in 1854 brought with them not only the name of their German hometown but also its customs. Fasching is observed here as merrily as anyplace in America.

New Ulm started out as a utopian planned community. While the idealism quickly faded, German identity grew stronger over the years. The local landmark, "Herman the German," a statue of Hermann the Cheruscan (known to students of classical history as Arminius), who defeated invading Roman armies in the Rhineland in A.D. 9, was erected in a burst of patriotic fervor in the 1890s. The state also clashed with local officials during World War I over suspected draft evasion, because of the strong German identity of the town. But New Ulm today, with its downtown

Hearty revelers sing at Fasching, a traditional German carnival designed to chase winter away. *(Courtesy of The Concord Singers)*

glockenspiel and its stores stocked with goods from Germany and Austria, is an outpost of more cheerful Old World tradition.

✳ **Location:** New Ulm is on U.S. 14, about 90 miles southwest of Minneapolis. ✳ **Events:** Costumed balls, food festival, parades, bonfires. ✳ **Contact:** Heritage Fest Office, P.O. Box 492, New Ulm, MN 56073, (507) 354-8850.

NORTHFIELD

 Defeat of Jesse James: Weekend after Labor Day.

The three strangers came riding into town on the morning of September 7, 1876, long linen dusters hiding their sidearms. They stopped for a leisurely breakfast and then went about their main item of business for the day—robbing the First National Bank of Northfield.

The men were Jesse James, Bob Younger, and Charlie Pitts—three of the most feared outlaws in the land. From their base in Missouri, the James gang had terrorized banks and trains across a huge swath of America. They ranged as far east as Kentucky and as far south as Texas. Mostly they went in anonymity. Although everyone knew their names, in this age before mass photographic reproductions hardly anyone knew what they looked like. The three bandits could just as easily have been who they said they were, prosperous cattle buyers.

Shots ring out in this exciting re-creation of the gunfight that broke up the notorious Jesse James gang. *(Courtesy of Northfield News)*

At a prearranged signal, five other members of the gang came swooping into Northfield on horseback. They were Jesse's brother, Frank James, two more Younger brothers, and two other associates, both of whom would lie dead in the streets of town before the morning was over. This tactic of creating a terrorizing diversion while the bank was being robbed had worked countless times for the gang. This time something went wrong.

First, the bank tellers refused to be cowed. They fought back, delaying the men inside the bank. While that was going on, the townspeople recovered, and under the leadership of a local medical student, Henry Wheeler, they got their guns and opened fire. A running gunfight erupted in the middle of Northfield. At the end, two were dead on each side and the bandits were in retreat, all of them badly wounded.

Jesse and Frank James managed to escape into the Dakota Territory but disappeared for three years before resuming their careers. Pitts was killed by a pursuing posse. All three Youngers were captured and sentenced to 25 years in the state prison. The Northfield raid ended one of the most notorious associations of outlaws in the West and signaled a clear warning about the hazards of robbing banks in Minnesota.

✳ **Location:** Northfield is just east of Interstate 35, about 45 miles south of Minneapolis. ✳ **Events:** Reenactment of the raid, rodeo, parade, outdoor art and food fair. ✳ **Contact:** Northfield Chamber of Commerce, P.O. Box 198, Northfield, MN 55057-0198, (800) 658-2548.

ST. PAUL

❖ **St. Paul Winter Carnival:** Last weekend of January and first week of February.

The residents of Minnesota's capital had to overcome many indignities in the course of the city's history, including the fact that the first name of their community was Pig's Eye. But none cut as deeply as the snide remark by a New York journalist in 1885 which described their city as "another Siberia, unfit for human habitation."

Taking that as a challenge, St. Paul immediately began making plans for a celebration of Minnesota's winter climate. Picking a time when the thermometer was at its nadir, they held the first Winter Carnival in 1886. The opening day weather was perfect—20 below. About four thousand people turned out to view the Ice Palace, a 106-foot-high building that transformed the wintry field into a northern fantasy.

The carnival was established as a tradition. Native son F. Scott Fitzgerald even placed one of his short stories, "The Ice Palace," in the setting. The story, written in 1918, did not have a happy ending. A southern girl, in St. Paul to meet her fiance's family, is trapped in the palace after closing and is so chilled by the experience that she breaks off the engagement and flees home to Georgia. Most visitors react much more positively. This is the best-attended celebration of its kind in America.

✳ **Location:** Citywide. ✳ **Events:** Pageants, coronation ball for the queen and king of the carnival, parades, ice sculpture, sled dog races, sporting events on ice, snowmobile races, ice-fishing contests. Tickets to some events must be obtained in advance. ✳ **Contact:** St. Paul Festival and Heritage Foundation, 322 Minnesota St., Ste. E-102, St. Paul, MN 55101, (612) 297-6953.

Ohio

❖ **National Cambridge Glass Show:** Last full weekend in June.

Glass was one of the great luxuries of late medieval times. Taxes in England were levied upon the number of windows in a home, since glass was usually an accurate accounting of the wealth in a household. Early British exploration parties to Virginia and Massachusetts were urged to look for stands of timber. Charcoal, which is made from the distillation of timber by fire, was essential as fuel for the manufacture of glass, and there were fears in the early seventeenth century that England's natural supply was running out. Reports from Virginia also enthusiastically stated that the local sand seemed well suited for glassmaking. In 1608, the year after the Jamestown landing, a glass operation already was functioning there, with experts imported from Europe to run it.

By the late nineteenth century, natural gas had replaced wood as the preferred heating agent in glass factories. With the discovery in the 1880s of vast fields of natural gas in Ohio, the industry quickly became centered in this state.

In Cambridge, the emphasis was on tableware and novelties. The Cambridge Glass Company opened in 1902 and over the next half century it turned out some of the most distinctively shaped and colored glassware in the country. Thousands of items were produced in its blowing rooms before the place closed its doors in 1954. But its products developed a life of their own, and collectors of Cambridge products have made this town the country's top meeting place for exhibits of historic glass.

✽ **Location:** At the intersection of Interstates 70 and 77, about 60 miles south of Canton and 50 miles west of Wheeling, West Virginia. ✽ **Events:** Historic glass displays, trading markets, glass-blowing demonstration, crafts booths. ✳ **Contact:** Museum of Cambridge Glass, (614) 432-4254; National Cambridge Collectors, P.O. Box 416, Cambridge, OH 43725-0416.

❖ While You're There:

There are several museums dedicated to Cambridge glass here, and a few glassmaking operations keep the tradition alive. The Museum of Cambridge Glass has what it claims to be the largest collection of locally-made glass in existence, with more than 5,000 items on display. This is the best place to compare the shades of difference in the unique colors that make Cambridge glass so highly prized.

The Degenhart Paperweight and Glass Museum exhibits the personal collection of M. Elizabeth Degenhart, whose family ran one of Cambridge's top glass companies. The Boyd family purchased the Degenhart factory shortly after Elizabeth's death in 1978, and their Crystal Art Glass continues to turn out several traditional and fanciful Degenhart designs, while adding new ones each year.

DAYTON

❖ Dayton International Air Show: Third weekend in July.

Their story was pure Americana. The two brothers running their bicycle shop, combing the public library to do research, and dreaming of a machine that could fly. The shop is now at Greenfield Village, near Detroit, Michigan, and the site of the first flight of a motor-driver aircraft is in North Carolina. But Dayton is heir to the spirit of its hometown Wright brothers.

Each man made two flights on that historic December day in 1903 at Kitty Hawk. Orville was at the controls for the first flight, and Wilbur made the longest one, a trip of 852 feet that lasted fifty-nine seconds. The shared credit marked their entire collaboration, one's ideas advanced by the other so seamlessly that it was impossible to say where any single concept had originated. But with the 1903 tests the brothers knew that they had solved the major problems with powered flight and all that remained was refinement.

Wilbur saw relatively little of the revolution he helped bring about. He died of typhus in 1912. But Orville survived until 1948 as Dayton's most beloved citizen. It was long enough for him to witness all the uses, in travel and trade and war, to which his invention would be put. Where else but in the Wrights' hometown would one of the country's top air shows be held?

✳ **Location:** The show goes on at Dayton International Airport, 10 miles north of the city, by way of Interstate 75 and westbound U.S. 40. ✳ **Events:** Air races, flying exhibitions, antique aircraft, balloons, gliders. Tickets must be purchased in advance. ✳ **Contact:** Dayton Visitors Bureau, 1 Chamber Plaza, Ste. A, Dayton, OH 45402, (800) 221-8235.

❖ While You're There:

The U.S. Air Force Museum, at Wright-Patterson Air Force Base just east of the city, has one of the finest collections of historic aircraft. Displays lay out the development of flying machines and celebrate the early heroes of flight. Just north of the base, on Ohio 4, is the Wright Brothers Memorial, erected in honor of the two inventors. A replica of their bicycle shop is in Carillon Park, south of downtown, off Interstate 75.

EAST LIVERPOOL

❖ Tri-State Pottery Festival: Third weekend in June.

No one paid much attention to the clay until James Bennett arrived. He was a young Englishman who had grown up in Staffordshire and was trained in that area's famous pottery works. While Bennett was on a steamboat trip up the Ohio River in 1838, a passenger happened to mention the unusual clay deposits at what was then called Fawcett's Town. Bennett investigated, and what he saw encouraged him to call on four leading citizens of the town. He said that they were sitting on enormous wealth and asked them to invest in a kiln. They agreed, and that was the start of an industry that would dominate American pottery production for a century.

So many English workers were imported to operate the 200 pottery plants here, including Bennett's two brothers, that the name of the town was changed to East Liverpool to honor the British city. Before the industry went into decline in the 1930s, the plants in the immediate area produced about half of the pottery made in the United States.

The Hall China Company continues its operations in East Liverpool. Other factories are scattered in nearby West Virginia and Pennsylvania. They join together for the Tri-State Festival to celebrate their common heritage.

✳ **Location:** East Liverpool is on the Ohio River, at the intersection of U.S. 30 and Ohio 7, about 40 miles south of Youngstown. ✳ **Events:** Pottery displays, pot-making Olympics, rose show, antique show, plant tours. ✳ **Contact:** East Liverpool Chamber of Commerce, P.O. Box 94, East Liverpool, OH 43920, (216) 385-0845.

❖ While You're There:

The Museum of Ceramics, on East 5th Street, has a complete display of locally-made pottery and information on how the industry shaped the history of the East Liverpool area.

GREENVILLE

❖ Annie Oakley Days: Last full weekend in July.

The song was wrong. You *can* get a man with a gun. And just about everything else, too. The life of Annie Oakley is testimony to that.

She was the top show-woman of the late nineteenth century. Her tours with Buffalo Bill's Wild West Show astonished audiences across North America and Europe. It seemed that there was no feat of marksmanship that could not be performed by this young woman from Ohio. She could hit improbably tiny targets from the back of a galloping horse. She could shoot the pips from a playing card tossed in the air before it could flutter to the ground. She bested Frank Butler, the shooting star of Pawnee Bill's rival show, and later married him—the basis of Irving Berlin's famous musical *Annie, Get Your Gun*.

She was born as Phoebe Mozee (Annie and Oakley were middle names) in 1860 at the nearby village of North Star. After her career was ended in a near-fatal train wreck in 1901, she returned to Greenville to spend the last twenty-five years of her life in retirement. But her hometown recalls its favorite gunslinger each summer.

✳ **Location:** Greenville is north of Dayton, about 20 miles west of Interstate 75, by way of U.S. 36. ✳ **Events:** Shooting contests, balloon rallies, old-time melodramas, parade. ✳ **Contact:** Annie Oakley Committee, P.O. Box 436, Greenville, OH 45331, (513) 548-3492.

❖ While You're There:

The Garst Museum in Greenville has displays relating to the careers of both Annie Oakley and another local favorite, newsman Lowell

*The astounding
shooting skills of
entertainer Annie
Oakley are recalled
with a summertime
festival in the town
where she spent her
last years.* (Archive
Photos, Inc.)

Thomas. Oakley left her prizes and mementoes of her fabulous career to the museum.

HINCKLEY

◈ Return of the Buzzards: Third Sunday in March.

Some places look for swallows. Others for robins. But in this north-eastern Ohio town, buzzards are the birds of spring. Each year on March 15, or thereabouts, they return from southern grounds to take up residence at a nearby lake.

"If I were reincarnated," William Faulkner wrote, "I'd want to come back as a buzzard. Nothing hates him or envies him or wants him or needs him. He is never bothered or in danger, and he can eat anything." Or, he might have added, anything that's dead. Buzzards are carrion-eaters and about as ugly a bird as any that fly. But with a six-foot wingspan, the birds are a majestic sight as they soar across the treetops.

Some local historians attribute the affinity of buzzards for Hinckley with a great slaughter of wild animals by settlers in 1818. The bodies were left to rot and the buzzards picked up on the invitation. Naturalists, however, say that is an unlikely scenario and that the buzzards probably ranged through the area on their flight path for many years. That was just the first time anyone noticed.

Buzzard Day had been a small local observance until 1957, when the birds were written up in a Cleveland newspaper. Since then it has become a major ornithological adventure for those who would never go bird-watching under ordinary circumstances but feel the pull of the buzzards.

✳ **Location:** Hinckley is on Ohio 303, just east of Interstate 71, about 20 miles southwest of Cleveland. ✳ **Events:** Pancake and sausage breakfast, walks led by park rangers who look for the buzzards and explain the birds' habits and habitat. ✳ **Contact:** Hinckley Chamber of Commerce, P.O. Box 354, Hinckley, OH 44233, (216) 278-2066.

ZANESVILLE

 Zane's Trace Commemoration: Third weekend in June.

Before there was a National Road, the first overland route to the West, Ebenezer Zane had blazed his own path through the wilderness of Ohio. Zane's Trace was more primitive, hardly more than ruts through the forest. But it got travelers from Wheeling to Maysville, Kentucky, starting in 1796, and for the few scattered settlers in the Ohio interior it was a lifeline.

Zane is regarded as the first permanent white resident of Ohio. He moved from across the Ohio River to what is now the town of Martin's Ferry shortly after the Revolutionary War. His wife was a heroine of that conflict. During the siege of Fort Henry, near Wheeling, Betty Zane ran from the besieged fort under fire to retrieve ammunition from a nearby house.

Zane received land grants along the route of his trace as payment, much in the way the railroads were given incentives to extend track into the western territories after the 1860s. Zanesville, where his road crossed the Muskingum River, was one of the more profitable grants. His descendants made their homes there for many years. Among them was Zane Grey, who wrote his first novel about the exploits of his illustrious ancestor, Betty Zane. Its success encouraged him to drop his career in dentistry and become the top-selling author of his time.

✳ **Location:** Zanesville is on Interstate 70 and U.S. 40, which is the route of both Zane's Trace and the National Road. It is about 55 miles east of Columbus. ✳ **Events:** Pioneer skills, parades on Zanesville's unique Y-shaped bridge, crafts, flea market. ✳ **Contact:** Zanesville Muskeum County Convention and Visitors Bureau, 205 North Fifth St., Zanesville, OH 43701, (614) 453-5004.

❖ While You're There:

The National Road-Zane Grey Museum, east of the city, has exhibits about the historic roads that came through this area and the life of the famous writer.

West Virginia

BERKELEY SPRINGS

◆ Apple Butter Festival: Columbus Day weekend.

When the western counties of Virginia divided from the mother state at the start of the Civil War, there was a definite geographic reason for the split. These counties lay west of the Appalachian Mountains, a formidable barrier from the rest of the state.

The Eastern Panhandle, however, was not part of the original West Virginia. This area is more like an extension of the Shenandoah Valley. Economically, culturally, and, in many ways, politically, it was more sympathetic to Virginia's secession from the Union. Because of the ease of access from the rest of Virginia, these counties also became a battleground, with armies moving back and forth in countless raids and campaigns. The Baltimore and Ohio Railroad, which had adopted a policy of neutrality, was outraged when Stonewall Jackson took some of its stock in one raid and diverted it to Virginia. The railroad, the most powerful financial force in the area, then threw its entire support to the North and in 1863 took the Eastern Panhandle with it, right into West Virginia.

Accents here are still more southern than mountain. Like the neighboring counties of Virginia, this is a great apple-growing region. As in Winchester (see Virginia), early landowner George Washington directed the tenants of his farms near Berkeley Springs to plant a certain number of acres in apple orchard. It remains the leading crop of the Eastern Panhandle. Apple butter is a top local specialty, and fanciers of the product come here to stock up on their supply.

The traditional process of making apple butter begins with apples simmering in a copper kettle over an open fire. (Courtesy of Stephen J. Shaluta, Jr.)

Washington was also an enthusiastic promoter of the springs as a health resort. He first visited them and took the waters as a teenaged surveyor in 1748 and returned repeatedly throughout the years. When the town was platted in 1777, even though Washington was occupied elsewhere with the colonial army, he still found time to buy a lot in Berkeley Springs, which then was called Bath. Its peak popularity among the wealthy began to fade in the 1830s, but it remains a charming resort town, still centered around the reputed curative powers of its mineral springs.

✳ **Location:** Berkeley Springs is on U.S. 522, about 35 miles north of Winchester, Virginia. ✳ **Events:** Demonstrations of apple butter-making in huge open kettles, street musicians, crafts fair. ✳ **Contact:** Berkeley Springs Chamber of Commerce, 304 Fairfax St., Berkeley Springs, WV 25411, (304) 258-3738.

ELKINS

❖ Mountain State Forest Festival: First weekend in October that includes a Thursday.

The oldest festival in West Virginia, this celebration is a combination of tributes to the state's mountain heritage, autumn foliage, and Appalachian culture. Elkins is surrounded by some of the finest scenery and highest mountains in West Virginia, most of which are part of the Monongahela National Forest. The town was shaped by two of the most formidable men in West Virginia's history: U.S. Sen. Henry Gassaway Davis and his son-in-law, Sen. Stephen Elkins. The two were virtually a political dynasty.

Davis was a brakeman on the Baltimore and Ohio Railroad. He came to the attention of company officials when he successfully completed the first night run in American rail history in 1848. Until then it was regarded as too dangerous to attempt. Davis rose through the ranks of company executives and was elected to the Senate in 1871. He was an ardent promoter of the commercial prospects of mountain valleys in this part of the state and worked consistently to get the railroad extended into this remote region. He finally succeeded in 1889 with the assistance of Elkins, who was then secretary of war in President Benjamin Harrison's cabinet. The town was named for him in 1890.

The railroad enabled lumbermen to exploit the enormous timber resources of the area and Elkins, the center of rail transportation, prospered. The man for whom it was named literally oversaw the place from his home atop a hill right outside Elkins. The town's Davis and Elkins College is named for its two primary benefactors, and the estates of the men are part of its campus. Some of the festival events are held there.

✳ **Location:** Elkins is at the junction of U.S. 33, 219, and 250, about 70 miles south of Morgantown. ✳ **Events:** Wood-chopping competitions, coronation of Queen Silvia (*Silvia* is Latin for forest), parade, crafts fair, jousting tournament, art show, display of forestry products, fiddle and banjo concerts, marksmanship contests. ✳ **Contact:** Mountain State Forest Festival, P.O. Box 369, Elkins, WV 26241, (304) 636-1824.

HARPERS FERRY

❖ Election Day, 1860: Second weekend in October.

As America moved towards the most portentous presidential election in its history, the town of Harpers Ferry was still in shock from events of

Speeches given by Southern politicians on the eve of the Civil War are heard again during the Election Day festival in Harpers Ferry. (Courtesy of Harpers Ferry National Historical Park)

one year before. In October 1859, John Brown and his raiders had seized the federal arsenal here in a poorly considered attempt to incite an uprising among Virginia's slaves. The raid was a total failure. The first man Brown's group killed was an African American. Ten members of the twenty-one-man group were killed, including two of Brown's sons, in an assault by U.S. Marines led by Col. Robert E. Lee and Lt. J. E. B. Stuart. Brown himself was captured, tried for treason, and hanged.

But the action left the South shaken and galvanized abolitionists. Attitudes on both sides hardened, making the descent towards war faster than before. It was apparent that decision would be made when the results of the 1860 election were learned.

National politics had divided into four segments in that historic campaign. Stephen A. Douglas was the candidate of traditional Democrats. John Breckenridge led the Southern wing of the party, where Secessionist sentiment was strongest. John Bell headed the Constitutional Union Party, based in the South but dedicated to preservation of the Union.

In this celebration, supporters of these three candidates walk the streets of Harpers Ferry and deliver campaign addresses, just as they would have done that fall. No spokesman for Abraham Lincoln appears, though. Harpers Ferry was part of Virginia then, and Lincoln's name did not appear on the ballot in any Southern state. Nonetheless, Lincoln's sweeping victory in the North gave him a clear margin in the Electoral College. While historians argue that there was no clear mandate resulting from the election, the inevitable conclusion in 1860 was that secession and war were at hand.

✳ **Location:** Harpers Ferry is on U.S. 340, at the junction of the Potomac and Shenandoah Rivers, about 60 miles northwest of Washington, D.C. ✳ **Events:** Political campaigning 1860-style, with traditional music and speeches, street entertainment, crafts. ✳ **Contact:** Harpers Ferry National Historical Park, P.O. Box 65, Harpers Ferry, WV 25425, (304) 535-6223.

❖ While You're There:

Harpers Ferry National Historical Park preserves most of the area relating to Brown's raid and its aftermath and also runs an excellent visitors' center that places the events of those years in perspective.

SISTERSVILLE

West Virginia Oil and Gas Festival: Second week in September.

The oil boom that flashed through this town is a memory now. It lasted for a generation, from the first discovery in 1889 to the closing of the last well in 1915. But it transformed this quiet Ohio River community and left it a legacy of fine old homes built by its temporary millionaires.

Sistersville was named for two members of its pioneer family, which had an oddly prophetic name for a future oil town. It was Wells. Charles Wells fathered twenty-two children to help populate the community. Daughters eighteen and nineteen, Sarah and Delilah, on whose farm the center of town was platted, are the sisters in its name. (Wells named his twentieth child Twenty and his twenty-first, Plenty. Then he went ahead and sired one more.)

Most of the original town was dislocated during the oil years, when derricks were hastily put up in backyards, along sidewalks, and through the middle of the main street. But the rigs are gone now and the architectural legacy remains.

✳ **Location:** Sistersville is on West Virginia 2, about 40 miles east of Parkersburg. ✳ **Events:** Parade, displays of vintage oil and gas equipment and

Sistersville's Oil and Gas Festival features a show of antique gas engines.

(*Courtesy of West Virgina Oil and Gas Festival*)

gas engines, crafts fair, fiddling contest. ✳ **Contact:** West Virginia Oil and Gas Festival, P.O. Box 25, Sistersville, WV 26175, (304) 652-3671.

WESTON

◆ Stonewall Jackson Heritage Jubilee: Labor Day weekend.

In the midst of territory that removed itself from Virginia rather than leave the Union, one of the Confederate Army's most brilliant leaders grew up. Thomas Jonathan Jackson spent his boyhood on the farm cleared by his grandfather, one of the founders of this community.

The memory of the Civil War lives on in the birthplace of Confederate leader Stonewall Jackson.

(Courtesy Stonewall Jackson Photo Club)

Jackson went on to West Point, served in the Mexican War, and became a teacher at Virginia Military Institute. When Virginia voted for secession in 1861 and residents were forced to choose sides, Jackson decided to cast his lot in with his state. He was appointed commander at Harpers Ferry (see above) after it was abandoned as indefensible by federal troops.

Jackson went on to acclaim as a brilliant leader of the Shenandoah campaign. He won his nickname through his stalwart leadership at First Manassas and was largely responsible for the victory at Second Manassas. Historians regard him as Lee's ablest lieutenant and his death at Chancellorsville in 1863 was a terrible blow to the Southern cause.

Weston changed hands several times during the war, although Jackson never returned to his hometown. The State 4-H Camp, the first in the country, was built adjacent to the former Jackson property. His family's mill is preserved as a display of rural life here at the time of Jackson's birth in 1824.

* **Location:** Weston is off Interstate 79, about 25 miles south of Clarksburg. The camp is 4 miles north on U.S. 19. * **Events:** Mountain crafts and music, traditional dancing, food booths, art fair, Civil War reenactment. * **Contact:** Stonewall Jackson Heritage Jubilee, P.O. Box 956, Weston, WV 26452, (304) 269-1863.

WILLIAMSON

 King Coal Festival: The week preceding the third Saturday in September.

They called it the "billion-dollar coalfield" and Williamson was right at its center. At one time, more than one hundred mines operated within a twenty-mile radius of the place, in West Virginia and across the Tug Fork of the Big Sandy River in Kentucky.

Coal has always been king in West Virginia. The first state seal depicted a miner with a pickax on his shoulder. The growth of the state's railroads was tied directly to discovery of new fields, the lines expanding like a web to penetrate the deep valleys and bring out the coal. It was only after the Norfolk and Western arrived here, in what used to be a cornfield, that Williamson grew up in the 1890s. It was named for local mine operator, Wallace J. Williamson.

This area was the scene of bitter union battles after World War I, with some of the most vicious chapters in American labor history written in Mingo County in battles between strikers and company guards. But statisticians have figured that the amount of coal mined in one nearby county in 1937 was greater than for the entire country of Canada. Production has slackened in recent years as alternate sources of energy are developed. But Williamson's Chamber of Commerce is still housed in a structure built in 1933 from sixty-five tons of coal.

* **Location:** Williamson is on U.S. 119, about 90 miles southwest of Charleston. * **Events:** Coal exhibits, crowning of King Coal, entertainment, dancing, theatrical productions based on the region's history, parade. * **Contact:** King Coal Festival, 28 Oak St., Williamson, WV 25661, (304) 235-5560.

Wisconsin

EPHRAIM

 FyrBal Fest: Weekend closest to June 21.

Norwegian immigration to Wisconsin began slowly in the 1840s. But within forty years this group of newcomers was exceeded only by the Germans in the state's foreign-born population. They left their mark throughout Wisconsin, but because of the ideals of one philanthropist, most memorably on this little Door Peninsula village.

Nils Otto Tank was a member of an aristocratic family. He was deeply interested in religious communities and was told about a group of Moravians who had come to Milwaukee and were looking for a place to settle. Attracted by their theories of religious communism, Tank arrived with $1.5 million in gold and bought land near Green Bay. He laid out the settlement personally and enthusiastically adopted their social and religious doctrines.

But distrust set in. A. M. Iverson, a young religion student, began to wonder about Tank's motives. Why was this wealthy man living in the Wisconsin woods and supporting a small religious group? Iverson suspected Tank of harboring notions of feudalism and demanded that he turn over title to their property to each family. Tank refused, saying that this was contrary to their own teachings. Led by Iverson, the Moravians picked up and left, settling in the present location of Ephraim. The town is now a resort community, but still celebrates many Norwegian traditions, including the midsummer holiday of the FyrBal, in which fires are kept burning all night.

✳ **Location:** Ephraim is on Wisconsin 42, about 75 miles northeast of Green Bay, near the north end of the Door Peninsula. ✳ **Events:** Lighting of the midsummer bonfire, traditional fish boil dinners, potluck, coronation of a FyrBal chieftain. ✳ **Contact:** Ephraim Visitor Center, P.O. Box 203, Ephraim, WI 54211, (414) 854-4989.

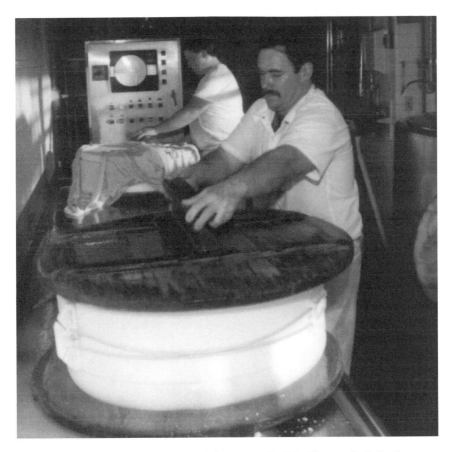

This 180-pound wheel of Swiss was made in a copper kettle in Monroe, the Swiss cheese capital of the U.S. (Courtesy of Studio Haus)

❖ While You're There:

Anderson Store was built to serve the Moravian community here in 1858. It has been restored to the appearance of a general store of the period, with many items unique to the Moravians.

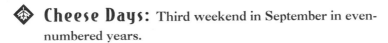

MONROE

❖ Cheese Days: Third weekend in September in even-numbered years.

You see them at football games, wearing ludicrous plastic cheese wedges atop their skulls. They are the Cheeseheads, and their headgear has become the unofficial emblem of the state of Wisconsin, replacing the time-honored badger as a symbol. Approximately half of the Swiss and Limburger cheese in America is produced in the area around Monroe, which must be considered Cheesehead Central.

Early settlers found the southern tier of Wisconsin particularly suited to dairy farming. The cheese industry got a foothold in the Swiss settlement of New Glarus (see below). Later arrivals from Switzerland chose to set up cheese production in this community, though, because of its better rail connections. Monroe soon became the state's top cheese producer, shipping its cheeses around the country.

According to local lore, an ordinance was once passed prohibiting the transport of Limburger through city streets in an open wagon. But since 1914 Monroe has happily celebrated all of its cheeses, the mild and the odorous, in this late summer festival.

✳ **Location:** Monroe is about 40 miles west of Interstate 90 from Beloit, by way of Wisconsin 81. ✳ **Events:** Cheesemaking exhibitions, cheese-tasting, Swiss folk dances and music, band concerts, traditional crafts. ✳ **Contact:** Green County Cheese Days, Inc., P.O. Box 606, Monroe, WI 53566, (608) 325-7771.

NEW GLARUS

Swiss Volksfest: First Sunday in August.

The cheesemaking success story celebrated by Monroe (see above) really began in this nearby village, the first significant Swiss settlement in Wisconsin. The Canton of Glarus in Switzerland organized an official immigration society after crop failures had brought hard times to the farm region in 1844. Two local residents were sent to the United States to find a place that would accommodate the sort of farming skills learned in Glarus.

The men searched the Midwest and finally settled upon this valley in southern Wisconsin. Unfortunately, their instructions back home were a bit vague, and the party of 193 emigrants landed in St. Louis, with no idea of where to proceed. It took four months to connect with the advance team, but in August 1845 they arrived in their new home.

Prosperity did not come soon. The Swiss were convinced that they should grow wheat. Only when its price collapsed after the Civil War did they adapt the dairying methods they knew in Switzerland to New Glarus. Their cheese won markets across the country and led directly to the establishment of the major industry in Monroe.

The art of alphorn blowing has not been forgotten in the Swiss community of New Glarus.
(Courtesy of New Glarus Chamber of Commerce)

New Glarus has remained a tiny community, still mindful of its Swiss heritage. Much of the town is decorated in Swiss rural style and old traditions that measure the pace of life are still carried on.

✳ **Location:** New Glarus is about 18 miles north of Monroe, and about 30 miles southwest of Madison, by way of Wisconsin 69. ✳ **Events:** Traditional songs and dances in Swiss costume, patriotic observances recalling the birth of the Swiss nation at this time of year in 1291, flag throwing, accordion music. ✳ **Contact:** New Glarus Chamber of Commerce, P.O. Box 713, New Glarus, WI 53574, (608) 527-2095.

❖ While You're There:

The Upright Embroidery Factory produces traditional lace, proving that the Swiss are capable of more than cheese. Imported Schiffli looms can be viewed in production.

RHINELANDER

❖ Hodag Festival: Second full weekend in July.

When things got slow in the North during the long winters, people would tell fantastic stories—about lumbering giant Paul Bunyan, and the Wendigo which raced through the woods with feet of flame. But

Rhinelander's very own tall tale was the Hodag, and the town treasures the beast.

The Hodag was something like the Bigfoot of its day, a fabulous animal that lived out in the swamps, seen only by a few. Nonetheless, a few residents of Rhinelander insisted that it was still out there. Then one day its carcass was discovered in a swamp outside of town.

It was brought into Rhinelander and caused a sensation. With its huge horns and claws and rows of teeth, it looked like something out of a nightmare. Trains came in bringing visitors who demanded to see this marvel. After weeks of mounting hysteria, local resident Gene Shepard finally confessed. He had made the thing out of an oxhide and some wood. Rather than being resentful, Rhinelander adopted the Hodag as its own. It nicknamed itself the Hodag Town, gave the name to its athletic squads, and celebrated the fact that it is fun to be fooled. Or maybe it was just relief that the thing wasn't real, after all.

✳ **Location:** Rhinelander is about 55 miles north of Wausau by way of U.S. 51 and Wisconsin 17. ✳ **Events:** Country music stage show, food booths. ✳ **Contact:** Hodag Festival Committee, 4743 Business Hwy 8, Rhinelander, WI 54501, (715) 369-1300.

❖ While You're There:

The Rhinelander Logging Museum has exhibits on the town's history as a lumbering camp and a replica of the hideous Hodag.

Great Plains

Iowa

Kansas

Missouri

Nebraska

North Dakota

Oklahoma

South Dakota

Texas

GREAT PLAINS

Iowa

1. National Hobo Convention, Britt
2. Steamboat Days, Burlington
3. Houby Days, Cedar Rapids
4. Glenn Miller Festival, Clarinda
5. Bix Beiderbecke Festival, Davenport

Kansas

6. Wah-Shun-Gah Days, Council Grove
7. Dodge City Days, Dodge City
8. Beef Empire Days, Garden City
9. Barbed Wire Festival, LaCrosse
10. International Pancake Race, Liberal
11. Messiah Festival, Lindsborg
12. Mini-Sapa Days, Oberlin

Missouri

13. Tom Sawyer Days, Hannibal
14. Maifest, Hermann
15. Santa-Cali-Gon Days, Independence
16. Lewis and Clark Rendezvous, Fete des Petites Cotes, St. Charles
17. Jour de Fete, Ste. Genevieve
18. Scott Joplin Ragtime Festival, Sedalia

Nebraska

19. Homestead Days, Beatrice
20. Oregon Trail Days, Gering
21. Arbor Day, Nebraska City

North Dakota

22. Roughriders Days, Ukrainian Festival, Dickinson

23. Frontier Army Days, Mandan
24. Norsk Hostfest, Minot
25. Bonanza Days, Wahpeton
26. Fort Union Rendezvouus, Williston

Oklahoma

27. American Indian Exposition, Anadarko
28. Will Rogers Days, Claremore
29. 89er Celebration, Guthrie
30. Creek Nation Festival, Pecan Festival, Okmulgee
31. Cherokee Strip Celebration, Perry
32. Cherokee National Holiday, Tahlequah

South Dakota

33. Gold Discovery Days, Custer
34. Days of '76, Deadwood
35. Corn Palace Festival, Mitchell

Texas

36. Charro Days, Brownsville
37. Chisholm Trail Roundup, Fort Worth
38. Fredericksburg Easter Fires Pageant, Fredericksburg
39. "Come and Take It" Days, Gonzales
40. Fiesta San Antonio, Las Posadas, San Antonio
41. World's Largest Rattlesnake Roundup, Sweetwater
42. Texas Rose Festival, Tyler
43. Texas Independence Day, Washington-on-the-Brazos
44. St. Anthony's Day, Ysleta

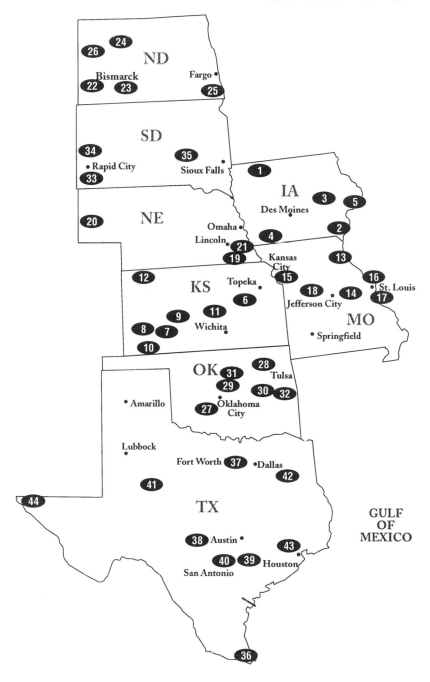

❖ February

Saturday before Ash Wednesday: **International Pancake Race,** Liberal, Kansas

Last weekend: **Charro Days,** Brownsville, Texas

◈ March

Weekend closest to March 2: **Texas Independence Day,** Washington-on-the-Brazos, Texas

Second weekend: **World's Largest Rattlesnake Roundup,** Sweetwater, Texas

◈ April

Saturday before Easter: **Fredericksburg Easter Fires Pageant,** Fredericksburg, Texas

Easter Week: **Messiah Festival,** Lindsborg, Kansas

Week including April 21 (unless it falls during Easter Week): **Fiesta San Antonio,** San Antonio, Texas

Last weekend: **Arbor Day,** Nebraska City, Nebraska

Last weekend: **89er Celebration,** Guthrie, Oklahoma

◈ May

First weekend: **Barbed Wire Festival,** LaCrosse, Kansas

Third weekend: **Houby Days,** Cedar Rapids, Iowa

Third weekend: **Maifest,** Hermann, Missouri

Third weekend: **Lewis and Clark Rendezvous,** St. Charles, Missouri

◈ June

First weekend: **Scott Joplin Ragtime Festival,** Sedalia, Missouri

First two weekends: **Beef Empire Days,** Garden City, Kansas

Second weekend: **Glenn Miller Festival,** Clarinda, Iowa

Second weekend: **Wah-Shun-Gah Days,** Council Grove, Kansas

Second weekend: **Will Rogers Days,** Claremore, Oklahoma

13: **St. Anthony's Day,** Ysleta, Texas

Week before Father's Day: **Steamboat Days,** Burlington, Iowa

Third weekend: **Creek Nation Festival,** Okmulgee, Oklahoma

Third weekend: **Fort Union Rendezvous,** Williston, North Dakota

Third weekend: **Frontier Army Days,** Mandan, North Dakota

Third weekend: **Homestead Days,** Beatrice, Nebraska

Third weekend: **Pecan Festival,** Okmulgee, Oklahoma

Last full weekend: **Bix Beiderbecke Festival,** Davenport, Iowa

Dates vary: **Chisholm Trail Roundup,** Fort Worth, Texas

◈ July

Weekend closest to July 4: **Roughriders Days,** Dickinson, North Dakota

Week of July 4: **Tom Sawyer Days,** Hannibal, Missouri

Weekend closest to July 15: **Oregon Trail Days,** Gering, Nebraska

Third weekend: **Ukrainian Festival,** Dickinson, North Dakota

Fourth weekend: **Gold Discovery Days,** Custer, South Dakota

Weekend beginning the last Friday: **Dodge City Days,** Dodge City, Kansas

❖ August

First full weekend: **Days of '76,** Deadwood, South Dakota

Second Saturday: **National Hobo Convention,** Britt, Iowa

Second full weekend: **Jour de Fete,** Ste. Genevieve, Missouri

Third full weekend: **Fete des Petites Cotes,** St. Charles, Missouri

Third week: **American Indian Exposition,** Anadarko, Oklahoma

❖ September

Labor Day weekend: **Bonanza Days,** Wahpeton, North Dakota

Labor Day weekend: **Cherokee National Holiday,** Tahlequah, Oklahoma

Labor Day weekend: **Santa-Cali-Gon Days,** Independence, Missouri

Second or third week: **Corn Palace Festival,** Mitchell, South Dakota

16: **Cherokee Strip Celebration,** Perry, Oklahoma

❖ October

First full weekend: **"Come and Take It" Days,** Gonzales, Texas

First full weekend: **Mini-Sapa Days,** Oberlin, Kansas

Second week: **Norsk Hostfest,** Minot, North Dakota

Second full weekend: **Texas Rose Festival,** Tyler, Texas

❖ November

First weekend: **Will Rogers Days,** Claremore, Oklahoma

❖ December

Second Sunday: **Las Posadas,** San Antonio, Texas

Iowa

❖ National Hobo Convention: Second Saturday in August.

It started as a gag in a rural Iowa newspaper in 1900. An editor wrote that there would be a national assembly of hoboes in this little town. When reporters showed up to cover the gathering, they found out it was all a hoax. But they decided to play along and wrote outlandish stories about the nonexistent event. It received such wide coverage that in the following year, hoboes actually did show up in Britt—a very early example of life imitating the media. The Hobo Convention has been held annually ever since.

With concerns about homeless people appearing in contemporary media daily, it is no longer proper to write lightly about tramps. But even in 1900, the situation was far weightier than the cartoon image of the carefree hobo—riding the rails and carrying his belongings in a knapsack over his shoulder. He was the Bum, the Little Tramp, the symbols of the Brooklyn Dodgers and Charlie Chaplin.

In reality, hoboes first appeared after the Civil War. Many uprooted veterans found that they could not return to the routine of their old life and took to traveling endlessly, hitching rides on boxcars. At first, the railroads felt it was their duty to allow these homeward-bound veterans aboard. Then things got ugly and security police were told to get rid of the men and to clean up their encampments, or hobo jungles, along the tracks. After the Panic of 1893, there were massive layoffs of people who had just left the farms to find work in the factories. With nowhere to go, they went on the road, too. By 1900, an estimated 65,000 homeless men wandered the land. They were romantic figures to some, but in many small towns they were blamed for most crimes and were frequently attacked by local police.

The Hobo Convention is more of a nostalgic look at these times than a genuine gathering of today's knights of the road.

✳ **Location:** Britt is on U.S. 18, about 21 miles west of Interstate 35. ✳ **Events:** Carnivals, talent shows, hobo parade, serving of mulligan stew, story telling. ✳ **Contact:** Britt Chamber of Commerce, P.O. Box 63, Britt, IA 50423, (515) 843-3867.

BURLINGTON

◈ **Steamboat Days:** Week before Father's Day weekend.

Many communities along America's great inland rivers recall their heritage with celebrations centered on the waterfronts. Especially on the Ohio, the Mississippi, and the Missouri, the river brought life. The waterway was the town's very reason for being.

Burlington, which climbs the Iowa bluffs above the Mississippi, puts on one of the best of these festivals. The place was the site of Native American encampments for years because of its flint deposits and strategic location. Later, it was the capital of the Wisconsin Territory, before Iowa was split off to form a territory of its own. In the years before the Civil War it was the chief port of embarkation for travelers bound for the state's interior. Because it served as this entryway, it also became a starting point for one of the first rail lines to the West. After the war, the river brought logs, floated down from Wisconsin for processing.

The town has retained much of the nineteenth-century look in its residential districts, especially those that lead down to the river. Snake Alley, a winding brick street that has seven curves in one block as it twists down the bluff, is the gateway to this historic area. On Memorial Day weekend, there is a bike race up this course. But during Steamboat Days, the fun is down on the riverfront.

✳ **Location:** Burlington is about 80 miles southwest of Davenport, by way of U.S. 34 and U.S. 61. ✳ **Events:** Concerts, regatta, parades, carnival, water-skiing, steamboat rides. ✳ **Contact:** Burlington Steamboat Days, P.O. Box 271, Burlington, IA 52601, (319) 754-4334.

CEDAR RAPIDS

◈ **Houby Days:** Third weekend in May.

When Czechs joined the throng of immigrants to America in the mid-nineteenth century, their primary destination was Iowa. Here in the

Polka dancing is one of the attractions of the Houby Days celebration of Czech heritage in Cedar Rapids. (Courtesy of Cedar Rapids Area Convention and Visitors Bureau)

rich, black soil of the Midwest, they put together a culture so vital that when composer Anton Dvorak came to America to write his "New World" Symphony, he spent much of 1893 in a small Iowa town to capture a Czech ambience while on these shores.

Cedar Rapids became a particular magnet for these newcomers. They clustered on the southwestern side of the city, making it into a community that was called "Little Bohemia." There was a Czech-language newspaper and a Czech bank, and much of the business was conducted in that language.

The area is preserved as Czech Village and it still maintains some of the old traditions. Among them is the hunt for "houby" (Czech for morel) mushrooms, an annual rite of spring in the old country.

✳ **Location:** Czech Village is concentrated along 16th Avenue, SW, just off downtown. ✳ **Events:** Mushroom hunt contests, Czech crafts and folk art, costumed dancers, traditional foods. ✳ **Contact:** Cedar Rapids

Convention and Visitors Bureau, P.O. Box 5339, Cedar Rapids, IA 52406, (800) 735-5557.

❖ While You're There:

The Czech and Slovak Museum, on 16th Street, is the finest collection in America of folk art, crafts, and national costumes from these lands.

CLARINDA

❖ Glenn Miller Festival: Second weekend in June.

Of all the big bands that flourished in the Swing Era of the 1930s and 1940s, the one led by Glenn Miller remains as the symbol of the times. Other bands might have had better musicians or more imaginative arrangements. But the Miller sound, unmistakable and romantic, with reeds carrying the melody, can never be forgotten by anyone who danced to it, whether fifty years ago or yesterday.

Miller was the first artist to sell over one million records of a song, with his version of "Chattanooga Choo Choo" in 1943. The band's recording of "In the Mood" has, over time, become the musical signature of the entire era. While the original Miller organization lasted just seven years—from 1937 until its leader's disappearance before Christmas of 1944 in a wartime flight across the English Channel—the sound has never really been gone. The band was reassembled by former personnel right after World War II and has gone on touring ever since.

Among the places it plays annually is the birthplace of its leader. This is one of the country's top nostalgia-fests, as big bands from around the world swing again in this Iowa town.

✳ **Location:** Clarinda is in southwest Iowa, about 90 miles southeast of Omaha, Nebraska, by way of Iowa 2, U.S. 59, and Iowa 92. ✳ **Events:** Big band concerts, tours of Miller's birthplace, Swing Era displays, dance, vocal and instrumental scholarship competition, presentations by original band members and associates. ✳ **Contact:** Glenn Miller Birthplace Society, P.O. Box 61, Clarinda, IA 51632, (712) 542-2461.

The house where big band leader Glenn Miller was born has been restored to its 1904 condition. (Courtesy of the Glenn Miller Birthplace Society)

DAVENPORT

◈ Bix Beiderbecke Festival: Last full weekend in July.

He was the prototype of the doomed jazz artist, a brilliant musician with a self-destructive drive that ran deeper than the Mississippi. Leon Bix Beiderbecke grew up in Davenport and heard the music. Just as the old cliche said, it was coming up the river from New Orleans. He learned to play it on the showboats that still wheeled along the river in the 1920s.

In those years, jazz was music played predominantly by black musicians. Formally trained whites seemed to lack the improvisational ability that lay at the heart of jazz. But Bix Beiderbecke was brilliant at it. His cornet solos and unique phrasing, heard on scratchy old discs more than

Bix Beiderbecke's influential jazz style developed out of musical influences he heard while growing up along the Mississippi River.

(Archive Photos, Inc.)

sixty years after their first recording, still have the power to charm. He inspired an entire generation of young composers and artists, among them Hoagy Carmichael and Benny Goodman.

His life, which was the model for the classic film *Young Man with a Horn,* was cut short at the age of twenty-eight. Filling the well of his talent with alcohol and riotous nights was more than his body could support. Davenport recalls its local jazzman with this musical tribute.

✳ **Location:** Most of the events take place in LeClaire Park, along the riverfront. ✳ **Events:** Concerts, riverboat races. ✳ **Contact:** Bix Beiderbecke Memorial Society, P.O. Box 3688, Davenport, IA 52808, (319) 324-7170.

Kansas

COUNCIL GROVE

❖ Wah-Shun-Gah Days: Second weekend in June.

A thick canopy of trees grew where the Santa Fe Trail crossed the Neosho River. This grove was the trail's jumping-off place, the last outfitting point before travelers crossed the wild, unsettled Plains between here and Santa Fe. It was also a place for parleys between whites and the Native Americans who lived in the area. These tribes were the Osage and the Kaw, or as they were also known, the Kansa. The remains of the oak under which the treaty of safe passage through their lands was signed in 1825 are still preserved here.

The Kansa were given reservation lands at Council Grove in 1847, and four years later the Methodist Church opened a mission here. But the Kansa were not interested in the religion. The Indian school which opened with high expectations was shut down. The Kaw Mission Museum still stands in the middle of town. The building did attain historic significance in 1854 when it reopened as the territory's first public school.

As the white presence in the area increased, the Kansa claim on their lands became shaky. Finally, in 1873, under growing pressure from settlers and local business, the tribe was removed to Indian Territory and left the state to which it had given its name. The Kansa dissolved as a legal entity in 1903 but have reestablished a tribal council at Kaw City, Oklahoma. This festival in their former home is named after the last Kansa chief and has been celebrated since 1983.

✳ **Location:** Council Grove is on U.S. 56, about 60 miles southwest of Topeka. ✳ **Events:** Indian encampment, parade, races, Santa Fe Trail rides. ✳ **Contact:** Council Grove Chamber of Commerce, 200 West Main, Council Grove, KS 66864, (316) 767-5882.

Riders at the Wah-Shun-Gah Days festival follow part of the same trail that nineteenth-century pioneers took to Santa Fe. (Courtesy of the Council Grove Chamber of Commerce)

DODGE CITY

❖ Dodge City Days: Weekend beginning the last Friday of July.

The greatest lawmen of the Old West tried to tame this town. Wyatt Earp and Bat Masterson, Bill Tilghman and Luke Short. Each strapped on his guns, kept the peace for a few months or a year, and then passed on to another of the West's wilder places. But Dodge City stayed as nasty as ever. What really tamed the town was the great blizzard of 1887. That ended the era of the great cattle drives, when Dodge City was the main railhead to the East for the ranches of the Southern Plains and trouble walked its streets with the arrival of every herd.

Dodge's wild time as a cowtown was brief, less than a decade. But the legend is among the most enduring in American history. Masterson and Short became dime novelists, and their experiences here provided much of their material. With the rise of the western movie, other writers adapted their earlier descriptions and embellished them. While the real Dodge City settled into a rather sedate anonymity, its roaring past blazed from the screen in dozens of films. The most successful western in television history, *Gunsmoke*, was also set in Dodge City, introducing an entirely new generation to the lore.

The local Rotary Club restored the town's Boot Hill graveyard and another civic effort did the same for Front Street, the notorious thoroughfare where gunslingers ate hot lead. Both restorations emphasize the legends rather than the history, but that's what most visitors to

Dodge City Days pays tribute to the mythical Old West with a reenactment of the Great Train Robbery. (Courtesy of the Dodge City Area Chamber of Commerce)

Dodge City want. This annual festival runs along the same lines, celebrating a past that is a lot more brave and glamorous in the retelling than it was the first time around.

✳ **Location:** Dodge City is at the junction of U.S. 50 and 283, about 90 miles south of Interstate 70. ✳ **Events:** Parades, rodeo, Old West entertainment and costumes, arts and crafts, street dances, barbecue cooking contest. ✳ **Contact:** Dodge City Convention and Visitors Bureau, P.O. Box 1474, Dodge City, KS 67801, (316) 225-8186.

Thrilling rodeo events highlight Beef Empire Days. (Courtesy of Beef Empire Days and F-Stop Photo)

GARDEN CITY

◈ Beef Empire Days: First two weekends in June.

As you can tell by its name, some of the early settlers of Garden City had been misinformed about the surrounding soil. This was fine grazing land for cattle. But the newcomers hoped to grow corn on the High Plains. The sparse rainfall on the Plains gave the farmers hardly any margin for error. While they managed to harvest a few crops, the drought of the late 1880s drove them off the land.

Then the wheat farmers arrived. Inspired by record market prices for the crop during World War I, and against the advice of veteran stockmen in the area, they plowed under much of the prime grassland to grow wheat. When the price plummeted in the 1920s, they were forced to turn still more land over to cultivation to stay even. Then the drought years returned in the 1930s, and one of the country's greatest ecological calamities, the Dust Bowl, was the result. With the protective grasses removed there was nothing to hold down the dry topsoil and it began to blow away, clouding the sky in huge, dark windstorms.

But a balance has been struck since then. Garden City now sits amid one of the great irrigation belts in Kansas, and a profitable sugar beet industry has been built up here. But cattle ranches are still the mainstay of the local economy. The western Kansas plains remain one of the nation's top beef-producing areas. There may be gardens at last in Garden City, but it's the beef that earns this celebration.

✳ **Location:** Garden City is at the junction of U.S. 50 and 83, about 50 miles west of Dodge City. ✳ **Events:** The first weekend features a rodeo. The second weekend features a number of other events, including a cattle show, chuckwagon cookouts, cowboy poetry readings, parade, western art, street dances. ✳ **Contact:** Garden City Chamber of Commerce, 1511 East Fulton Terrace, Garden City, KS 67846, (316) 276-3264.

LA CROSSE

◈ Barbed Wire Festival: First weekend in May.

The days of the open range, when cattle wandered freely and twice a year cowboys rode out to round them up and brand the new calves, is a treasured part of western lore. This communitarian system developed out of necessity. On the Plains, there wasn't enough wood to build fences. Line riders patrolled the borders of each ranch but most cattle grazed on common pastureland controlled by the federal government.

But with the production of barbed wire in the mid 1870s, those days came to an end. Ranchers now had a practical way of enclosing their land. There had been wire fences before, but they were easily knocked down by determined cattle. The barbs made this fencing permanent. The line rider was replaced by the fence rider, who endlessly rode the perimeter of the wire to make repairs where weather had damaged it.

The coming of barbed wire made it much more difficult and riskier to build up one's herd by rustling cattle. Many substantial herds were created by such activity on the open range. But the wire also touched off range wars in some states. Outraged small ranchers regarded it as a plot to drive them off the best pastureland, and they resorted to night raids on the fences, cutting them down to give their cattle access. It became a political issue, with the Greenback Party siding with the cutters and accusing the big ranchers of trying to turn their small competitors into serfs. Moreover, some of the fencers illegally put their wire across public roads. It took a decade to work out a fair solution in the legislatures of many Plains states.

On the Kansas Plains, La Crosse recalls that era with its Barbed Wire Museum. It contains the earliest sample of the wire, dating from 1854, as well as international styles and a sample of barbed wire used during trench warfare in World War I. This celebration salutes barbed wire in all its varieties and its significance in the development of the West.

✶ **Location:** La Crosse is on U.S. 183, about 25 miles south of Interstate 70, from the Hays exit. ✶ **Events:** Collectors' meet, splicing contests, community cookouts, public auction. ✶ **Contact:** Barbed Wire Museum, P.O. Box 716, 201 West First, La Crosse, KS 67548, (913) 222-9900.

LIBERAL

 International Pancake Race: Saturday before Ash Wednesday.

The custom originated in Olney, England, sometime during the fifteenth century. According to local lore, a housewife making pancakes with the last of her cooking fat, which was forbidden during Lent, lost track of the time. She was still baking when she heard the bells ring for the start of worship. She raced to the church with her apron still on and her skillet in her hand.

From that incident, a competition developed among the women of Olney. Starting at the village well, they would run the 415 yards to the church through the winding streets of the village carrying their skillets. A custom developed that pancakes had to be flipped when the race began and as a contestant crossed the finish line, as proof that she still had the cakes. If a pancake was dropped, a runner had to stop and retrieve it.

In 1950, the president of the Liberal Jaycees read about this custom and decided that it was just the thing for his town. R. J. Leete cabled the British organizer of the race and challenged Olney to a competition. While Liberal is laid out in a grid like most western towns, a 415-yard zigzag course, identical to the one in England, was plotted through its streets. Liberal's contestants dress in traditional aprons and headscarves, although in Kansas the kiss for the winner is not given by the church bell-ringer as it in Olney. For the American event, the British consul for the area is called in to perform that duty.

✻ **Location:** Liberal is in southwestern Kansas, at the junction of U.S. 54 and 83, about 80 miles southwest of Dodge City. ✻ **Events:** Pancake race, community pancake breakfast, parade, eating and flipping contests, amateur talent show. ✻ **Contact:** Liberal Chamber of Commerce, 1021 South Pennsylvania, Liberal, KS 67901, (316) 624-3855.

LINDSBORG

◈ Messiah Festival: Easter Week.

The town was settled entirely by Swedish pioneers in 1869 and named for three community leaders. Their names were Lindgren, Lindell, and Linde. It maintained a strong ethnic character over the years, a little slice of Scandinavia in the midst of the wheat belt. But Lindsborg met its destiny when Dr. Carl Swensson arrived in 1878 as pastor of Bethany Church.

Swensson was a graduate of the Swedish Lutheran Church's Augustana College in Illinois. While he was there, he came under the influence of a music teacher who was determined to perform Handel's *Messiah* oratorio at the school. He never accomplished that but did give a number of choral recitals, which inspired Swensson. When he arrived in Kansas he decided to try to further this work at the proper time.

The impetus came with the founding of Bethany College here in 1881, with Swensson as its first president. To raise funds for the school, he organized a choral group and gave concerts in neighboring towns. On Easter Sunday, 1882, Swensson brought in his former music teacher from Augustana along with the school orchestra to lead his new choral group of farmers and merchants in a triumphant performance of the *Messiah*.

The presentation has been repeated ever since, expanding to Palm Sunday in 1889. Oratorios by J. S. Bach also are performed, and outstanding guest soloists are invited to sing with the chorus each year. Its home has moved from the old Bethany Church into the college's Presser Hall, a gift from a music publisher who was awed by the level of the chorus's artistry. A week-long festival has grown up around the performances.

✻ **Location:** Lindsborg is off Highway 81 on Interstate 135, about 70 miles north of Wichita. ✻ **Events:** Concerts, art exhibitions. ✻ **Contact:** Bethany College, Office of Special Events, 421 North First St., Lindsborg, KS 67456, (913) 227-3311.

✜ While You're There:

The Birger Sandzen Memorial Gallery, on the Bethany campus, features works of art by Swedish-American painters from this community.

The McPherson County Old Mill Museum contains displays of Swedish pioneer life.

OBERLIN

 Mini-Sapa Days: First full weekend of October.

The plains of western Kansas were thickly populated by Native Americans when white settlers arrived in the region. When the Indian wars intensified in the 1860s, the area became a battleground. Indian raids were met with army retaliation all across the Kansas plains.

The end came in 1878. The Northern Cheyenne had been defeated by the army in a series of fights in the fall of 1876. Although the Northern Cheyenne were recognized by treaty as a separate group, the Indian Bureau arbitrarily removed them to an Oklahoma reservation with the tribe's southern branch. In unfamiliar land with no way of supporting themselves, the northern group suffered forty-one dead over the winter; two-thirds of the remainder fell ill from the effects of starvation and poor medical care. Two bands of Northern Cheyenne broke away late in the summer of 1878 and made a run for their former homes. Under the leadership of Dull Knife and Little Wolf, they raced north through western Kansas with the U.S. Fourth Cavalry right at their heels.

While the two leaders tried to make this a peaceful campaign, they could not control all their young men. There were raids along the way, some of them murderous. The last town hit in Kansas was Oberlin. On September 28, as the Cheyenne came through, nineteen settlers were killed. The Indians galloped on into Nebraska, where they divided. Dull Knife was captured near Fort Robinson and killed in January 1879, during an attempted breakout with sixty-four of his men. But Little Wolf surrendered peacefully and his group was allotted lands for the Northern Cheyenne reservation in Montana.

Oberlin commemorates the last Indian raid in Kansas with this festival, which recalls the slain settlers and the town's pioneer past. The Last Indian Raid Museum displays artifacts from that event.

✳ **Location:** Oberlin is at the junction of U.S. 36 and 83, about 60 miles north of Interstate 70 at the Kansas 23 exit. ✳ **Events:** Arts festival, Indian encampment, pioneer crafts, antique show, museum open house. ✳ **Contact:** Last Indian Raid Museum, 258 South Penn, Oberlin, KS 67749, (913) 475-2712.

Missouri

❖ Tom Sawyer Days: Week of July 4.

The greatest of Mark Twain's books, if you took a vote of intellectuals, would be *Huckleberry Finn*. If you asked journalists, the winner might be *Life on the Mississippi* or *Roughing It*. But if you inquired among average readers, the easy winner would be *The Adventures of Tom Sawyer.*

While Huck was a symbol of the American spirit, always ready to head out for the frontier to find freedom, it was his pal, Tom, who captured the essence of boyhood. Wearing his straw hat, carrying his fishing pole, a gleam of mischief in his eyes which go all gooey at the sight of Becky Thatcher, Tom Sawyer was an immediate hit when he first appeared in 1876, and his popularity never waned.

Twain placed Tom and Huck in an idyllic town called St. Petersburg. It was obviously modeled after his boyhood home of Hannibal, where he grew up as young Samuel Clemens, with the wide Mississippi River at his front door and the deep forest at his back. "Nothing touches this serenity," Twain's biographer Bernard DeVoto wrote about this portrait of mid-nineteenth-century small-town America. "The steamboats bring pageantry, not pressure from the world outside. The village is ignorant of that world—which is hardly a rumor, hardly a dream."

Tom Sawyer distilled the experiences of boyhood and placed them in the purified village of Twain's memories. The success of the book brought Twain international fame and a degree of financial comfort, although this was always a struggle for him. He was urged to revive Tom in subsequent books, which he did in *Tom Sawyer Abroad*. While almost unread today, aside from Twain scholars, the book sold so well in early editions that it still ranks seventh in the author's all-time sales.

A whitewashing contest straight from the pages of Tom Sawyer takes place each year in Hannibal, Missouri, the birthplace of author Mark Twain. (Courtesy of Hannibal Visitor's Bureau)

The young shrewdness of Tom as he persuades his friends to whitewash Aunt Polly's fence has become the most endearing episode of *The Adventures of Tom Sawyer*, the one that defines his character. The ritual whitewashing is a central feature of this celebration of Hannibal's past and its fictional son.

✳ **Location:** Hannibal is on the Great River Road, U.S. 61, about 115 miles northwest of St. Louis. ✳ **Events:** Whitewashing competition, jumping frog contest, tomboy games, Mississippi mud volleyball tournament, fireworks, tours of Hannibal sites associated with Twain and Tom Sawyer. ✳ **Contact:** Hannibal Visitors' Bureau, 505 North Third, Hannibal, MO 63401, (314) 221-2477.

✧ While You're There:

Samuel Clemens's boyhood home, built in 1843 and now a museum of his life, is in the middle of Hannibal. Nearby is Mark Twain Cave, scene of many of Tom's adventures. A sculpture of Tom and Huck stands on the riverfront.

HERMANN

◈ **Maifest:** Third weekend in May.

As the great waves of German immigrants came pouring into America in the 1830s and 1840s, there were some who hoped that a German-speaking state could be carved out of the wilderness in the West. A Philadelphia-based group, the German Settlement Society, wanted at the very least to plant colonies. The hope was that once free of the crowded eastern cities, with their jumble of ethnic groups, the colonists could preserve a purity of German language and culture.

Hermann was one such colony. The settlers arrived in 1837, but all the planning was done in Philadelphia. The design for the town had been drawn up there, with public squares in each of its quarters, as well as plans for the proper German cultural organizations. Within two years, the Hermann settlers grew tired of all that and cut their ties with Philadelphia. But the town did retain much of its ethnic character for generations. Its easygoing tolerance for Sunday entertainment and shopping even brought Hermann into conflict with the state legislature, which shut down the stores and taverns in 1905. (The so-called "blue laws" have long since been rescinded and Sunday is again a day of enjoyment.)

The settlers were skilled at winemaking and made it the basis for the local economy. The Stone Hill and Hermannhof wineries, both founded before 1852, are still in operation. Stone Hill was once the third largest winery in the country, but was put out of business by Prohibition and didn't resume operation until 1965. The traditional Maifest commemorates the town's ethnic roots and its dedication to the art of wine.

✳ **Location:** Hermann is on the Missouri River, at Missouri 19, about 45 miles east of Jefferson City. ✳ **Events:** Parade, street entertainment, crafts fair, tours of historic homes, ethnic dancing, food and wine. ✳ **Contact:** Hermann Tourism Group, 306 Market, Highway 19, Hermann, MO 65041, (314) 486-2744.

❖ **While You're There:**

The Historic Hermann Museum has displays about the town's early years and the steamboat era on the Missouri.

INDEPENDENCE

◈ **Santa-Cali-Gon Days:** Labor Day weekend.

"We're going west tomorrow with our fortunes in our hands." That's the way one writer summed up what Independence means in American history. This is where the hopes of a new life finally got to look out on the realities of the hard voyage ahead. Independence was where the three great trails to the western frontier—Santa Fe, Oregon, and California—began. For thirty years, the wagon trains assembled here. The first of the overland stages clattered through its streets. The steamboats brought in the next round of pioneers, headed for new land beyond the Rockies or the California gold diggings.

The Santa Fe Trail originated several miles down the Missouri River, in the town of Franklin. The existence of an overland route to Santa Fe had been known since 1792 when a French trader, Pierre Vial, had shown up in St. Louis with a load of goods from New Mexico. But Spain was not cordial to the idea of American traders in its territory. So not until 1821, when Mexico had declared its independence, did a group of daring Missouri traders, led by William Becknell, leave for the Southwest. When they returned home with tales of a warm welcome, and lots of money too, the Santa Fe Trail came alive. In 1822 the first wagon train was on its way.

Independence didn't assume its place as the start of the trail until 1830, when steamboat travel was extended this far up the Missouri. Afterwards, right up to the eve of the Civil War, Independence was where the trails began. The Oregon Trail was developed after 1840 with the discovery that wagons could get through the Rockies at South Pass. The California Trail followed the Oregon to Fort Hall, Idaho, and then branched south into Nevada's Washoe Valley and over the Sierra Nevada.

This festival combines the history and lore of all three trails and recaptures the days when the West began at Independence.

✳ **Location:** Independence is about 10 miles east of Kansas City. ✳ **Events:** Wagon encampment, pioneer enactment with demonstrations, entertainment, pioneer crafts and artisans, western food, costumed historical figures, carnival. ✳ **Contact:** Independence Chamber of Commerce, P.O. Box 1077, Independence, MO 64050, (816) 252-4745.

❖ While You're There:

The National Frontier Trails Center has displays and a multimedia presentation on the history of the trails that began in Independence. This was also the hometown of President Harry S Truman and the library and museum devoted to his presidency, 1945–52, is the town's biggest attraction.

ST. CHARLES

◈ Lewis and Clark Rendezvous: Third weekend in May.

❖ Fete des Petites Cotes: Third full weekend in August.

The place was known as Petites Cotes, the "little hills," long before the Lewis and Clark expedition stopped by on its way west in 1804. Missouri had come under American rule as part of the previous year's Louisiana Purchase. But its major towns, such as St. Charles, were still solidly French in language and in culture.

It had been settled by Louis Blanchette in 1769, who selected the place because it was the first high ground on the Missouri River west of its meeting with the Mississippi. It was he who called the bluffs in the area the little hills. The town was mostly a home for hunters and trappers, but after it was formally surveyed in 1787, it began to emerge as a town. The Spanish authorities changed its name to San Carlos four years later, a name that was Anglicized after the Purchase.

For Lewis and Clark, this was the last vestige of the known world before they headed up the Missouri into the Northwest. They stopped here to gather final provisions before embarking on the epic journey. Individual trappers had penetrated this wilderness for decades, but no systematic mapping or exploration of the Missouri and Columbia valleys had ever been attempted. Americans had no idea how vast a territory they had just bought. The expedition brought home to them the unimaginable size of the continent west of the Mississippi. It also opened Missouri to Anglo settlement and made the state the great jumping-off point for western-bound travelers. Meriwether Lewis was later appointed governor of the territory. The annual festival here in May recalls the state's debt to him and his partner in exploration.

Only fourteen years after Lewis and Clark returned from their voyage, Missouri's population qualified it for statehood. St. Charles prospered and served as the state capital from 1820 to 1826. But as population growth shifted westward, the government followed it to Jefferson City. The town's ethnic tone also began to change by the end of the 1820s.

German immigrants rushed into the area. They brought with them a feel for business and a period of economic prosperity. By 1870, the local population was about two-thirds German and most of the old French traditions were forgotten.

The Petites Cotes Festival is a reminder of the older heritage and also a tribute to St. Charles as a frontier outpost.

✳ **Location:** St. Charles is now a St. Louis suburb, about 25 miles northwest of that city on Interstate 70. ✳ **Events:** The Lewis and Clark Rendezvous features a reenactment of the 1804 encampment, a black powder shoot, pioneer crafts and entertainment, fife and drum parades. The Fete des Petites Cotes has many of the same features, with a greater emphasis on traditional crafts of this area and early nineteenth-century entertainment and dancing. ✳ **Contact:** Greater St. Charles Convention and Visitor Bureau, 230 South Main, St. Charles, MO 63301, (800) 366-2427.

❖ While You're There:

The Lewis and Clark Center, on Riverside Drive, considers the achievements of the great expedition that began here. Multimedia presentations try to capture the world into which the explorers ventured. The First State Capitol is now a museum of Missouri life in the 1820s, when the government was in St. Charles.

STE. GENEVIEVE

❖ Jour de Fete: Second full weekend in August.

As with St. Charles (see above), Ste. Genevieve began as a thoroughly French community which later became a center of German immigration. But while St. Charles rose to political and economic prominence, Ste. Genevieve remained a small, secluded place that was able to preserve more of its ethnic past. As one walks its streets today, French roots are still evident. Many historic homes still bear the names of their first French owners and some corners of town feel like a part of French Canada.

This is the oldest European community in Missouri, although the date of settlement is uncertain. When land grants were first made here in the 1750s, there were already twenty-seven inhabitants, and some historians say Ste. Genevieve grew up near lead mines that were being worked in the vicinity as early as 1715. Descriptions of the place on the eve of American settlement in the late eighteenth century found it very much like a small town in Quebec, with a tiny central area and most of the homes lining one main road. At that time, it was larger than St. Louis and was the economic center of Missouri.

But constant flooding was a problem, and in time the currents of trade moved to other places. Ste. Genevieve declined into a backroad place, but its homes and churches retained the look of France well into the 1840s, far longer than other Missouri towns founded by Gallic settlers. Many of the old customs are revived in this annual celebration.

✳ **Location:** Ste. Genevieve is situated on the Mississippi River, off Interstate 55, about 65 miles south of St. Louis. ✳ **Events:** Artists and crafts people demonstrate the work that would have been performed here during colonial days. Tours of historic homes, art show, antiques booths, French market, folk dancing. ✳ **Contact:** Great River Road Interpretive Center, 66 South Main, Ste. Genevieve, MO 63670, (800) 373-7007.

SEDALIA

❖ Scott Joplin Ragtime Festival: First week in June.

This was a rough and rollicking railroad town when a young black musician published a new tune, named in tribute to the local saloon in which he worked. "The Maple Leaf Rag" by Scott Joplin appeared in 1897 and it changed American music forever.

Ragtime was already starting to be heard in some of the more daring night spots in the South and Midwest, but it was still unacceptable in respectable middle-class homes. Its ragged meter was an open invitation to dance ... and who knows what that would lead to? Shameless, said the ministers and moralists, and they urged that it be suppressed.

But the white audience went wild when they heard Joplin's tune. Within six months, "Maple Leaf Rag" had sold an unprecedented 75,000 copies of sheet music and this dangerous sound was suddenly being heard on parlor pianos everywhere. It made Joplin enough money to move to St. Louis, where he continued to write the rags that were an inspiration to composers like the young Irving Berlin. The style was the dominant force in popular music for the next twenty years.

Joplin, however, was a serious musician, who aspired to grand opera. But the public was unwilling to listen to symphonic compositions written by African Americans, and what he regarded as his masterpiece, *Treemonisha*, went unproduced in his lifetime. He died in 1919, bitter, broke and obscure, in New York. His work was rediscovered decades after his death, however, and a heightened appreciation for his skills as a composer grew after new recordings of his music were made in the 1970s. Many of his

Scott Joplin's wildly popular "Maple Leaf Rag" brought ragtime out of the saloons and into the homes of America.

(The Bettman Archive)

rags were used as the score for the hit movie *The Sting*, which brought his work to a wider audience. Finally, in 1972, at Atlanta's Morehouse University, *Treemonisha* was given its first performance.

Sedalia never forgot the genius who once played piano here. Although the Maple Leaf Bar is long gone, the music written there lives on. This festival brings together some of the finest ragtime artists in the country and celebrates the legacy of Joplin.

✳ **Location:** Sedalia is south of Interstate 70, at the U.S. 65 exit, about 60 miles west of Jefferson City. ✳ **Events:** Concerts (both free and paid), dancing, street entertainers, Ragtime Ball. ✳ **Contact:** Scott Joplin Festival, 116 East Main, Sedalia, MO 65301, (816) 826-2271.

❖ While You're There:

The Ragtime Archives, with rare sheet music and taped interviews with ragtime artists, are housed in State Fair Community College.

Nebraska

 Homestead Days: Third weekend in June.

Daniel Freeman was a young soldier home on leave from the Civil War with some urgent business to attend to. It was New Year's Day, 1863. The previous spring, Congress had passed the Homestead Act. It guaranteed that any settler who lived on and improved the land for five years could gain title to 160 acres free of charge. The act followed years of agitation from western interests to open up the territory by allotting public lands in this manner.

Much of this land already was occupied by squatters, unsure of what their rights were. Freeman was among them. Wanting to legalize his claim to land he had worked on Cub Creek, he persuaded a clerk to open the local land office right after midnight on January 1, as soon as the act went into effect. When Freeman filed, he became the first claimant under the new act and took his place in history. Freeman's farm is now part of Homestead National Monument, just northwest of this Nebraska city.

It is estimated that the act opened up 270 million acres of new land to settlers and was one of the most powerful boosts to the westward movement after the Civil War. In Nebraska alone, approximately 100,000 people came into the state to take advantage of the free land. Throughout the West, the number was more than one million. On the Freeman property, the pioneers who staked their claims and made the land bountiful are saluted in this celebration.

✳ **Location:** Beatrice is on U.S. 77, about 40 miles south of Lincoln. ✳ **Events:** Pioneer crafts, demonstrations of skills required by a typical homesteading family, sheepshearing competition, musical entertainment. ✳ **Contact:** Homestead National Monument, P.O. Box 47, Beatrice, NE 68310, (402) 223-3514.

GERING

❖ Oregon Trail Days: Weekend closest to July 15.

In the spring of 1813, a bedraggled group of men, led by Robert Stuart, stumbled into St. Louis with tales of an incredible journey. They had left the fur-trading post in Astoria, Oregon, at the mouth of the Columbia River, almost a year before. They were searching for a way to reach the East by traveling overland. The party had discovered a new and easier crossing of the Rockies in Wyoming, which came to be known as South Pass. They also learned that by following the valley of the North Platte River, they could reach the Missouri.

The journey of the Stuart party was one of the great epics of western exploration. It had blazed what would become the Oregon Trail. For the next half century, it was the main highway to the West. This is the way the Mormons went to Utah and the 49ers and Pony Express to California. It was also the route the railroads would follow. At its peak, in the words of one observer, it was "the greatest traveled highway in the world, wider and more beaten than a city street, with hundreds of thousands of people passing over it."

There were many starting points on the trail. Some came from Independence, Missouri, and some from Council Bluffs, Iowa. The branches converged near Grand Island and then followed the route which Interstate 80 now parallels through much of Nebraska.

West of Ogallala, though, the Oregon Trail is traversed by U.S. 26. This is the way taken by Jean Sublette, one of the craftiest of mountain men, as he guided the first westbound wagon train along the trail, in the summer of 1830. On July 17, they camped near Gering, at the base of the towering Scotts Bluff. This was the most important landmark on the route and every westward traveler who left a written impression of the journey mentions it prominently. It was the first break in the monotony of the Plains and a promise of the mountains ahead. Gering recalls those who came this way to build a nation with this celebration, held on the weekend closest to the anniversary of Sublette's first campfire here.

✳ **Location:** Gering is on Nebraska 82, across the North Platte from the town of Scottsbluff and about 120 miles west of Ogallala. ✳ **Events:** Parades, Indian gathering, cooking contests, pioneer crafts, community barbecue, quilt and art shows, bike races. ✳ **Contact:** Gering Civic Center, P.O. Box 222, Gering, NE 69341, (308) 436-6886.

❖ While You're There:

Scotts Bluff National Monument towers 800 feet above Gering. There is an Oregon Trail Museum at the monument headquarters, and you can see portions of the original trail within the park, wagon ruts still clearly visible. A road to the summit leads to a remarkable view over western Nebraska and deep into Wyoming.

NEBRASKA CITY

 Arbor Day: Last weekend in April.

He was born near Lake Ontario, in the thickly forested land of upstate New York. So when J. Sterling Morton arrived in Nebraska with his bride in 1855, the thing they both missed most in their new home was the trees.

Morton was a squatter, but he picked a choice piece of property on which to perch. It overlooked the Iowa bluffs on the Missouri River, at what was then the most widely used point of entry into Nebraska. The town of Nebraska City grew up nearby, and within a few years Morton was one of the state's most prominent citizens. His splendid home, Arbor Lodge, was always kept well-shaded with a variety of trees chosen by the Mortons.

At this time, Nebraska was still known as the Great American Desert. It was a name given to it by an early explorer on the Plains. While it applied only to the western half of the state, Nebraskans still felt that its reputation retarded settlement. Morton decided to do something about that. While president of the State Board of Agriculture, he had the governor declare an official day of tree-planting, Arbor Day. Eleven years later, the Legislature declared it an official holiday and designated Morton's birthday, April 22, as the date. The celebration at Nebraska City, however, is held on the last weekend in the month.

Morton later went on to be Secretary of Agriculture in the cabinet of President Grover Cleveland and did his best to promote Arbor Day on a national scale. But while it is observed haphazardly in many places, in Nebraska it remains an official holiday and planting a tree is regarded as an almost sacred duty.

✳ **Location:** Nebraska City is on U.S. 75, about 50 miles south of Omaha.
✳ **Events:** Ceremonial tree-planting, parade, art festival, food exposition, environmental programs. ✳ **Contact:** Nebraska City Chamber of Commerce, 806 1st Ave., Nebraska City, NE 68410, (402) 873-3000.

A parade celebrates Arbor Day, a holiday born in Nebraska City. *(Courtesy of Nebraska City Chamber of Commerce)*

❖ While You're There:

Arbor Lodge, the home of the Mortons, is a 52-room mansion surrounded by acres of plantings. The son of the Arbor Day founder went on to establish the Morton Salt Company and the home is a Nebraska showplace.

North Dakota

DICKINSON

❖ **Roughriders Days:** Weekend closest to July 4.

❖ **Ukrainian Festival:** Third weekend in July.

Dickinson held its first Fourth of July celebration in 1886, when the town was barely six years old. There were horse races, dancing, and fireworks. The featured speaker was a rancher from nearby Medora, the Honorable Theodore Roosevelt, former assemblyman from New York.

Roosevelt's ranch was about 50 miles away, and it was while living in this area that he made the friends who would serve with him in one of the most famous groups ever assembled by the U.S. Army. The First Volunteer Cavalry of the Spanish-American War came to be known as the Roughriders. It was a term that Roosevelt was familiar with from his days on the North Dakota frontier. It referred to ranch hands with the toughest jobs, riding the unbroken horses. Roosevelt's unit, which charged into immortality up the slopes of Cuba's San Juan Hill, was drawn from many western states. But he always had a particular affinity for North Dakota.

The future president arrived here in 1883, in poor health and mourning the loss of his wife and his mother, who had died just days apart. His ranching career was not successful financially, but it restored him physically and emotionally. His election as head of the local stockmen's association was also the first step back on a political career that would lead, eighteen years later, to the White House.

Roosevelt returned to New York after the disastrous winter of 1887, which killed off cattle ranching in a good part of the Dakotas. It was after the huge blizzards of that year that Ukrainian farmers began to settle the land around Dickinson. They still make up the strongest ethnic presence in the area and celebrate their traditions each summer.

✴ **Location:** Dickinson is on Interstate 94, about 100 miles west of Bismarck. ✴ **Events:** Roughrider Days features rodeos, mounted parades, dances, beer gardens, power pulls, an outdoor concert and fireworks. The focus of the Ukrainian Festival is traditional music and dances played on authentic instruments, displays of folk art, and crafts booths. ✴ **Contact:** For Roughrider Days: Roughrider Commission, P.O. Box C, Dickinson, ND 58602-C; Dickinson Chamber of Commerce, (701) 225-5115. For the Ukrainian Festival: Ukrainian Cultural Institute, 1221 Villard St. W, Dickinson, ND 58601, (701) 225-1286.

❖ While You're There:

Theodore Roosevelt National Park preserves the president's Maltese Cross Ranch and his cabin. It is located at the entrance to the park's South Unit, near Medora.

MANDAN

❖ Frontier Army Days: Third weekend in June.

In May 1876, Gen. George A. Custer, commanding officer of Fort Abraham Lincoln on the Missouri River, set off for Montana with his 7th Cavalry. He was to put down problems with Sioux raiders. A Hunkpapa leader named Sitting Bull, unhappy with white infringements on reservation lands in the Black Hills, had declared himself unrestricted by treaties and was attacking Crow settlements. Custer had caused much of the problem himself by leading a military-sanctioned gold expedition into the Sioux lands two years before. Now he was being sent off to fix it.

Custer and his wife, Elizabeth, had arrived at this fort in 1873. It was regarded as a key appointment, since the outpost controlled commercial access to the northwest. Mrs. Custer rode out on the first day of the march, spent the night's encampment with her husband, and then returned to the fort. They never saw each other again. It would be two months before she learned of Little Big Horn, the most controversial battle in the entire scope of the Indian Wars. The wounded of Maj. Marcus Reno's regiment brought the news as they were returned by riverboat from the battlefield. Twenty-six women at the fort would be told on that day that they were widows. It also was from this fort that the first telegraph reports of the defeat went out to the nation. In its national impact, the shock and disbelief was much the same as when the country heard of the attack on Pearl Harbor, sixty-five years later.

During Frontier Army Days, visitors can observe life at Fort Abraham Lincoln as it would have been for General Custer's 7th Calvary before its fateful engagement at Little Big Horn.
(Courtesy of North Dakota Tourism Department)

The fort has been restored to its appearance of 1876, including the house occupied by the Custers. During this historic festival, Fort Abraham Lincoln functions much as it would have then, with authentically outfitted troops reenacting the roles they played in that fateful year.

✴ **Location:** The fort is directly across the river from Bismarck, off Interstate 94. ✴ **Events:** Cavalry charges, drills, cannon firing, military encampment, Custer House tours, scholarly lectures. ✴ **Contact:** Foundation Offices, 401 West Main, Mandan, ND 58554, (701) 663-4758.

MINOT

 Norsk Hostfest: Second week in October.

Just as the plains of North Dakota were opening to settlement, a political conflict on the far side of the Atlantic was heating up. Norway, after 500 years of union with Denmark and then Sweden, was pressing for independence and a separate identity. The Swedish government was not always sympathetic to Norse concerns about its rural economic policies or compulsory military service. As a result, the greatest tide of emigration in Norwegian history began heading for the new lands of North Dakota.

In the first three decades of the twentieth century, this state had the highest percentage of foreign-born rural population in America. One-third of them traced their roots to Norway. For a time, Norwegian Independence Day, May 17, was observed as a state holiday.

Over the years, that sense of connection with the old country had weakened. But most of North Dakota's cities still have large Norwegian populations. Minot, which began as a Great Northern Railroad campsite in 1887, grew up just as the wave of Norse immigration was peaking. Its Norsk Hostfest celebrates all the Scandinavian cultures, but the emphasis is on the heritage of Norway.

✴ **Location:** The State Fairgrounds in Minot. ✴ **Events:** Traditional Scandinavian music, dancing, crafts, and foods; top-name entertainment. ✴ **Contact:** Norsk Hostfest Offices, P.O. Box 1347, Minot, ND 58702, (701) 852-2368.

WAHPETON

◈ Bonanza Days: Labor Day weekend.

The bonanza farms of North Dakota symbolized one of the most spectacular eras in American agriculture, when it seemed that there were no limits to what research, technology, and mechanization could accomplish. The farms were created in the 1870s by the board of the Northern Pacific Railroad, which was convinced that the only way the railroad could make a profit out of its holdings here was to get people on the land.

The railroad had been given land grants along its route, but the government was still handing out free parcels to all comers—with very few takers. Farmers were unconvinced that crops ever could be grown profitably in the rigorous Dakota climate. So the Northern Pacific enabled some of its leading stockholders to assemble enormous packages of land, selling it to them at forty cents an acre. The purpose was to demonstrate its potential. These parcels, some of which were as large as 65,000 acres, became known as the bonanza farms.

Their only crop was wheat. Using economies of scale, the farm managers brought in new machinery. They took advantage of recent discoveries in milling and plant genetics, developing a more rugged strain of wheat. Because they could work enormous acreage with just one crop, the bonanza farms were on the cutting edge of technology, producing yields unheard of in older agricultural areas. By 1906, farms here were selling for $40 an acre and newly-arriving settlers were pouring across the land. With their publicity mission accomplished, the owners began breaking up the bonanza farms into smaller parcels. There were only a few left by the 1930s.

This celebration is held on the last of the bonanza farms and is meant to capture the ambience of what those days were like.

✴ **Location:** Wahpeton's Bagg Bonanza Farm is west of Interstate 29, about 40 miles south of Fargo. ✴ **Events:** Demonstrations of old-time farm equipment, reunion of former bonanza farm workers, music, ice cream social. ✳ **Contact:** Bagg Bonanza Farm, P.O. Box 702, Mooreton, ND 58061, (701) 274-8989.

WILLISTON

 Fort Union Rendezvous: Third weekend in June.

As fur traders slowly opened up all the hidden places of the American West, John Jacob Astor, owner of the American Fur Company, was struck with a wonderful idea. If a trading post stocked with the most sought-after goods could be opened farther west than those of his rivals, he would get first crack at the best pelts. So in 1828 his company built Fort Union, where the Missouri flowed into the Yellowstone River. It was the only such post in a thousand miles and established a virtual monopoly with the Crow, Blackfoot, and Assiniboine. In the house of the bourgeois, or overseer, gentlemen dressed for dinner and ate off fine china. The effect was intended to awe the trappers and Indians who came here to trade. Fort Union dominated the area and for years was the strongest outpost in the Northwest.

Astor sold out his interests in 1833 when on a trip to London he noted that fashionable men were wearing hats made of silk instead of beaver. But the fort thrived for another 30 years. As less scrupulous traders took control, though, relations with the Native Americans deteriorated and by the 1860s they had reached outright hostility with the Sioux. On an 1864 visit, Gen. Alfred Sully was so disgusted by what he found here that he recommended the fort be closed and its function taken over by a U.S. Army outpost. Within two years, Fort Buford was built a few miles downriver. Much of the material used to construct it was taken from the abandoned Fort Union.

In recent years, archeological exploration has revealed the outlines of the old fort and much of it has been rebuilt according to descriptions of traders and travelers who saw it in the 1850s. The rendezvous recreates the sights and sounds of a trading post at the edge of the frontier, with trappers gathering after months of isolation to celebrate the only touch of comfort they'd have in the next year.

✳ **Location:** Williston is about 125 miles west of Minot on U.S. 2, with Fort Union southwest of town on North Dakota 1804. ✳ **Events:** Demonstration of skills and crafts of the Old West, including smithing and cooking. Frontier games, with costumed participants competing in tomahawk throws, pit sawing, buffalo chip tosses. ✳ **Contact:** Fort Union Trading Post, R.R. 3, Box 71, Williston, ND 58801, (701) 572-9083.

Oklahoma

❖ American Indian Exposition: Third week in August.

This town grew up as an administrative center for the so-called unsettled tribes. These were Native Americans, mostly from the Southern Plains, who had not previously been allotted lands in the Indian Territory. Among them were the Wichita, Kiowa, Comanche, Caddo, and Apache. Later on they were joined by the Delaware, who had been driven all the way across the country from their ancestral home around Delaware Bay and ended up landless. They were given a share of the Wichita lands here in 1960.

The Wichita arrived here first in 1859, but they were caught up in the bitter feuds arising out of the Civil War. The Wichita were Union sympathizers and were driven back into Kansas by other tribes who were allied with the Confederacy. They returned in 1867 and were soon joined by the other unsettled tribes. The Kiowa are now the most populous group in the area.

A Bureau of Indian Affairs regional office was set up in Anadarko, and a rich amalgam of Native American cultures developed in the area. The tribes cooperate in running several historical facilities, including the Museum of the Southern Plains Indian and the American Indian Hall of Fame. This mid-summer gathering is one of the largest in America and attracts members from all of the Southern Plains tribes.

✳ **Location:** Anadarko is on U.S. 62, about 60 miles southwest of Oklahoma City. ✳ **Events:** Traditional ceremonial dances and contests, horse racing, Native American crafts, grand parade, National War Dance competition, all-Indian rodeo. ✳ **Contact:** American Indian Exposition, P.O. Box 908, Anadarko, OK 73005, (405) 247-6948.

CLAREMORE

 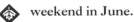 **Will Rogers Days:** First weekend in November and second weekend in June.

Several states honor their famous sons with festivals. But the relationship between Oklahoma and Will Rogers is a bit closer than most. Oklahomans view Rogers as the embodiment of their state—a man with Indian blood in his veins whose wry humor and unaffected way of life seemed to typify the spirit of this country.

He was born near this northeastern Oklahoma town when it was still Indian territory and spoke with pride about his Native American forebears. "My ancestors didn't come over on the Mayflower," he joked, "but they were there to meet the ship." He had been a working cowboy on a ranch, and a lariat was part of his act when he worked in the Ziegfeld Follies. He did rope tricks and talked, not telling jokes but finding laughs in the absurdities of life and the pretensions of the famous.

Rogers was a prototypical stand-up comic, commenting on the news of the day in a deceptively simple style that actually cut right through to the core. As the most popular movie star of the early 1930s, he was famous for making up his own dialogue, simply getting a feel for who the character was and improvising lines on his instinctive knowledge of such people. His instincts were seldom wrong.

While he owned elaborate homes in California and New York, he always regarded Oklahoma as home. Oklahoma returns the favor in this annual birthday festival. He may have died in an Alaskan plane crash in 1935, but in Oklahoma they figure that they don't have to believe that if they don't want to.

✳ **Location:** Claremore is about 20 miles northeast of Tulsa by way of Interstate 44, the Will Rogers Turnpike. ✳ **Events:** Entertainment, parade, pony express races, wreath-laying at Rogers's gravesite. ✳ **Contact:** Claremore Chamber of Commerce, 419 West Will Rogers Blvd., Claremont, OK 74017, (918) 341-2818.

❖ While You're There:

The Will Rogers Memorial is a museum of his life, situated in a ranchhouse on property he owned and where he intended to build a home. There are memorabilia of his career and his personal collection of western items.

Claremore native Will Rogers made a name for himself on the stage and screen with his down-to-earth brand of humor. (The Granger Collection)

GUTHRIE

◈ **89er Celebration:** Last weekend in April.

The Unassigned Lands sat in the middle of Indian Territory like a huge, unopened treasure box. They were a two-million-acre rectangle of land lying just to the west of the tribal territories, well-watered by the Cimarron and Canadian Rivers. The lands were regarded as part of the tribal lands but were occupied by none of the Indian nations. That hazily defined status was an open invitation to white settlers. Cattlemen were given grazing rights on the Unassigned Lands through the 1880s and pressure on Congress to open them up to settlement was increasing irresistibly. An organization called the Boomers grew up on the Kansas frontier. They claimed a right to settle the lands and a few of their members had to be forcibly removed by federal troops when they tried to come in and occupy the area.

In early 1889, the Creek and Seminole nations decided to break the stalemate and offered to accept cash payments for their claims in the Unassigned Lands. A bill was rushed through Congress by March, authorizing settlement of the lands, and was signed reluctantly by President Grover Cleveland in his last days in office. His successor, President Benjamin Harrison, then designated noon, April 22, as the day for opening the Oklahoma Territory for land claims.

By the evening before that date, an estimated 50,000 people had camped out along the borders of the territory or at one of the intended townsites, waiting for the firing of the starting gun the next day. The wild scramble across the frontier on horseback, covered wagons, bicycles, anything that could move, has been commemorated in several films, most notably *Cimarron*.

Guthrie had been designated by Congress as the future capital of the territory to be formed after the land rush. On April 22, there were more applicants for sites in Guthrie than there was land. Guthrie went from a dot on the map, a land office on the Santa Fe Railroad, to a booming city of 10,000 people, literally, in a single day.

From the foundation of the Territory to the move of the capital to Oklahoma City in 1910, Guthrie was the center of Oklahoma's political life. Congress had stipulated that it was to remain the capital until 1913, but that did not sit well with Oklahomans. They decided to place their capital where they saw fit, and in a statewide referendum voted to move it three years early and see what Congress wanted to do about it. The result was to turn Guthrie into a museum of Territorial days. Ninety percent of its original buildings are still standing. The town is no bigger now than on the day it was born and preserves much of the atmosphere of old Oklahoma, as well as its most historic structures. This celebration recalls the birth of the town and the state in one of the wildest episodes in American history.

✳ **Location:** Guthrie is about 30 miles north of Oklahoma City by way of Interstate 35. ✳ **Events:** Parade of 89ers, rodeo, pioneer crafts, entertainment. ✳ **Contact:** American Legion Post 58, P.O. Box 69, Guthrie, OK 73044, (405) 282-2589.

OKMULGEE

◈ **Creek Nation Festival:** Third weekend in June.

◈ **Pecan Festival:** Third weekend in June.

The Creeks were among the most politically active of the nations in the Indian Territories. Their leaders dreamed of forming a Native American confederacy, an alliance with the Cherokee, Choctaw, Chickasaw, and Seminole. These were the so-called Five Civilized Tribes that had been transported here from the southeastern states in the early nineteenth century and promised the land forever.

When they occupied their ancestral lands in Alabama and Georgia, the Creeks organized themselves into a confederacy. It was a form of government that came naturally to them. In the 1870s, the Creeks began inviting representatives of the other tribes to their capital, Okmulgee, to discuss plans for self-rule, independent of Washington. This alarmed the federal government, which made it clear that it had the power to nullify any plans passed by the tribes.

The notification made it absolutely clear to the tribes that their days of nationhood were numbered. Eventually, they would be absorbed into the white-run government. Nonetheless, the issues of self-rule continued to be debated here right up to the eve of statehood, when the Indian nations were dissolved and blended to form Oklahoma.

The Creeks continued to prosper, and their capital is now an oil-refining center. The area around it is also one of the top pecan-growing regions in the country. The two festivals, celebrating the history of the Creeks and their largest crop, share these dates each June.

✳ **Location:** Okmulgee is on U.S. 75, about 40 miles south of Tulsa. ✳ **Events:** The Creek Nation Festival features Creek ceremonials, parade, rodeo, crafts and food booths. The Pecan Festival features pecan baking contests, arts and crafts, entertainment, and the Pecan Wood Derby. ✳ **Contact:** For the Creek Nation Festival: Creek Nation Offices, P.O. Box 580, Okmulgee, OK 74447, (918) 756-8700. For the Pecan Festival: Okmulgee Chamber of Commerce, 112 North Morton, Okmulgee, OK 74447, (918) 756-6172.

PERRY

 Cherokee Strip Celebration: Weekend nearest September 16.

Four years after the great rush into the Unclaimed Lands in 1889 (see Guthrie, above), Oklahoma opened more territory for white settlement in the same way along the Cherokee Strip. This was a sixty-mile-deep band of territory that ran west from the Cherokee Nation, from the 96th to the 100th meridians. It contained more than 6 million acres and was leased by cattle ranchers for its grazing land.

The Cherokee and the ranchers were satisfied with the arrangement. But homesteaders wanted settlement rights on the land and they managed to get a rider attached to the bill by which Congress opened up the Unclaimed Lands in 1889. This brought the Cherokee Strip into the package and authorized the payment of $1.25 an acre. The cattlemen promptly offered $3 an acre and the tribe decided that sounded a lot better to them.

But President Benjamin Harrison issued a proclamation barring any further grazing concessions on the land and obtained opinions from two U.S. attorneys-general that indicated the Cherokee had no right to make their own deal. The tribe, with no real alternative, had to accept the government's offer, although it was clearly in violation of the land rights they had been granted.

The Cherokee Strip was opened in 1893 amid scenes that repeated the experience of 1889. Perry was the administrative center of these lands, and the town relives the excitement of the rush onto the Strip at the end of each summer.

✳ **Location:** Perry is about 60 miles north of Oklahoma City, on Interstate 35. ✳ **Events:** Parade, rodeo, street dancing, entertainment, county fair. ✳ **Contact:** Perry Chamber of Commerce, P.O. Box 426, Perry, OK 73077, (405) 336-4684.

❖ While You're There:

The Cherokee Strip Museum in Perry displays memorabilia from the land run and the early days of settlement on the Strip.

TAHLEQUAH

❖ Cherokee National Holiday: Labor Day weekend.

At the end of the infamous Trail of Tears, Tahlequah was born in 1839 as the capital of the new Cherokee Nation. A portion of the Cherokees had come to terms voluntarily with the federal government and accepted removal into the Indian Territories. But the majority of the Cherokees, relying on the rule of law and the promises of the U.S. government, held on to their lands in Georgia, Tennessee, and Alabama. Even a decision in their favor by the U.S. Supreme Court, however, could not slow their expulsion. President Andrew Jackson simply ignored it and the governor of Georgia sold the land out from under them and forbade them to occupy it.

By 1838, the last of the Cherokees (aside from a small remnant who hid out in the Great Smoky Mountains and remain there still on their own lands) had been removed, often with great cruelty and suffering, to the new territory. This was the most assimilated of all the eastern tribes. Most were fluent in English and practiced Christianity. Even after their expulsion, the Cherokee still felt such loyalty to their ancestral home that many of them fought on the side of the South when the Civil War was carried into Oklahoma.

The portion of the tribe that had arrived here first had set up their capital in Gore. But the two groups were reunited in Tahlequah, which functioned as their national capital until the coming of statehood. The tribal administrative offices are still located in the former capitol, built in 1867. The town is filled with many other monuments of the Cherokee Nation and the Cherokee Heritage Center, a living museum of tribal culture and history. That is where this festival is held.

✳ **Location:** Tahlequah is located on U.S. 62, about 40 miles northeast of Muskogee. The Heritage Center is 4 miles south of town. ✳ **Events:** Parade, rodeo, tribal rites, Native American crafts, traditional games. ✳ **Contact:** Cherokee Nation, P.O. Box 948, Tahlequah, OK 74465, (918) 456-0671.

South Dakota

CUSTER

❖ Gold Discovery Days: Fourth weekend in July.

The Black Hills had been guaranteed to the Sioux forever by treaty. But on July 27, 1874, a prospector named Horatio Ross, traveling with an exploring expedition into the Hills led by Gen. George Custer, spotted gold in French Creek. The chain of events touched off by the find turned out to be a curse for everyone involved. Almost exactly two years later, Gen. Custer and his troops were wiped out at Little Big Horn in the uprising caused by his incursion onto Sioux ground. Ross barely made a nickel from his discovery and died a pauper. The Sioux lost all claims to their land here. And Custer, the town that had sprung up around Ross's find, was abandoned almost overnight when even richer deposits were discovered the following year in Deadwood (see below).

Custer did recover, though (the town, not the general). While its population never again approached the five thousand who clustered here during the first gold strike, it survived as a ranching center and tourist stop. It is now the southern gateway to the Black Hills. Just north of town is the memorial to Crazy Horse, another historical figure who won immortality because of the events set in motion by the army's gold-hunting expedition here.

Gold is still mined commercially in this area, although among rockhounds Custer is more famous for its rose quartz. But on the weekend closest to the date of the original discovery, the town recalls its golden era.

✳ **Location:** Custer is on U.S. 16, about 40 miles southwest of Rapid City. ✳ **Events:** Parade, pageant about the early days of the gold camp, hot air balloon rally, street fair, carnival. ✳ **Contact:** Custer Chamber of Commerce, 447 Crook, Custer, SD 57730, (605) 673-2244.

DEADWOOD

❖ Days of '76: First full weekend in August.

Even by the standards of western mining towns, behavior in Deadwood during the summer of 1876 was excessive. After the discovery of gold in the Black Hills at Custer in 1874 (see above) the government made a few feeble efforts to respect Native American claims and keep the miners out. But treaties could not stand up for long against a lust for riches. First in a trickle and then in a wave, the gold-seekers flooded across the Black Hills in 1875. Late that autumn, John B. Pearson made a strike in Deadwood Gulch. He kept it a secret over the winter, but by spring of 1876 the word was out, and within weeks Deadwood was a roaring mining camp of 25,000 people. Not many of them were believers in the law.

Among those drawn to the town was James B. Hickok. Born in Illinois, Hickok went West as a young man and saw service as a scout for the Union Army during the Civil War and later for Gen. George Custer. He won notoriety on the frontier, and the indelible nickname of Wild Bill, as the marshal of Abilene and Hays, in Kansas. A feared marksman, he killed about two dozen men in his line of work, some of them intentionally.

Hickok, apparently, came to Deadwood to try his luck in the goldfields. He also wanted to supplement his income at poker, a game he excelled at even during his days as a lawman. But Hickok's arrival made some members of the Deadwood business community nervous. Money was pouring in and they were not eager to have a tough marshal start enforcing the law. They feared Hickok might get that job. There is evidence to suggest that they bribed a local ne'er-do-well, Jack McCall, to shoot him. Others insist McCall just wanted the notoriety of killing a famous gunman. But whatever the motive, Hickok was shot in the back of the head while playing poker. The cards he held, pairs of aces and eights, were known from then on in American lore as the "dead man's hand."

McCall was acquitted in a kangaroo court called by the very miners who had encouraged his actions. But he was later arrested by a U.S. marshal, tried again in the territorial capital at Yankton, and hung. The gold boom went on in Deadwood until heavy floods damaged most of the mines in 1883. But new strikes near Lead kept a measure of prosperity in the area.

In recent years, Deadwood has traded on its colorful past and become a center of legalized gambling. Its casinos now ring up profits that match anything ever taken out of the ground at the gold mines. Days of '76, first celebrated in 1923, is one of the oldest historical celebrations in the West, and it continues to relive the most eventful year in Deadwood's history.

✳ **Location:** Deadwood is about 40 miles northwest of Rapid City, by way of Interstate 90 and U.S. 14. ✳ **Events:** Parades; reenactments of famous events in the town's past with actors portraying Hickok, McCall, Calamity Jane, and other fabulous characters; rodeo; "Trial of Jack McCall" stage show. ✳ **Contact:** Deadwood Chamber of Commerce, 735 Main, Deadwood, SD 57732, (605) 578-1876.

MITCHELL

◈ Corn Palace Festival: Second or third week of September.

When the citizens of this community inquired how much it would take to hire John Philip Sousa's band to play for a week, his manager told them that they couldn't afford it. They persisted. $7,000, Sousa's representative wired back, thinking that would stop the nonsense. In 1904, that was more than most musicians made in a year. But Mitchell guaranteed that amount, even delivering it in cash to a dubious Sousa when he arrived by train.

The appearance of the renowned bandmaster, and the publicity he received for performing in this far-flung outpost for a solid week, elevated the Corn Palace Festival into a major American event. It had started in 1892 as a way for civic boosters to get Mitchell some publicity and show off the richness of its soil. The town was then and still remains at the center of the Midwest's most productive corn belt. The farms of eastern South Dakota pace the country in terms of productivity.

The festival worked so well that for a time a statewide movement tried to get the capital transferred here from Pierre. That plan fell short, but the Corn Palace kept getting bigger. It started out as a rather plain building that was easily adorned. But the present structure, a Moorish fantasy of domes and minarets, is covered with some three thousand bushels of corn and grass in the harvest season. Much of it is dyed and arranged to form designs, with each festival having a different theme. During the rest of the year, the Palace, which seats about 4,500 people, is used for civic and athletic functions.

✳ **Location:** Mitchell is on Interstate 90, about 70 miles west of Sioux Falls. ✳ **Events:** Name entertainment, carnival, agricultural displays and demonstrations. ✳ **Contact:** Mitchell Chamber of Commerce, 604 North Main, Mitchell, SD 57301, (605) 996-7311.

The Corn Palace, twice rebuilt, is decorated with the natural colors of native corn, grains, and grasses at harvest time. (Courtesy of Mitchell Chamber of Commerce)

Texas

 Charro Days: Last weekend in February.

This a city whose ties to Mexico are stronger, perhaps, than any other in the United States. Its economic life is completely intertwined with its sister community across the Rio Grande, Matamoras. Brownsville was even created by the Mexican War, originating as a fort on the river and named for an officer killed in the Mexican attack upon it in May of 1846.

Brownsville was periodically caught up in the political strife that swept the neighboring country. Robert E. Lee was stationed here for a time in the 1850s after turmoil spilled across the river and deserters from the Mexican Army raided the town for loot. Gen. Philip Sheridan also served here immediately after the Civil War, when the emperor Maximilian's European troops massed in the northern part of the country and it appeared that hostilities might break out.

Porfirio Diaz planned the campaign that led him to the dictatorship of Mexico in a Brownsville house in 1877. When the border country was in chaos again during the revolutionary days of the Pancho Villa era, in 1916, the National Guard was sent here.

It was during this period, when soldiers from around the country served here, that the city's potential as a warm weather resort and port was first publicized. When tranquility returned to Mexico, the Brownsville-Matamoras area embarked on the most prosperous era of its existence, as an outlet for the vast farming region of the adjacent Rio Grande Valley. The two cities began observing Charro Days jointly in 1938 as a salute to the shared Hispanic culture of the border country. Charro refers to the horsemen who work the brush country along the river.

✳ **Location:** The events are citywide on both sides of the border. ✳
Events: Costume parties, street dancing, entertainment, Mexican rodeo,

carnival, parade, jalapeno-eating contest. ✳ **Contact:** Charro Days, Inc., P.O. Box 3247, Brownsville, TX 78523-3247, (210) 542-4245.

FORT WORTH

◈ Chisholm Trail Roundup: In June, dates vary.

"To go north with a herd on the Chisholm Trail was the ambition of every Texas ranch-raised boy," wrote an historian of the West. This was the ultimate for a cowboy, riding the long trail from the heart of Texas to the railheads of Kansas. It was a journey of more than a thousand miles, filled with hazards at every turn. Bad weather and river crossings and stampedes and rustlers—all of them were the routine stuff of the trail.

There had been a few long drives before the Civil War. Many of them ran along a route from San Antonio to Abilene, Kansas, pioneered by a Texas trader named Jesse Chisholm. The war stopped this trade almost totally. But the existence of Chisholm's well-blazed trail, with wagon ruts visible in many places, encouraged the Kansas Pacific Railroad to construct huge stockyards in Abilene in 1867. The first large-scale drives from Texas began heading north, and by the end of that year 35,000 head of cattle had moved on the Chisholm Trail. The next year the number doubled. By 1871, the peak year on the trail, Abilene handled 1.5 million head. Other railroads had copied the rail stockyard concept by then and rival trails were established. The rails were also being extended across Texas, into the heart of the cattle country.

Fort Worth had been situated right along the route of the Chisholm Trail, and it grew up as a cowtown. As the railroads arrived, its stockyards became the great shipping point for Texas beef. Many Texans once insisted that a line ran between Fort Worth and Dallas, and on the Fort Worth side of the line was where the West began. That isn't true anymore. This city is as high tech as any other Texas metropolis. But Fort Worth's legacy is the bellowing of the big herds on the long drive and this celebration of its days on the greatest of the cattle trails helps it recapture that past.

✳ **Location:** The celebration is centered in the city's Stockyards National Historic District, north of downtown. ✳ **Events:** Parade, street dancing, cowboy cooking competition, rodeo, Comanche pow-wow, armadillo and pig races, arts and crafts, fiddler's contest, cowboy poets. ✳ **Contact:** Chisholm Trail Roundup, P.O. Box 4815, Fort Worth, TX 76164-0815, (817) 625-7005.

One thousand people ride 26 miles on horseback to kick off Fort Worth's celebration of its history as a stop on the Chisholm trail. (Courtesy of Chisholm Trail Roundup)

FREDERICKSBURG

◈ fredericksburg Easter fires Pageant: Saturday before Easter.

The German colonists who arrived in this isolated part of central Texas in 1846 had no idea what they were in for. The settlement association that had brought them to Texas ran out of money to support them. Sickness swept the town during its first winter, striking down more than one-fourth of the 600 settlers. The land was also claimed by the Comanches, who occasionally struck without warning.

During their first Easter in Fredericksburg, the settlers carried on peace negotiations with the tribe. The Comanche camped in the surrounding hills, awaiting the outcome of the talks. Seeing their campfires, children in one family nervously asked their mother what they were. To reassure them, she made up a story that they were lit by the Easter rabbit to boil the eggs he would be leaving on the holiday. When the peace talks were successful, the village had a real holiday to celebrate.

Fredericksburg still carries on many of its Old World ethnic traditions. But the story of the Easter Fires, a Texas original, has become a local legend and the entire community turns out to celebrate its message of courage in the face of fear.

✶ **Location:** Fredericksburg is on U.S. 290, about 80 miles west of Austin. ✶ **Events:** Lighting of the fires on the hillsides, historical pageant, religious services. ✶ **Contact:** Gillespie County Fair Association, P.O. Box 526, Fredericksburg, TX 78624, (210) 997-2359; Fredericksburg Chamber of Commerce, (210) 997-6523.

❖ While You're There:

Among the German families who settled the town were the Nimitzes, who built one of its first hotels. One of their descendants went on to become the chief U.S. naval commander in the Pacific during World War II. The Admiral Nimitz Museum is housed in the hotel built by his grandfather.

GONZALES

 "Come and Take It" Days: First full weekend in October.

The battle at Gonzales was the Lexington and Concord of Texas's struggle for independence. The first shots fired in the war were heard here in 1835, from the mouth of a brass cannon that was a gift from the Mexican authorities.

The settlement of Gonzales received the cannon in 1826 to help in the defense from Indian attacks. When the Anglo community there got into a dispute with a nearby Mexican colony, the authorities sent out a courier from San Antonio to ask for the return of the cannon. The local officials stalled and secretly sent messengers to ask for help.

A force of 100 Mexican cavalry arrived at the far side of the river on September 20 and again demanded the weapon. But the men of Gonzales had hidden all the boats and the troops had no way to get across. By this time, enough Anglos had streamed into the town to even the numbers. So the cannon was rolled out and a huge white banner attached to it that read: "Come and Take It."

The Mexicans protested that they had not been ordered to fight, only to take the cannon. Nevertheless, they lined up in battle formation and the Americans opened fire. They managed to kill one of the opposing soldiers, and the rest decided to withdraw. The battle, fought five months before the fall of the Alamo, is regarded as the opening engagement of the war. The first Texas army was organized here, and Gonzales also sent thirty-two men to join the already besieged garrison at the Alamo in February, 1836.

✳ **Location:** Gonzales is on U.S. 183, south of Interstate 10, about 70 miles east of San Antonio. ✳ **Events:** Battle reenactment, costumed parade, street dancing, tour of historic homes, crafts fair. ✳ **Contact:** Gonzales Chamber of Commerce, P.O. Box 134, Gonzales, TX 78629, (210) 672-6532.

S A N   A N T O N I O

◈ **Fiesta San Antonio:** The week including April 21 (unless it falls during Easter week).

❄ **Las Posadas:** Second Sunday in December.

No other big city in the United States has quite the flavor of San Antonio. A booming Texas metropolis, in its soul it remains a little Spanish town of glowing lanterns and soft guitars. While the city's most revered monument, the Alamo, commemorates a bitter defeat to the Mexican Army, in its traditions and pace of life San Antonio treasures the heritage of its Mexican past.

The struggle that began at the Alamo in February 1836 ended less than two months later when the Texans under Sam Houston routed the Mexican forces at San Jacinto. Houston had lured Gen. Antonio Lopez de Santa Anna further and further from his supply base, more than 200 miles east of San Antonio, refusing to fight until he had the strategic advantage. Then Houston struck, destroying a force that outnumbered his by almost two-to-one and winning independence for Texas.

On the fifty-fifth anniversary of that battle, in 1891, President Benjamin Harrison paid a visit to San Antonio. The city's welcome included a battle of flowers, with participants throwing spring blooms at each other in the streets in front of the Alamo. That was such a success that the celebration has been repeated every year since then as the Fiesta San Antonio. It

Spanish dancing in front of the Alamo at the Fiesta San Antonio. *(Courtesy of Al Rendon)*

is now a citywide event that attracts an estimated three million people, a blend of Mardi Gras, the Tournament of Roses, and nights in the gardens of Spain.

In the Christmas season, San Antonio lovingly preserves another centuries-old Mexican tradition. The city is decorated with luminaria, sand-filled bags in which a candle is placed. There are thousands of them, clustered especially along the River Walk, to light the way for the Holy Family, whose arrival is then reenacted in Las Posadas, or the rests. A procession of singers, costumed as the participants in the Nativity, walks from station to station and is turned away from each one as they symbolically seek a room at the inn. It is one of the most moving of all holiday rituals. The lanterns and music and the passing of the ceremonial procession transport the viewer into a fantasy of the past.

✳ **Location:** Both events are citywide. The focus of Fiesta San Antonio is La Villita, a restoration of the original mission village, located south of the central business district. Las Posadas takes place along the River Walk, which winds through the heart of downtown. ✳ **Events:** The Fiesta still features its Battle of Flowers, as well as four parades, including one on the river. There are also ethnic festivals with music and food, concerts, flower show, fashion show, art shows. Las Posadas has candlelit

A snake handler displays a western diamondback at Sweetwater's Rattlesnake Roundup.
(Courtesy of Sweetwater Chamber of Commerce)

processions, mariachi music, traditional carols, folk dancing, pinata party.
✳ **Contact:** For Fiesta: Fiesta Committee, 122 Heiman, San Antonio,
TX 78205, (210) 227-5191. For Las Posadas: Conservation Society, 107
King William St., San Antonio, TX 78204, (210) 224-6163.

SWEETWATER

 World's Largest Rattlesnake Roundup: Second
weekend in March.

They do not care much for rattlers in Nolan County. But people in
West Texas have a direct way of dealing with critters that they regard
as pests.

In earlier days, they used to conduct rabbit drives. Men of the community would divide into two groups. One would advance, guns at the
ready, across the fields in a straight line. The others would flush out the

animals. Afterwards, there would be a community rabbit feast. The same method was used in clearing the fields of prairie dogs, except that the dinners were omitted. The hunters insisted that the slaughter was necessary because of the damage these animals inflicted on crops.

In 1958, diamondback rattlers joined the list of Sweetwater's unwanted. The first rattlesnake roundup was held that year. It has grown since then into an event that takes in 12,000 pounds of live snakes annually during the hunt. This is an area in which rattlesnakes are almost as familiar as cattle. The pass through the hills west of this area is called Rattlesnake Gap. There are a lot fewer of them, however, than there used to be.

✳ **Location:** Sweetwater is on Interstate 20, about 160 miles west of Fort Worth. ✳ **Events:** Rattlesnake hunt, parade, demonstrations of snake-handling and venom-milking, fried snake dinner and eating contest, beauty pageant, carnival, flea market. ✳ **Contact:** Sweetwater Chamber of Commerce, P.O. Box 1148, Sweetwater, TX 79556, (915) 235-5488.

TYLER

 Texas Rose Festival: Second full weekend in October.

There is no actual proof that the Confederate marching song, "Yellow Rose of Texas," was written about a young lady from Tyler. But the circumstantial evidence is abundant. This part of East Texas has been famous for its rose gardens and nurseries for more than a century. And not only yellow. Just about any hue that the flower comes in can be found in the fields around Tyler. Most of the new varieties developed in America are first grown here.

This area produces more than half of the field-grown roses in the country. A drive along U.S. 69 in blooming season is like a journey into a Disney feature, with huge squares of dazzling color running off in every direction. Mild climate and rich soil combine to promise a rose garden to everyone who lives here.

The Municipal Rose Gardens are among the largest in the world, featuring 38,000 plantings and 500 different varieties. The city has held this festival at the peak of blooming season since 1934.

✳ **Location:** Tyler is on U.S. 69, south of Interstate 20, about 95 miles east of Dallas. ✳ **Events:** Rose show, garden tours, art show, queen's coronation, parade, exhibit of china, concerts. ✳ **Contact:** Rose Festival Contact Office, P.O. Box 8224, Tyler, TX 75711, (903) 597-3130.

WASHINGTON-ON-THE-BRAZOS

◈ **Texas Independence Day:** Weekend closest to March 2.

Four days before the fall of the Alamo, in 1836, delegates from Anglo Texas streamed into this village, which then became the capital of the newly declared Republic of Texas. In one sitting they drafted a declaration of independence and a constitution, adopted on March 17, or 15 days after the declaration was signed, and formed a government.

There was no paint on the walls of the one-story shack in which they met, and the wind blew in through paneless windows. But the delegates were not planning to stay long. Along with the rest of the new republic, they had to join Sam Houston's flight east, to the Sabine River, where the Texans wheeled on the pursuing Mexican army and defeated it at San Jacinto.

Washington had one more brief run as the republic's capital. An invading Mexican army captured San Antonio in 1842, and the government moved back here for a few months. But on February 16, 1846, the last president of the republic, Anson Jones, lowered the lone star flag in Austin and raised the Stars and Stripes as Texas joined the Union.

Jones's house still stands in Washington, which is now a state historic park. There is also a replica of the town's Independence Hall and a museum that contains exhibits on the twelve-year life of the Republic of Texas.

✳ **Location:** Washington-on-the Brazos is off Texas 105, about 75 miles northwest of Houston. ✳ **Events:** Uniformed militia units drill, music and dancing from the period of the Republic, crafts, meals served from the hearth of Anson Jones's house, entertainment, living history demonstration. ✳ **Contact:** Star of the Republic Museum, P.O. Box 317, Washington, TX 77880, (409) 878-2461.

YSLETA

◈ **St. Anthony's Day:** June 13.

In 1680 the Indian pueblos of New Mexico rose in revolt against the harsh Spanish rule and for a period of twelve years kept the Europeans out of their country. But not all the pueblos joined the revolt. One group remained loyal to the Spanish and joined them in their retreat into Mexico.

They became known as the Tigua after settling along the Rio Grande near El Paso in 1682. The name probably came from their language, Tiwa, which is still spoken in many of the New Mexico pueblos. The Tigua Reservation community is now regarded as the oldest continuously inhabited place in Texas, although it heads the list on a technicality. Originally on the Mexican side of the Rio Grande, it became a part of Texas when the river changed its course. Much of the original pueblo construction is still in use.

The Tigua are not usually included among the other pueblo cultures, but they have retained a strong identification with the practices of those groups. The dances performed here at the Mission of Nuestra Senora del Carmen on St. Anthony's Day have been traced back to the mid-seventeenth century. There is also a museum, a crafts shop, and a restaurant which serves bread from the original ovens in the settlement.

✳ **Location:** Ysleta is about 14 miles east of El Paso by way of the Zaragosa Road exit of Interstate 10, then east on Alameda to Old Pueblo Road. ✳ **Events:** Dances, rituals, traditional foods. ✳ **Contact:** Tribal Offices, 119 South Old Pueblo Rd., El Paso, TX 79907, (915) 859-7913.

West & Pacific

Alaska

1. Fur Rendezvous, Anchorage
2. Alaska Day, Sitka

Arizona

3. Lost Dutchman Days, Apache Junction
4. London Bridge Days, Lake Havasu City
5. Territorial Days, Tombstone
6. Gold Rush Days, Wickenburg
7. Bill Williams Rendezvous, Williams
8. Navajo Nation Fair, Window Rock

California

9. Fandango Day, Alturas
10. Calaveras County Fair and Jumping Frog, Angels Camp
11. Garlic Festival, Gilroy
12. Date Festival, Indio
13. Flower Festival, Lompoc
14. Bok Kai Festival, Marysville
15. Tournament of Roses, Pasadena
16. National Orange Show, San Bernardino
17. Chinese New Year, San Francisco
18. Swallows Day, San Juan Capistrano
19. Old Spanish Days, Santa Barbara
20. Danish Days, Solvang
21. Valley of the Moon Vintage Festival, Sonoma

Colorado

22. World's Championship Pack Burro Races, Fairplay
23. Gold Rush Days, Idaho Springs
24. Boom Days, Leadville
25. Pikes Peak Road Race, Manitou Springs
26. Hardrockers Holiday, Silverton

Hawaii

27. Coffee Festival, Kailua-Kona

Montana

28. Crow Indian Fair, Crow Agency
29. The C. M. Russell Auction of Original Western Art, Great Falls
30. Little Big Horn Days, Hardin
31. Bucking Horse Sale, Miles City

Nevada

32. Nevada Day, Carson City
33. Cowboy Poetry Gathering, Elko
34. National Basque Festival, Elko
35. Pony Express Days, Ely
36. Jim Butler Days, Tonopah

New Mexico

37. Bat Flight Breakfast, Carlsbad
38. Cimarron Days, Cimarron
39. Artist and Craftsman Show, Eight Northern Pueblos
40. Inter-Tribal Indian Ceremonial, Gallup
41. Apache Maidens' Dances, Mescalero
42. Santa Fe Fiestas, Indian Market, Santa Fe
43. Green Corn Dance, Santo Domingo
44. San Geronimo Feast Day, Taos

Oregon

45. Chief Joseph Days, Joseph
46. Pear Blossom Festival, Medford
47. Roundup, Pendleton
48. Rose Festival, Portland

Utah

49. Peach Days, Brigham City
50. Driving of the Golden Spike, Promontory

Washington

51. Lummi Stommish Festival, Bellingham
52. Irrigation Festival, Sequim
53. Chief Seattle Days, Suquamish

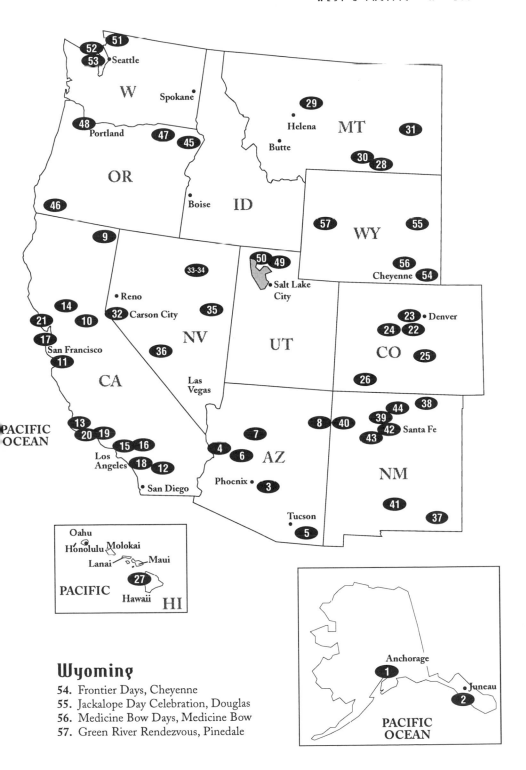

Wyoming

54. Frontier Days, Cheyenne
55. Jackalope Day Celebration, Douglas
56. Medicine Bow Days, Medicine Bow
57. Green River Rendezvous, Pinedale

❄ January

1: **Tournament of Roses**, Pasadena, California

Last week: **Cowboy Poetry Gathering**, Elko, Nevada

According to Chinese lunar calendar: **Chinese New Year**, San Francisco, California

❄ February

First weekend: **Fur Rendezvous**, Anchorage, Alaska

Second weekend: **Gold Rush Days**, Wickenburg, Arizona

Begins Friday before Presidents' Day: **Date Festival**, Indio, California

Last weekend: **Lost Dutchman Days**, Apache Junction, Arizona

End of February or early March, according to Chinese lunar calendar: **Bok Kai Festival**, Marysville, California

❖ March

First weekend: **Territorial Days**, Tombstone, Arizona

19: **Swallows Day**, San Juan Capistrano, California

Weekend closest to 19th: **C. M. Russell Auction of Original Western Art**, Great Falls, Montana

❖ April

Second weekend: **Pear Blossom Festival**, Medford, Oregon

❖ May

First weekend: **Irrigation Festival**, Sequim, Washington

10: **Driving of the Golden Spike**, Promontory, Utah

Third weekend: **Bucking Horse Sale**, Miles City, Montana

Third weekend: **Calaveras County Fair and Jumping Frog Jubilee**, Angels Camp, California

Memorial Day weekend: **Bill Williams Rendezvous**, Williams, Arizona

Memorial Day weekend: **Jim Butler Days**, Tonopah, Nevada

Dates vary: **National Orange Show**, San Bernardino, California

❖ June

Memorial Day weekend through mid-July: **Rose Festival**, Portland, Oregon

Third full weekend: **Jackalope Day Celebration**, Douglas, Wyoming

Weekend closest to 25th: **Little Big Horn Days**, Hardin, Montana

Fourth weekend: **Medicine Bow Days**, Medicine Bow, Wyoming

Last full weekend: **Flower Festival**, Lompoc, California

Dates vary according to tides: **Lummi Stommish Festival**, Bellingham, Washington

❖ July

4: **Apache Maidens' Dances**, Mescalero, New Mexico

4: **Pikes Peak Road Race**, Manitou Springs, Colorado

First weekend: **Fandango Day**, Alturas, California

First weekend: **National Basque Festival**, Elko, Nevada

Second weekend: **Gold Rush Days**, Idaho Springs, Colorado

Second weekend: **Green River Rendezvous**, Pinedale, Wyoming

Third weekend: **Artist and Craftsman Show**, Eight Northern Pueblos, New Mexico

Last full weekend: **Chief Joseph Days,** Joseph, Oregon

Last full weekend: **Garlic Festival,** Gilroy, California

Last full weekend: **World's Championship Pack Burro Races,** Fairplay, Colorado

Last full week: **Frontier Days,** Cheyenne, Wyoming

❖ August

4: **Green Corn Dance,** Santo Domingo, New Mexico

First full weekend: **Boom Days,** Leadville, Colorado

First week: **Old Spanish Days,** Santa Barbara, California

Second Thursday: **Bat Flight Breakfast,** Carlsbad, New Mexico

Second weekend: **Hardrockers Holiday,** Silverton, Colorado

Five days after the second Tuesday: **Inter-Tribal Indian Ceremonial,** Gallup, New Mexico

Third weekend: **Chief Seattle Days,** Suquamish, Washington

Third weekend: **Crow Indian Fair,** Crow Agency, Montana

Third weekend: **Indian Market,** Santa Fe, New Mexico

Last two weekends: **Pony Express Days,** Ely, Nevada

❖ September

Labor Day weekend: **Cimarron Days,** Cimarron, New Mexico

Wednesday through Saturday after Labor Day: **Navajo Nation Fair,** Window Rock, Arizona

Weekend after Labor Day: **Peach Days,** Brigham City, Utah

Weekend after Labor Day: **Santa Fe Fiestas,** Santa Fe, New Mexico

Second full week: **Roundup,** Pendleton, Oregon

Third weekend: **Danish Days,** Solvang, California

Last weekend: **Valley of the Moon Vintage Festival,** Sonoma, California

29–30: **San Geronimo Feast Day,** Taos, New Mexico

❖ October

18: **Alaska Day,** Sitka, Alaska

Last full week: **London Bridge Days,** Lake Havasu City, Arizona

31: **Nevada Day,** Carson City, Nevada

❖ November

Second week: **Coffee Festival,** Kailua-Kona, Hawaii

Alaska

ANCHORAGE

❄ Fur Rendezvous: First weekend in February.

Anchorage is among the youngest big cities in America. It wasn't founded until 1914 when it grew out of a construction camp on the Alaska Railroad. Even in 1950 it had only 11,000 inhabitants, a figure it would increase 20 times over by 1990.

So while this is very much a booming urban area, it is a city that is still in touch with its roots. The fur trade was responsible for the settlement of many cities across the country's Great Lakes and Northwest. But in those cities fur is only a distant echo in a history book. In Alaska, it is still an element in the state's economic life.

The pursuit of fur is why the Russians entered Alaska in the late eighteenth century. The Russian America Company, given exclusive trading rights by the czar in 1799, ruled the area as a private fiefdom for the next 65 years. It was not a benevolent rule. Native people were virtually enslaved, and British and American traders were barred from Alaska for several years. But when Americans first began discussing the possibility of buying Alaska, it was representatives of the fur trade who pushed hardest. The Alaska Commercial Company purchased all the rights and property of its Russian predecessors and remained in operation until 1890.

It is oil rather than pelts that now drives the Alaskan economy, but this celebration of how the state used to be reflects a history that is still within living memory. While it is held in mid-winter, this is not usually a harsh season in Anchorage. It is compared most often to Denver's winter climate, where it can snow deeply but melts quickly.

✳ **Location:** Events are held city-wide. ✳ **Events:** Fur sales, sled dog races, pioneer contests, Native American crafts. ✳ **Contact:** Anchorage Convention and Visitors Bureau, 1600 A St., Suite 200, Anchorage, AK

This fur auction is a reminder that the sale of pelts was an important element of Alaska's economic development. (Courtesy of Grant Klotz)

99501-5162, (907) 276-4118; Greater Anchorage Inc., 327 Eagle St., Anchorage, AK 99501, (907) 277-8615.

SITKA

◈ Alaska Day: October 18.

On October 18, 1867, the Russian flag was lowered at the governor's house here, as a noblewoman wept at a second story window, and the American flag was raised in its place. Sixty-eight years of Russian rule in Sitka had come to an end, and Alaska was officially, and surprisingly, a territorial possession of the United States.

Alaska seemed to have been acquired in a temporary burst of enthusiasm that soon settled back into total indifference. The transcontinental telegraph had reached Sitka in 1865. That act of connecting the region's communications to the rest of the country seemed to fire up old expansionist dreams. Secretary of State William H. Seward completed a purchase agreement for $7.2 million and Russia considered itself well rid of this farflung territory. It has been pointed out many times that the great mystery of the transaction was not why Russia wished to sell Alaska but why the United States wanted to buy it.

The Russian stay here had been brutal. Conflict with the Tlingit nation raged for decades. The first Russian party to go ashore in the area, in 1741, disappeared and was never heard from again. The Russian fort was attacked in 1802 and its occupants killed. But in 1804, the Russians returned with heavy artillery and simply blasted the Tlingit into submission. The site of that battle, the last sustained Native American resistance to European expansion in Alaska, is preserved in the Sitka Historical Park.

For a time, Sitka was reputed to be the most attractive port on North America's Pacific Coast, with its mix of Russian and frontier cultures. But it became too costly for the Russians to sustain the North American branch of their empire, and they were only too happy to unload Alaska when the United States made an offer. In fact, stories persisted for years afterwards that congressmen were paid off by agents of the czar to make the price a little sweeter.

America really wouldn't start paying attention to this territory until gold was discovered in the Klondike in 1897. But this date is celebrated in Sitka as the day Alaska became part of the country.

✳ **Location:** Sitka is on Baranof Island, in the southeastern panhandle, and can be reached by the Alaskan ferry system. ✳ **Events:** Costumed reenactment of the flag-raising, parade, historical exhibits. ✳ **Contact:** Sitka Convention and Visitors Bureau, P.O. Box 1226, Sitka, AK 99835, (907) 747-5940.

Arizona

❄ **Lost Dutchman Days:** Last weekend in February.

There are some who say it is merely folklore, that it never really existed. Every mining area has its legends about fabulous lost fortunes, troves of unimaginable wealth out there for the finding. All you need is the luck, the drive, and maybe an old tattered map.

The Lost Dutchman Mine, somewhere in the Superstition Mountains, is easily the best known of them all. This is, truly, the stuff that dreams are made of. Its location hidden for more than a century, with death and treachery all around it, the Lost Dutchman still has the power to stir the imagination.

The legend goes back to the 1850s, when this land was still part of Mexico. A desperate fugitive entered the mountains, which were Apache country and usually avoided. According to the Apaches, during the time of a great flood the mountains had harbored a remnant of the human race. The gods had shown them this sanctuary on the condition that they make no sound. But as the waters receded they forgot the promise, started to talk, and were turned to stone. You can still see them there, the Apaches claim, in the fantastically shaped rocks among the mountains. One of these formations, a tall, thin column, was called Weaver's Needle, after frontier scout Pauline Weaver. It is near the Needle that the Lost Dutchman is supposedly hidden.

The man who first discovered it returned to his village and came back here with a few hundred grateful neighbors to take the riches home. But they were ambushed by the Apaches on their way out and killed to the last man, except for two little boys who hid under a bush and escaped. They returned twenty years later as adults, having memorized the way to the mine. On the way, they met a white-bearded prospector, Jacob Wolz.

They all went into the mountains together, but only Wolz was ever seen again. When he did reappear, he was toting gold.

From time to time, Wolz would show some of the gold he had taken from the mine and swear that he would never reveal its location. The Dutchman claimed to have killed eight men who followed him into the mountains, trying to learn his secret. Finally, on his deathbed in the 1880s, he gave the directions to a friend. But certain landmarks were not as Wolz had described them. The mine could never be found. Whether it exists or not, thousands of people have been driven to search for it over the decades. And each February this town at the base of the Superstition Range salutes the legend at its doorstep with this festival.

✳ **Location:** Apache Junction is about 30 miles east of Phoenix, on U.S. 60. ✳ **Events:** Parade, rodeo, street entertainment, music, western art show, carnival. ✳ **Contact:** Apache Junction Chamber of Commerce, P.O. Box 1747, Apache Junction, AZ 85217-1747, (602) 982-3141.

LAKE HAVASU CITY

◆ London Bridge Days: The last full week of October.

This must be one of the strangest of all American festivals. In the middle of the desert, a bridge built in 1831 to cross the Thames River in the heart of London is the centerpiece of a celebration to mark its rebirth in an Arizona resort in 1971.

This town, on a lake formed by the Parker Dam on the Colorado River, was part of a development planned by manufacturer Robert McCulloch. Wanting to save on taxes by relocating from California, McCulloch knew he couldn't just plop down a new factory in the middle of the desert and expect to attract a stable workforce. So the resort was built around the new plant to create the desired amenities.

Still, Lake Havasu was pretty much out of the way and unknown. Then McCulloch had his inspiration. He read that London was about to tear down this outmoded bridge. Everyone, he reasoned, had heard of London Bridge. So if he rescued it, wouldn't everyone want to come to Lake Havasu to see it?

The old bridge was disassembled and packed up in crates to be shipped to Arizona. There it was put back together again, although fifty-three feet had to be chopped from its length to fit the new location. It cost McCulloch $2.4 million, but it was brilliant. Lot sales at his development doubled, the bridge turned into the state's second biggest attraction (after the Grand Canyon) and Lake Havasu City was truly on the map. On the anniversary of its reopening, a grateful town turns out to celebrate its splendid span.

✳ **Location:** Lake Havasu City is 23 miles south of Interstate 40, by way of Arizona 95. ✳ **Events:** Parade, traditional western and British entertainment, art fair, horseshoe and golf tournaments, band competition. ✳ **Contact:** Lake Havasu City Chamber of Commerce, 1930 Mesquite, Suite 3, Lake Havasu City, AZ 86403, (800) 242-8278.

TOMBSTONE

◆ Territorial Days: First weekend in March.

It bills itself as "the town too tough to die." Plenty of people did pass into the beyond within the city limits of this community, either at the wrong end of a revolver or a rope. But Tombstone itself, unlike other rough mining camps that are now only decaying shacks in the hills, survives to celebrate its past. In fact, it takes every opportunity to relive it and to salute the odd and deadly characters who once walked its streets.

"All you'll find out there will be your tombstone," Ed Schieffelin was told when he went into Apache country to look for silver in 1877. He found, instead, the Lucky Cuss mine, touching off one of Arizona's greatest booms. Within three years, 14,000 people were crowded into the Tombstone area. Many of them did not get along. Lawmen could turn into gunmen at the drop of a dollar, and last year's marshal could be holding up the stage this year. The Earp family and Doc Holliday engaged in their famed gunfight at the O.K. Corral, with the outgunned members of the Clanton family and several of their ranch hands losing the draw. Texas John Slaughter later kept the peace in a less frenzied but more effective manner, simply suggesting that miscreants disappear or face the consequences. Very few took him up on the challenge. And the tombstones kept climbing up Boot Hill, with the rarest of burials being those resulting from natural causes.

But in 1887 underground water began seeping into the mines, and the cost of pumping it out made them unprofitable. By the 1890 census, only 1,875 people remained here. But the town held on, sustained by the county government which it kept until 1931—possibly because other communities were too scared to try to take it away.

Then in 1963 an attorney from Grosse Pointe, Michigan, drove through the place while on vacation. Over the next twenty years, Harold

Love invested tens of thousands of dollars to restore its best-known buildings—its bars and bawdy houses and even its newspaper office—to recapture a sense of what Tombstone was like in its wildest era. The entire place is now a National Historic Site and probably the best-preserved major mining camp in the Southwest. The former courthouse has an excellent museum of the town and some of Tombstone's liquid assets still flow in the Bird Cage Theatre and Crystal Palace Saloon. Territorial Days commemorates the town's founding and re-creates, in a sanitized manner, the ambience of the 1880s.

✳ **Location:** Tombstone is 26 miles south of Interstate 10, by way of Arizona 80. ✳ **Events:** Traditional western festival with fire cart races, staged shootouts, street entertainment, music, pet parade, gun show. ✳ **Contact:** Tombstone Tourism office, P.O. Box 917, Tombstone, AZ 85638, (602) 457-2211.

WICKENBURG

❖ **Gold Rush Days:** Second weekend in February.

While there is some doubt that the Lost Dutchman gold mine ever existed (see Apache Junction), the Vulture mine is an authentic part of Arizona history. Gold was discovered there by Henry Wickenburg in 1862, and before the mine was played out something like $20 million was extracted from it.

The mine turned this town, named for the prospector and largest landowner in the vicinity, into one of Arizona's biggest communities. People were getting rich so fast that no one wanted to take the time to build one of the necessary amenities of a typical mining town—a jail. So lawbreakers were simply chained to a tree in the middle of town until they promised to mend their ways or could be transported to the territorial prison in Yuma. The Jail Tree still stands on Center Street.

But the Vulture's luck turned very bad in later years. A dam broke on the Hassayampa River in 1890 and buried most of Henry Wickenburg's property in sand and rocks. Eighty people drowned in the flood, one of the worst disasters in Arizona's history. It turned Wickenburg into a broken old man; a few years later he walked out of his house into a walnut grove and shot himself in the head.

Happier days in Wickenburg are recalled in this Old West celebration.

✳ **Location:** Wickenburg is at the junction of U.S. 60 and 93, about 60 miles northwest of Phoenix. ✳ **Events:** Gold panning, rodeo, parade,

Participants pan for gold in Wickenburg, the site of a mine that produced $20 million in gold in its heyday. (Courtesy of Wickenburg Chamber of Commerce)

entertainment, street dancing, carnival. ✳ **Contact:** Wickenburg Chamber of Commerce, Drawer CC, Wickenburg, AZ 85358, (602) 684-5479.

WILLIAMS

◈ Bill Williams Rendezvous: Memorial Day weekend.

Even among the mountain men, William Sherley Williams was regarded as something of an odd character. A former circuit-riding minister from Missouri, Williams became one of the toughest of the frontier scouts. A contemporary described him as a man who could "trap more beaver, kill more horses by hard riding, drink more liquor, swear harder and longer, shoot higher and deeper" than any of his colleagues.

He was probably the first trapper to venture into the Arizona mountains and was respected even by the Apache, who jealously guarded this land. He also had his enemies, including the explorer John Fremont, who accused Williams of getting one of his expeditions lost and, besides incompetence, also accused him of cannibalism.

At the age of 62, Williams met his end at the hands of a tribe with whom he had once lived, the Utes. He stole some of their money, wasted it on riotous living, and then led soldiers in an attack on their settlement. Still, this unlovable individual had a mountain in northern Arizona named for him, and this town, which is at the mountain's foot, also bears his name. The Rendezvous is meant to be a re-creation of the years of the mountain men.

✳ **Location:** Williams is along Interstate 40, about 30 miles west of Flagstaff. ✳ **Events:** Roping competition, parade, black powder shoot, cowboy food and barbecue, western arts show, arts and crafts carnival, music and dancing. ✳ **Contact:** Williams Chamber of Commerce, 200 West Railroad Ave., Williams, AZ 86046, (520) 635-4061.

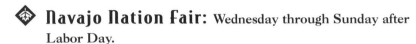

WINDOW ROCK

◈ Navajo Nation Fair: Wednesday through Sunday after Labor Day.

The Navajo are one of the great comeback stories among America's native people. Forcibly removed by the U.S. Army from lands they had occupied for 600 years and marched deep into New Mexico, the tribe was on the verge of eradication in the 1860s. Their numbers were down to 8,000, and those who survived lived in crushing poverty.

But the Navajo now number 200,000, the largest Native American group in the United States. Their reservation, which is the size of West Virginia, sits on extensive oil and natural gas reserves. The income from those resources has enabled the Navajo to set up a model tribal government, which balances the forces of tradition with the necessities of modernization. Within their lands are some of the top attractions in the Southwest, including Monument Valley, the Four Corners, and several national monuments.

The people came to this area in the thirteenth century, ending a long migration from Canada. They were deeply influenced by the Hopi, who already were on the land and whose reservation is now entirely surrounded by the Navajo. They also borrowed many cultural elements from the Pueblos and from the Mexican residents of the area, especially the craft of silver-working. But each borrowing received its own unique twist, giving the Navajo one of the most complex and accomplished ways of life of any tribal group.

Window Rock, named for a red sandstone formation with a hole at its center, is right on the New Mexico line and is the reservation's administrative center. The Tribal Museum, opened here in 1961, is a massive compi-

In the social dance competition, one of the Navajo Nation Fair's most popular events, contestants perform traditional Navajo dances. (Courtesy of Dawn Ferguson)

lation of Navajo history and art. The annual fair is the largest tribal gathering and exhibition in the country, a joyous celebration of Navajo life.

✳ **Location:** Window Rock is about 28 miles north of Interstate 40, by way of Reservation Road 12. ✳ **Events:** Traditional dances, crafts, all-Indian rodeo, games, parades, historical exhibits, pow-wow, archery and horseshoe tournaments, carnival.✳ **Contact:** Window Rock Fair offices, P.O. Box 2370, Window Rock, AZ 86515, (520) 871-6478.

California

ALTURAS

❖ Fandango Day: First weekend in July.

This merry celebration, falling near the great patriotic holiday of July 4, has a rather tragic origin. It commemorates a massacre of settlers by a local Native American tribe.

A group of California-bound settlers had just made the difficult crossing of the Warner Mountains on a seldom-used branch of the Oregon Trail. The trail through the pass had been blazed by scout Lindsey Applegate in 1846 and was far more difficult than the pioneers had been led to suspect. Their joy was so great at making it safely to California that they held an impromptu celebration. The Spanish term "fandango," which means a lively sort of dance, was just coming into common usage then due to the Mexican War. So that's what they called the party.

Watching the revelry, however, were the Modoc, a native people who were not at all happy to see newcomers on their lands. The Modoc were a tough and resilient people and resisted inroads on their territory until 1873, when a concerted U.S. Army campaign was launched against them.

As the fandango went on, no attention was paid to defense: no pickets were posted, no barricades were put up. The Modoc attacked and wiped out the settlers. The site of the Fandango Massacre is marked on a back road leading to the pass, which has also been named Fandango.

✳ **Location:** Alturas is on U.S. 395, in the northeastern corner of California, about 40 miles south of the Oregon border. ✳ **Events:** Parade, dances, fireworks, crafts show. ✳ **Contact:** Alturas Chamber of Commerce, 522 South Main St., Alturas, CA 96101, (916) 233-4434.

A frog on the starting pad at the Jumping Frog Jubilee, which has been held every year since 1928. (Courtesy of Jumping Frog Jubilee)

ANGELS CAMP

◈ Calaveras County Fair and Jumping Frog Jubilee: Third weekend in May.

The years that Mark Twain spent as a newspaperman and wanderer in the mining camps of California and Nevada shaped his style. They also led to his first published success, the short story "The Celebrated Jumping Frog of Calaveras County."

Twain put the action for his 1865 story in Angels Camp, a Gold Rush town that was assuredly not named for the disposition of its inhabitants. It bore the last name of an early miner at the camp. Historian Bernard

DeVoto has traced published versions of this tale of the frog, so loaded with buckshot that he could not jump in a critical contest, to ten years before Twain's story appeared. He concluded that it was a well-known frontier legend that Twain enriched with his own wit and sense of the unlikely.

The reception given to his story puzzled and then annoyed the author. In a letter to his mother, he complained: "To think that after writing many an article a man might be excused for thinking tolerably good, those New York people should single out a villainous backwoods sketch to compliment me on!" Nonetheless, the Jumping Frog survives as a well-loved part of the Twain canon. This contest based on the story has been held annually since 1928. In a twist that Twain might have admired, it was disrupted in the late 1970s when a Sacramento entrant imported a giant African tree frog, which jumped all opposition into oblivion. A rules change eventually excluded him, but the inspiration was in the spirit of the tale.

✳ **Location:** Angels Camp is on California 49, the Gold Rush Highway, about 50 miles east of Stockton. ✳ **Events:** Jumping frog competition, parades, rodeo, livestock show, fireworks, cow-milking contest. ✳ **Contact:** Agricultural Association offices, P.O. Box 489, Angels Camp, CA 95222, (209) 736-2561.

GILROY

◈ Garlic Festival: Last full weekend in July.

From a seasoning known for leaving a diner with breath so foul it could end marriages, garlic suddenly turned into the miracle drug of the 1990s. Doctors advocated its use to treat high cholesterol, fight many kinds of cancer, lower blood pressure, and enhance the immune system. It also kept vampires away. Cornell University Medical School, in New York City, set up a Garlic Hot Line to answer questions about it, and garlic pills, popular for many years in Germany and Japan, broke strongly into the American market.

Some food historians feel that medical science was simply catching up to the wisdom of the ancients. Garlic was used as an all-purpose cure in the Egypt of the Pharaohs and in China. As recently as 1900 it was employed in the treatment of tuberculosis, cholera, and typhus. The bulb contains the chemical S-allyl cysteine, the benefits of which are still being

Flaming calamari is just one of the dishes highlighting garlic at the Gilroy Garlic Festival.
(Courtesy of Bill Strange)

explored. Louis Pasteur found in 1858 that it killed certain bacteria, and many doctors now prescribe it for early symptoms of a cold or flu.

There are those killjoys, however, who point out that its smell is very bad and lingers for days. The Japanese tried to come up with an odorless variety in 1987, but purists scoffed. One chef who had exhibited his garlic dishes many times at this festival responded: "Garlic without the smell is like going to bed with your shoes on."

Gilroy is regarded as the garlic capital of the nation. Growing conditions in California's coastal climate are almost ideal, and garlic has been the major local crop since the end of the nineteenth century. The festival, celebrated since 1979, is not a place for the sensitive of smell. But chefs come from as far away as Paris to compete in the cooking competition here. Food booths featuring garlic in everything from oysters to pizza stretch on for several blocks.

✳ **Location:** Gilroy is on U.S. 101, about 35 miles south of San Jose. ✳ **Events:** Food displays and competitions using garlic, entertainment, cooking demonstrations. ✳ **Contact:** Garlic Festival offices, P.O. Box 2311, Gilroy, CA 95021, (408) 842-1625.

INDIO

 Date Festival: Begins Friday before Presidents Day.

No stretch of land in the United States looked less promising for agriculture than the Coachella Valley. One of the hottest places on earth, temperatures here routinely rise to 120 degrees in summer. But shortly after 1900, Southern Pacific Railroad officials reasoned that dates might make it there. After all, they had been grown commercially for centuries in the deserts of the Middle East, where it gets just as hot. If they could do it in Egypt, why not California? So the railroad practically gave land away to farmers willing to try, in the hopes that their success would give the railroad a new product to ship.

Early date farmers wrapped themselves in towels drenched in cold water to survive in the heat. But they established the industry. Marketing the fruit wasn't always easy, though. "The candy that grows on trees" enjoyed a small but devoted market in this country. But for many years California's supply outstripped the demand. Many consumers simply believed that imported varieties were superior and passed on California brands. That changed during World War II, when dates were substituted for candy bars on grocers' shelves because of sugar shortages. Since then, the biggest problem the area's date-growers have faced is the rapid expansion of the adjacent Palm Springs resort area onto their lands.

This festival traditionally has an Arabian Nights theme, in a nod to the region from which the fruit came. Burnooses flow and camels are everywhere, and during this mid-winter celebration, weather in the torrid Coachella is almost perfect.

✳ **Location:** Indio is on Highway 111 and Arabia Street, off of Interstate 10, about 30 miles east of Palm Springs. ✳ **Events:** The festival, which runs for 10 days, features camel and ostrich races, food booths, Arabian Nights pageantry, flower and garden show, arts exhibits. ✳ **Contact:** Date Festival offices, 46350 Arabia, Indio, CA 92201, (619) 863-8245.

LOMPOC

 Flower Festival: Last weekend in June.

This town served as a running gag for W. C. Fields, who was intrigued not only by the comic possibilities of its name but also by the fact that it was the first community in California to enforce Prohibition.

Lompoc was settled in 1874 as the result of a program run by the California Immigrant Union. While it is hard to imagine now in this most populous of states, there was concern in the late nineteenth century that not enough people would make the long journey to fill up California's empty spaces. The Union managed to wrap up several Spanish land grants and sell them off in lots. A high-minded organization, the Union thought that a ban on alcohol also would be beneficial for the new town.

The nearly ideal climate of the area has developed the country's largest floral industry and turned Lompoc into a city of gardens. Fields surrounding the town produce more than half of the world's supply of flower seeds. There are also test gardens in the middle of Lompoc, at which visitors can see new kinds of flowers as they are being developed. This festival celebrating Lompoc's flowers was first held in 1953.

✳ **Location:** Lompoc is located off of California 1, about 50 miles northwest of Santa Barbara. ✳ **Events:** Floral parade, flower shows, entertainment, bus tours of surrounding fields, art show, carnival. ✳ **Contact:** Flower Festival office, 113 North I St., Lompoc, CA 93436, (805) 735-8511.

MARYSVILLE

 Bok Kai Festival: End of February or early March, according to Chinese lunar calendar.

This Chinese celebration was first celebrated in the United States here in Marysville in 1881 and is among the oldest of its kind in America. The Chinese have lived in Marysville almost since its start as an outfitting point for the gold diggings on the Feather River in 1854.

The town began as a trading post on the Oregon-California Trail and was later named in honor of local resident Mary Murphy Covillaud. She was a survivor of one of the most harrowing journeys ever taken on that trail, that of the Donner Party, trapped in the winter snows in the Cascades in 1846.

At the height of the Gold Rush, Marysville was the third largest city in California. Its position at the junction of the Feather and Yuba Rivers brought prosperity, but it also brought grief in the form of repeated floods. A huge system of levees now protects Marysville and hydraulic engineering has actually raised the bed of the river higher than the town. The Chinese settlers, wary of the ways of rivers, built a temple dedicated to the river god, Bok Kai, in 1879. The god is supposed to watch out for people who live along water and bring them good luck. The temple is now right on the levee, at D Street, and is open to visitors.

✳ **Location:** Marysville is about 45 miles north of Sacramento, on California 70. ✳ **Events:** Lion dances, parade, Chinese art and food, "Lucky Bombs" fireworks display. ✳ **Contact:** Yuba-Setter Regional Arts Council, P.O. Box 468, Marysville, CA 95901, (916) 742-2787.

PASADENA

❖ Tournament of Roses: January 1.

New Year's Eve may belong to Times Square in Manhattan. But there is no question where the focus of America settles on the first day of the year. With its floral parade and football game, the one that announcers love to describe as "the granddaddy of all bowl games," sedate Pasadena is the symbol of another year's beginning.

Pasadena was settled in the 1870s by earnest midwesterners who felt their community should have a name reflecting an Indian origin. Although it sounds vaguely Spanish, Pasadena is actually an amalgam of the first syllables of four Chippewa words suggested by a missionary to that tribe. The words supposedly meant "Crown of the Valley."

By 1890, however, the warm California sun had turned Pasadena's residents a bit more playful. On New Year's Day, they decided to revel in the beauty of the climate by decorating some carriages with flowers and holding burro races. They had a good time and also sent pictures to the folks back home to show them what a paradise Pasadena was—the same achievement that television pulls off today.

Within five years, the Tournament of Roses had attained much of its present form, with numerous flower-bedecked floats and a Rose Queen. In 1902, they decided to add a football game. In the first Rose Bowl, Michigan came out to the West Coast and throttled Stanford, 49–0. That discouraged the Californians, and for the next fourteen years they limited it to a parade and a few chariot races. But the football games resumed in 1916 and, aside from one year during World War II when travel restrictions forced its removal to North Carolina, the Rose Bowl has been an intrinsic part of the festivities.

✳ **Location:** Pasadena is northeast of downtown Los Angeles. The parade is held on its main commercial thoroughfare, Colorado Boulevard. ✳ **Events:** Longest floral parade in the world, with participants coming from around the globe. The parade lasts around two and a half hours. ✳ **Contact:** Tournament of Roses Parade offices, 391 South Orange Grove Blvd., Pasadena, CA 91184, (818) 449-4100; also (818) 449-7673 (24-hour recording).

Lavish floral floats are the hallmark of the Tournament of Roses Parade. (Courtesy of Pasadena Tournament of Roses)

❖ While You're There:

The Rose Bowl itself is off Arroyo Boulevard by way of Interstate 210. It can be visited on days when no events are scheduled.

SAN BERNARDINO

◈ National Orange Show: In May, dates vary.

Before there was a Hollywood or a Golden Gate Bridge, the national symbol of California was the orange grove. In the last quarter of the nineteenth century, most of Florida was still undeveloped swamp and Arizona was a desert. The overwhelming majority of Americans lived in rigorous winter climates. The image of oranges growing on trees in Californians' own backyards was irresistible. The appearance of orange shipping crates while winter still gripped the East Coast and Midwest was the best advertising the state could get.

There is evidence of oranges being cultivated at the Mission San Gabriel as early as 1804. Cuttings from those trees were the basis of much of the state's early orange industry. A settler from Kentucky, William Wolfskill, is given credit for starting the first commercial grove in 1841. But it was the importation of navel oranges from Brazil in 1873 by Elijah Tibbetts that was the start of large-scale cultivation.

The Tibbetts grove was in Riverside, just across the hills to the south of San Bernardino. This area was the heartland of orange production for decades, and the first Orange Show was held here in 1915. In recent years, though, the relentless eastern growth of metropolitan Los Angeles has embraced these communities and turned them essentially into bedroom suburbs, where affordable housing can still be found. The groves have moved further south and east. It is still San Bernardino, however, that hosts the annual celebration of the state's onetime signature industry.

✳ **Location:** The focus of the celebration is the San Bernardino County Fairgrounds, at Mill and E Streets. ✳ **Events:** Citrus exhibits, rodeo, entertainment. ✳ **Contact:** National Orange Show, 689 South E St., San Bernardino, CA 92408, (909) 888-6788.

SAN FRANCISCO

 Chinese New Year: Late January or early February, according to Chinese lunar calendar.

The Chinese began settling in San Francisco before the city even was part of America. The first recorded arrival was in 1840, while this was still a province of Mexico. When the official statehood parade was held ten years later, there were fifty representatives of the city's Chinese community in the line of march.

Immigration didn't begin on a large scale, however, until the beginning of the transcontinental railroad project in the 1860s. The Central Pacific portion of the line was built almost entirely by laborers brought in from China. When the project was completed in 1869, however, the new arrivals were thrown onto the labor market. Within three years, it was estimated that half of the factory jobs in San Francisco were held down by Chinese workers. The early labor movement in the state capitalized on the resentment of native workers and the fears that their wages were

The dragon parade is one of the highlights of the Chinese New Year celebration. (Wide World Photos)

being driven down by Chinese who were willing to work for less. That was the origin of anti-Asian sentiment in California and of the persistence of anti-immigration politics in the state.

The Chinese soon established themselves as model capitalists, however, efficiently investing in the buildup of their own community. San Francisco's Chinatown has remained the largest such ethnic enclave in America, even though the original community was almost wiped out by the 1906 earthquake. It is one of the city's largest tourist attractions and Grant Avenue, its main thoroughfare, is a nationally recognized street. During the annual New Year's celebration, the streets of Chinatown come alive with traditional dancers and music, foods and fireworks. The celebration takes different forms, depending on which of twelve symbolic animals the year is dedicated to.

✳ **Location:** The streets of Chinatown. ✳ **Events:** Cultural displays, street fair, flower market, traditional songs and dances, lion parade, fireworks, Chinatown USA pageant and fashion show, the climactic dragon parade. ✳ **Contact:** Chinese Chamber of Commerce, 730 Sacramento St., San Francisco, CA 94108, (415) 982-3000.

SAN JUAN CAPISTRANO

◇ Swallows Day: March 19.

California's famed mission builder, Fr. Junipero Serra, arrived here about four months after the signing of the Declaration of Independence, on November 1, 1776. He must have missed the swallows by just nine days. They leave San Juan Capistrano each year on October 23 for their winter homes, 6,000 miles away in Argentina.

It is their return, however, that is the cause for celebration. The swallows always come back to Capistrano on March 19, harbingers of spring on the wing. Their voyage has become America's most famous bird migration, indicating that Capistrano was holy ground to the avian world long before Fr. Serra ever arrived.

The small church the padre built here in 1778 is still in use. It is regarded as the oldest building in California. But a far more ambitious project, a cross-shaped edifice with five domes, fared less well. Six years after its completion in 1806, it collapsed during an earthquake and has remained a ruin ever since. The sight of the little birds nesting amid the old ruins evoke the long sweep of California's traditions and history.

✳ **Location:** San Juan Capistrano is off Interstate 5, about 30 miles south of Anaheim. ✳ **Events:** Parade, traditional dances, art show. ✳ **Contact:** San Juan Capistrano Chamber of Commerce, P.O. Box 1878, San Juan Capistrano, CA 92693, (714) 493-4700.

SANTA BARBARA

◈ Old Spanish Days: First week in August.

The Spanish arrived in the Santa Barbara Channel on December 4, 1602, and named the body of water and adjacent coastline after the saint's day. But they didn't come to stay until 1782. The Spanish court, alarmed at Russian ambitions on California's South Coast, ordered that a fort be set up. For the next sixty years, the most romantic traditions of Old California became rooted here.

Of all the cities in the state, Santa Barbara has managed to hold on best to the ambience that made California part of the fabric of the American dream for so long. Through strict zoning ordinances staunchly supported by its residents, Santa Barbara has avoided the worst excesses of

The sight of a costumed dancer evokes the spirit of Santa Barbara's colorful Spanish heritage. (Courtesy of Jeffrey Cords)

California's hyper-growth. It still retains much of the texture of a Spanish village by the sea. Mission Santa Barbara, which is usually referred to as "The Queen of the Missions," overlooks the town from its hillock above the business district as it has since 1820. Preservation of the waterfront area has successfully restored many historic structures.

Old Spanish Days has been a part of the city's life since 1924. The few local families who can trace their roots back to royal land grants, and newcomers who have just arrived, all turn out to celebrate a heritage that is slowly slipping away in other places.

✳ **Location:** The festival is citywide. ✳ **Events:** Reenactment of events in the city's history, the largest all-equestrian parade in the nation, featuring antique carriages and wagons, rodeo, Spanish marketplace, two Mexican marketplaces, entertainment, arts and crafts fair. ✳ **Contact:** Old Spanish Days, P.O. Box 21557, Santa Barbara, CA 93121-1557, (805) 962-8101.

SOLVANG

◈ Danish Days: Third weekend in September.

It is not terribly unusual to find ethnic communities scattered throughout the Midwest. During the years of large-scale immigration from Northern Europe, the land in the prairie states was just opening up. Several organizations promoted the formation of entire towns based on an ethnic or religious identity in the broad band of states ranging from Michigan to Kansas. Many of them retain that cultural identity to the present day.

It is rare, however, to find such places in the West. Solvang is one of them. It was formed by a group of Danish settlers from the Midwest who banded together in 1911 in hopes of setting up a California settlement that would preserve their culture.

They gave it the name of Solvang, which means "sun meadow," and set about re-creating the look of a Danish town in the warmth of southern California. Incongruous as it may sound, the community works: Solvang has become a major tourist attraction, with its cross-timbered business district and Danish-style bakeries and restaurants, even the artificial storks on its chimneys. Motels in the vicinity bear names like "Hamlet," "Kronborg Inn," and "King Frederik," while the pea soup made by one of its restaurants has become a state tradition. This festival is the ultimate Danish salute in America.

✳ **Location:** Solvang is off U.S. 101, about 40 miles northwest of Santa Barbara. ✳ **Events:** Danish folk dancing and singing by costumed performers, parade, band concerts, crafts fair. ✳ **Contact:** Visitor's Bureau, P.O. Box 70, Solvang, CA 93464, (805) 688-0701.

SONOMA

◈ Valley of the Moon Vintage Festival: Last weekend in September.

When a young botanist named Luther Burbank arrived in the Sonoma Valley in 1875, he could barely contain his joy. "It is the chosen spot of all the earth as far as nature is concerned," he wrote home to Massachusetts. "I almost have to cry for joy when I look upon this lovely valley."

The Hungarian nobleman, Col. Agaston Haraszthy, had been a bit more restrained when he came to this area nineteen years earlier. But he immediately saw the possibilities for wine production. Within two years, he managed to plant 85,556 vines, using cuttings imported from every important wine-producing area of Europe. His Buena Vista Winery, opened at Sonoma in 1858, is regarded as the birthplace of California's booming wine industry. This area of the Sonoma Valley is known as the Valley of the Moon, a name popularized when Jack London used it as the title of a locally-set novel.

While there are records of wine being made at the San Diego mission as early as 1770, Haraszthy was the first to put it on a systematic basis. He introduced the red Zinfandel variety, and cuttings from his growths were the foundation for the rest of California's vineyards. The original Buena Vista wine cellars are still in existence (although the actual winemaking process has been moved elsewhere) and may be visited for tours and tasting. Several other quality vineyards also remain in the Sonoma area.

The town is also interesting historically as the location of the Bear Flag Revolt. The California Republic was declared here at the start of the Mexican War on June 14, 1846. The Republic lasted twenty-five days before being absorbed by the United States.

✳ **Location:** Sonoma is located on California 12, about 15 miles east of the U.S. 101 exit at Petaluma and 55 miles north of San Francisco. ✳ **Events:** Parade, grape-stomping, wine tasting, blessing of the grapes, entertainment. ✳ **Contact:** Valley of the Moon Festival Association, P.O. Box 652, Sonoma, CA 95476, (707) 996-2109.

❖ While You're There:

Sonoma State Historic Park in the center of town preserves the home of Gen. Mariano Vallejo and sites associated with Bear Flag Revolt. Jack London State Historic Park, west of town on California 12, contains the cottage, gravesite, and ruins of the mansion built but never occupied by the famous writer.

Colorado

◈ World's Championship Pack Burro Races: Last full weekend in July.

South Park was a place of wonder to the mountain men who entered Colorado in the 1830s. This valley within the Rockies, forty miles long and thirty miles across, had been the hunting ground of the Utes. Hemmed in by towering peaks, it was treated with reverence by the Indians. It was a feeling shared by the first whites—trappers and miners—who came there. "It was a paradise," wrote Bernard DeVoto in his history of the fur trade, *Across the Wide Missouri.* "It was the last place in the mountains where the old life could be lived to the full."

This was the spirit that the settlers of Fairplay brought to their new community at the northern edge of South Park. They were gold miners who were indignant about being driven out of the Tarryall camp in 1859 by earlier arrivals who claimed more ground than they could work. So they called their town Fairplay, where everyone could stake a fair share, then watched in satisfaction as their older rival played out and the new town prospered.

One of the early heroes of the town was Prunes, a burro reputed to have worked every mine in the area. The burros were constant companions of Colorado's miners. Sure-footed and strong, they toted the supplies and equipment to the mountain mining sites, inaccessible by any other means of transport. They also pulled the trains that brought the ore back out. This annual race to the crest of Mosquito Pass celebrates the durability and intelligence of the little animals.

✳ **Location:** Fairplay is on U.S. 285, about 85 miles southwest of Denver.
✳ **Events:** Burro and llama races, western entertainment and food, arts and crafts. ✳ **Contact:** Town clerk, Fairplay Town Hall, P.O. Box 267, 400 Front St., Fairplay, CO 80440, (719) 836-2622.

A loaded burro and its human teammate cross the finish line of the World's Championship Pack Burro Race. (Courtesy of Gary E. Nichols)

❖ While You're There:

South Park City museum is a restoration of a mining town of the 1860s and contains thousands of items associated with the history of South Park.

IDAHO SPRINGS

❖ Gold Rush Days: Second weekend in July.

There is some dispute over which town can claim to be the first gold mining camp in Colorado. Central City maintains that its claims were the first to be worked in 1859. But Idaho Springs retorts that the claim here was the first to be filed.

George Jackson was a prospector working this canyon in the fall of 1858. While putting out his campfire one morning, he noticed flecks of gold in the embers. Realizing that it was too late in the season for any further investigation, he quietly filed his claim in Denver and waited for spring. When he went back, the rush was already on at Central City, and it soon spilled over to his diggings in Clear Creek Canyon.

There are still more than 200 mines in the vicinity, including a training facility used by the Colorado School of Mines. The five-mile long Argo Tunnel, built through the mountains to carry ore from Central City to the refining center here, is still in operation. Even while Idaho Springs was still a mining camp, though, its radium hot springs were refreshing weary prospectors. The springs made the place into a spa, a tourist attraction the town still exploits today.

✳ **Location:** Idaho Springs is off Interstate 70, about 35 miles west of Denver. ✳ **Events:** Gold panning, drilling contests, parade, food booths, horseshoe contest. ✳ **Contact:** Idaho Springs Chamber of Commerce, 2200 Miner St., Idaho Springs, CO 80452, (303) 567-4382.

❖ While You're There:

The Argo Gold Mill and Double Eagle Mine are still in operation in Idaho Springs and both welcome visitors.

LEADVILLE

 Boom Days: First full weekend in August.

Not many places ever reached the heights of Leadville. Not only was it situated 10,400 feet up in the Rockies, twice as high as Denver, but the fortunes and the characters that wandered through its mine were the stuff of legend. Or, at least, opera and musical comedy. *The Ballad of Baby Doe* and *The Unsinkable Molly Brown*, two landmark musical works, drew their inspiration from the events and personalities of Leadville.

Baby Doe was the teen-aged bride of Horace Tabor, the town postmaster who struck it rich in gold and became the wealthiest man in Colorado. He parlayed one mine into even richer ones and his luck was extraordinary. Once he was sold a "salted" mine, a shaft determined to be worthless but seeded with a layer of ore by swindlers. Tabor kept drilling and hit the Chrysolite lode, another bonanza. He acquired the Matchless, the richest silver mine in Colorado, which earned $100,000 a month. Tabor became a political kingmaker in the state. He then unhitched himself from his first wife and married Elizabeth McCourt Doe in a ceremony attended by President Chester A. Arthur in 1883.

But ten years later, Tabor's luck ran out. The price of silver collapsed, his real estate holdings in Leadville became worthless, and he died broke. His last words to his wife were: "Hold on to the Matchless." Taking him literally, she refused to sell it even when starving in an unheated shack. She held on until 1935, when she was found frozen to death. The story is the basis of Gian Carlo Menotti's opera.

Leadville Johnny Brown was another of Leadville's big shooters and the golden wealth that flowed from his Little Johnny mine gave him and his wife, Molly, the wherewithal to try to crash Denver society. Their story supplied the plot line for Meredith Willson's musical.

The town now has fewer than 4,000 residents, compared to a peak of 30,000 in the 1880s, when it trailed only Denver in wealth and influence in Colorado. Boom Days recaptures the flair of its great historic era.

✳ **Location:** Leadville is on U.S. 24, about 25 miles south of Interstate 70 by way of Colorado 91. ✳ **Events:** Parades, drilling competition, street entertainment, carnival. ✳ **Contact:** Leadville Chamber of Commerce, 809 Harrison, Leadville, CO 80461, (719) 486-3900.

❖ While You're There:

Horace Tabor's home, the Matchless Mine, and the opera house he built here may all be visited. In addition, the Healy House, another restored Victorian mansion, serves as a museum of Leadville's richest days.

MANITOU SPRINGS

❖ Pikes Peak Road Race: July 4.

Most people are nonplussed to learn that Pikes Peak is merely the twentieth-eighth-highest peak in Colorado. In the public mind, it is the best known and the tallest in the Rockies. Even the man for whom it is named, Zebulon Pike, who spotted it from far off in the Colorado plains on his expedition of 1806, estimated its height at 18,000 feet, and predicted that it would never be climbed.

Actually, Pikes Peak measures 14,110 feet in altitude, and it was climbed just fourteen years after Pike first saw it. Its secret is that it stands alone, in majestic isolation, with no other high mountains nearby. So it became a symbol of America's westward movement, and the slogan "Pikes Peak or Bust" was a national catchphrase during the gold rush to Colorado of the late 1850s.

It was from its summit that Katherine Lee Bates wrote the poem that became the United States' alternate national anthem, "America, the Beautiful." She made the ascent by cog railroad in 1893, two years after the line was opened. The Pikes Peak Highway opened in 1915, so that the supposedly unclimbable mountain could be conquered in the comfort of a private car. Ever since 1923, the race to the summit from the town of Manitou Springs has been an annual event, an endurance test for machines and a gut check for drivers. It is now the second-oldest auto race in the country. Only the Indianapolis 500 has been held more often.

✳ **Location:** Manitou Springs is on U.S. 24, about 6 miles west of Colorado Springs. ✳ **Events:** Road race, parade, antique cars, community dinners. ✳ **Contact:** Pikes Peak Auto Climb Headquarters, 135 Manitou Ave., Manitou Springs, CO 80829, (719) 685-4400; Manitou Springs Chamber of Commerce, (719) 685-5089.

SILVERTON

 ## Hardrockers Holiday: Second weekend in August.

Despite the name, this is not a musical event. Silverton is proud of its heritage and the fact that it is still a mining town. In fact, its slogan is: "The mining town that never quit." Since 1871, when the first silver mine was discovered here, the ore has just kept on coming. The entire center of Silverton is a National Historic District, but while its vintage hotel and public buildings certainly evoke an earlier era, the place is no museum.

Silverton occupies one of the most scenic corners of the state. The Million Dollar Highway, U.S. 550, running north to Ouray, is a storied road through the rugged San Juan Mountains. The Silverton and Durango narrow-gauge railroad runs south and it, too, is known as one of the most spectacular rides in the West.

There are also jeep tours to ghost towns throughout the surrounding hills. Amid all this splendor, a mining festival may seem a bit gratuitous. But the hardrockers take pride in their skills, which are still called into use on a daily basis. The celebration links today's mines to those from which 65 million dollars in silver ore was taken in the past.

✳ **Location:** Silverton is on U.S. 550, about 50 miles north of Durango. ✳ **Events:** Mining competitions, such as drilling, tug-of-war and handmucking; food booths; crafts. ✳ **Contact:** Silverton Chamber of Commerce, (303) 387-5654.

Hawaii

◈ **Coffee Festival:** Second week in November.

In the rain shadow of 13,677-foot high Mauna Loa, the west coast of Hawaii's Big Island has climatic conditions unique in the United States. Dewy mornings are followed by sun-filled days, and then clouds and showers in the late afternoon.

The combination has made the island's Kona Coast the only place in the country in which coffee is grown commercially. The Kona variety makes a dark, full-bodied roast. About 650 small farms in the area grow the beans, and it is a $4.5 million annual industry for the state.

Coffee was first planted here in the 1840s, and the area's school year used to be organized around the harvest. Classes were dismissed in early November until all the coffee was brought in. Now school stays in session but a festival is held, instead, celebrating the crop's historic importance in Hawaii.

✳ **Location:** Kailua-Kona is on the west coast of the Big Island of Hawaii, about 100 miles from Hilo. Most events are held in the bayside Hale Halauai Recreational Pavilion, south of the city. ✳ **Events:** Coffee tasting, beauty contest and coronation, food booths, art shows. ✳ **Contact:** Current Events, 75-5751 Kuakini Hwy, Ste. 202, Kailua-Kona, HI 96740, (808) 326-7820.

In the rigorous Cupping Competition at the Kona Coffee Cultural Festival, expert judges evaluate the best of the local brews. (Courtesy of Current Events)

Montana

❖ **Crow Indian Fair:** Third weekend in August.

In the years of the Indian wars in the northern Plains, the Crow found themselves caught between two stronger forces. They knew that the whites, eventually, would take their lands. But their immediate enemies were the Sioux, who wanted to take their land now.

It was land worth having. It was called by the name the Crow gave themselves, Absaroke. The meaning is "good country," because it contained everything needed to sustain life. The Crow, who were excellent horsemen and hunters, had come to the country between the Yellowstone and Bighorn Rivers in the late eighteenth century after a migration from the Lake Winnipeg area of Manitoba. They were sometimes allies and sometimes enemies of the stronger Sioux. But in the 1860s, the Crow made their choice and decided to ally themselves with the U.S. Army, serving as scouts throughout the years of warfare.

The reward was a remnant of Absaroke, along Bighorn Canyon. The Custer Battlefield is part of the reservation land. The Crow Fair is the biggest on the northern Plains and the collection of tipis that goes up here for the events is the largest such gathering in the country.

✳ **Location:** Crow Agency is off Interstate 90, about 60 miles south of Billings. ✳ **Events:** Rodeo, crafts fair (especially beaded horse decorations), traditional dances, tribal encampment. ✳ **Contact:** Crow Tribe Administration Bldg., Public Relations Dept., Crow Agency, MT 59022, (406) 638-2601.

A bronze sculpture of galloping horses goes up for bids at the annual auction of western art held to commemorate artist Charles Russell. (Courtesy of The C. M. Russell Auction of Original Western Art)

GREAT FALLS

◈ The C. M. Russell Auction of Original Western Art: Weekend closest to March 19.

Charles Russell was born in 1864, when the country was already linked by telegraph and the transcontinental railroad was just five years from completion. The Old West was passing away. The great, unexplored emptiness that then existed within the memories of most living Americans was being populated, cultivated, demystified.

Brought up in St. Louis, Russell was determined to do what he could to make a visual record of the remnants of the earlier era. Against his parents' wishes, he left for Montana in 1880, ostensibly to work on a sheep ranch. Without any formal training in art, he began to draw what he saw there, guided only by a strict sense of discipline and his emotional reaction to the color of cowboy life. He arrived early enough to still see buffalo stampeding across the plains and Indians riding in pursuit. Wagon trains still churned along the dusty trails, and cow towns filled up with big herds at the railheads.

Russell always traveled with modeling clay in his pocket, and as he talked or observed he made figurines to use as models. He caught a priceless moment in the nation's history, and at his home and studio in Great Falls he transferred it to canvas. By his death in 1926, highways were penetrating Montana's plains, the buffalo were a memory, and isolated ranchers could pick up the World Series on their radios. But the West he knew lives on in his paintings. This celebration of western art is his adopted hometown's way of expressing appreciation.

* **Location:** The Heritage Inn, 1700 Fox Farm Road. * **Events:** Art exhibits and auctions, seminars and displays of western art, reception at the Charles Russell Museum, dance. * **Contact:** The C. M. Russell Auction of Original Western Art, P.O. Box 634, Great Falls, MT 59403, (800) 803-3351; Charles Russell Museum, (406) 727-8787.

HARDIN

 ## Little Big Horn Days: Weekend closest to June 25.

To Native Americans, it provided a hero, the great war leader Crazy Horse. To whites, it left a martyr, Gen. George A. Custer, who, over time, has turned into something of a villain. The battle of the Little Big Horn still has the capacity to raise deep passions. Even the official renaming of the battlefield in 1991 stirred a national debate, as Indians insisted that Custer's name be dropped from the title.

Since the June day in 1876 when Custer split his command and led 225 men into a force that outnumbered him 18 to 1, the Little Big Horn has been an object of passionate debate. As the nation celebrated its centennial and marvelled at the telephones and steam engines on display at the Philadelphia Exposition, a people supposedly left behind by progress was annihilating American soldiers in Montana. The shock of this news compared to any event in the nation's history. There was disbelief, horror, and then a grim, inexorable revenge. Within months, the alliance of Plains tribes had been shattered, Crazy Horse was dead, and Sitting Bull was in exile in Canada.

More books and movies have been plotted around this battle than any other of the West's historical events. Historians still debate Custer's strategy and whether he was a victim of poor scouting or his own bravado.

The Battle of Little Big Horn is reenacted each year at Hardin, Montana. (Courtesy of Karen Simpson)

The battlefield itself is a haunting place—bare, brown ridges dotted with tombstones for each of the soldiers who fell. If ever there was a candidate for an historic reenactment, the Battle of the Little Big Horn fills the bill. It is the centerpiece of this celebration in Hardin, which is just a few miles from the actual site of the battle.

✳ **Location:** Hardin is on Interstate 90, about 45 miles east of Billings. ✳ **Events:** Battle reenactment, western entertainment, roping competition, traditional crafts and food, rodeo, traditional costume military ball, street dance, parade. ✳ **Contact:** Hardin Chamber of Commerce and Agriculture, 219 North Center Ave., Hardin, MT 59034, (406) 665-1672.

MILES CITY

◈ Bucking Horse Sale: Third weekend in May.

The town is named for the general who was sent to Montana after the defeat of Custer to restore order. It grew into Montana's rowdiest cowtown, the end point of the longest trail from Texas in the 1880s. Surrounded by the endless plains of eastern Montana and the processor of about one-quarter of livestock sales in the state, Miles City remains a place that is steeped in western atmosphere.

Nathan Miles arrived at this point on the Yellowstone River two months after Custer was wiped out. Within a few months, he was able to divide the Indian alliance that had defeated Custer and in separate engagements routed the forces of Crazy Horse and Sitting Bull. Fort Keogh, which he built here, was Miles's base, and the city grew up around it. The old fort, which was deactivated in 1908, is now part of the Range Riders Museum, which preserves several historic structures of the frontier era.

The Spring Roundup was still a major event in the life of Miles City well into this century. The Bucking Horse sale grew out of it, starting in 1951. One of the country's largest livestock auctions, Miles City takes the opportunity to celebrate its western heritage in the streets around the sale.

✳ **Location:** Miles City is on Interstate 94, about 150 miles east of Billings. ✳ **Events:** Rodeo, livestock sales featuring bucking horses and bulls, street dances and entertainment, Old West dress and food, art show, and quick draw. ✳ **Contact:** Miles City Chamber of Commerce, 901 Main, Miles City, MT 59301, (406) 232-2890.

Nevada

CARSON CITY

◈ Nevada Day: October 31.

To California-bound settlers and miners, Nevada was just the big, empty space that had to be crossed before they reached the Sierra. It was claimed by Utah as part of its territory, although not many cared. One Nevada community even was called Ragtown, because it was there that wagon trains dumped off every bit of excess baggage in order to make it across the Sierra Nevada mountain range. For years afterwards, the place was littered with this cast-off property. The thought of staying put and saving themselves the trip never was considered.

Then the Comstock Lode came in. There had been some mining done in the streams that flowed east from the Sierra Nevada mountains, but settlements were sparse and the yield was disappointing. Then, in 1859, Henry Comstock went riding into Six Mile Canyon, saw gold in the bottom of his pan, and bluffed everyone else in the area off "my claim." Eventually, one billion dollars in silver and gold came out of the Comstock. Within two years of its discovery, Nevada had become a territory, and three years later, in 1864, it was a state. The transformation from emptiness to statehood occurred faster than in any other place in United States history.

Carson City, which was then called Eagle Station, was one of the few permanent settlements that existed before the Comstock came in. So it became the state capital, almost by default. For more than a century, it had the least population of any capital. But now it has climbed all the way to the thirty-eighth spot, which is reflective of what has happened with the rest of the state. The first legislative sessions here were held in a hotel room, with a curtain hung down the middle to make it bicameral. But the silver-domed capitol was completed in 1871 and still houses Nevada's state government. This festival commemorates Nevada's sudden rise to statehood and its frontier legacy.

✳ **Location:** Carson City is at the junction of U.S. 50 and 395, about 30 miles south of Reno. ✳ **Events:** Parade, street entertainment, Grand Ball, Old West music and crafts, historical exhibits. ✳ **Contact:** Nevada Day Committee, P.O. Box 999, Carson City, NV 89702, (702) 882-2600; Carson City Chamber of Commerce, (702) 882-1565.

ELKO

Cowboy Poetry Gathering: Last week of January.

Cowboys have a lot of time for deep contemplation. Under the open sky, far from crowds that are madding or otherwise, with long hours of solitude, they can address the riddles of existence and the beauties of the land through which they ride. These things lend themselves to poetry.

Many of their poems have been set to music and are an important part of the American cultural package. Don't forget the musical genre is still known as country and western—although in recent years the western part of the program has been pretty much neglected in favor of Nashville glitz. Cowboy music, which had its origin in the practice of singing to calm a jittery herd, still is going strong out on its home turf.

In recent years, former folksingers, such as Ian Tyson, have returned to their western roots to continue the cowboy tradition. Tyson is a frequent guest teacher and performer at these gatherings, in which thoughts set down in the high lonesome find a sympathetic audience. The event is scheduled at this chilly time of year because most of the participants are working cowboys, and this is their only time off.

✳ **Location:** Elko is on Interstate 80, about 110 miles west of the Utah line. ✳ **Events:** Entertainment, poetry readings, seminars in songwriting, rawhide braiding, silver smithing, western cooking. ✳ **Contact:** Elko Chamber of Commerce, 1601 Idaho St., Elko, NV 89801, (702) 738-7135; Western Folklife Center, P.O. Box 888, Elko, NV 89803-0888, (702) 738-7508.

◈ National Basque Festival: First weekend in July.

When political changes forced them from their homeland in the Pyrenees region of Spain, the Basques, like most European people, looked

Two cowboy poets share their verses during a break between scheduled readings at the Cowboy Poetry Gathering. (Courtesy of Western Folklife Center)

for a part of America that seemed familiar. They were one of the few, however, to choose Nevada.

The mountain-rimmed high desert country of northern Nevada and southern Idaho, with its endless open grazing lands, was ideal for sheep raising. And the Basques, who were used to rugged living, adapted quickly. Their move here began in the 1870s, when the Castilian government revoked the autonomous privileges the Basques enjoyed and their language lost its legal standing. Echoes of this ancient conflict still go on in Spain, with occasional acts of violence marking the resistance of the Basque people to cultural subjugation.

In Nevada, several towns hold annual Basque festivals. Elko's is the largest and the oldest, dating to 1964. It features several competitions in skills unique to the culture and a rare look into one of the country's lesser-known ethnic groups.

✳ **Location:** See above. ✳ **Events:** Traditional contests in wood-chopping, weight lifting, Basque yelling, and handball. Lamb and steak barbecues, traditional songs and dances, sheepdog exhibitions. ✳ **Contact:** Elko Chamber of Commerce, (see above).

The short-lived but much romanticized Pony Express took its riders through some of the most desolate areas of the West. (Ewing Galloway)

ELY

◆ Pony Express Days: Last two weekends in August.

The Pony Express was in operation for only eighteen months, between April of 1860 and October of 1861, before going out of existence. It had proven to be financially disastrous and was also technologically outmoded by completion of the cross-continental telegraph. But in its brief time it left a permanent image on the American imagination.

The picture of the young rider galloping into a remote relay station somewhere in the vastness of the West, dismounting, throwing his pouch across the flanks of a fresh horse, then speeding off again into the distance has endured for more than a century. The idea was conceived by California political leader William Gwin, who was concerned at the gap in communications between his state and the rest of the country. This was a critical time. War seemed to be drawing closer every week. But California was far out of touch. It took three weeks to get mail there by stagecoach, more than a month by ship. Gwin envisioned an express service that could deliver the mail from Missouri to Sacramento in half that time.

The freight firm of Russell, Majors and Waddell decided to take on the project. The course would run 1,996 miles and stations would be built ten miles apart, each of them requiring a tender. There would also be 500 topflight horses and eighty of the best riders in the country. The project was $100,000 in the hole before the first riders ever left. But when they got through in just ten and a half days, the country was aghast.

But the business could not be sustained. The horses and riders simply could not endure the incessant pounding. Weather and Indians were constant problems over much of the route. Subscribers did not match expenses. When the first message went singing across the telegraph wires, the Pony Express was history.

On many places along its route, though, especially in Nevada, the legacy survives. The riders followed two routes across the territory, one of them paralleling the present-day Interstate 80, and the other across U.S. 50. The first was along the Humboldt Valley and was the classic pioneer route. The second crossed nothing but emptiness. U.S. 50 is, in fact, still nicknamed "The Loneliest Road in America." Ely, at the eastern end of that road in Nevada, pays tribute with this celebration to a fabulous era in American history and to the riders who passed this way.

✳ **Location:** Ely is at the junction of U.S. 50 and 93, about 65 miles west of the Utah line. ✳ **Events:** Western parade, horse-racing, pioneer crafts and food, pari-mutuel betting, fair. ✳ **Contact:** White Pine Chamber of Commerce, 636 Aultman, Ely, NV 89301, (702) 289-8877.

T O N O P A H

◈ **Jim Butler Days:** Memorial Day weekend.

In May of 1900, a part-time prospector named Jim Butler wandered into a nearby canyon looking for some runaway burros. He chipped some rock from a shelf because it looked a lot like silver ore. But Butler was too broke to do more than wonder. He didn't have the money to have the rock assayed, and the local assayer was not handing out any freebies.

Butler was inclined to just let it ride, but a friend convinced him to send the sample up to the school superintendent in Austin, who did a little assaying on the side. The message came back that Butler better get back and file a claim because he had found silver. The superintendent then quit his job and rushed off to Butler's find, as did the original assayer who had passed on testing the sample. Butler's wife decided to call his mine Mizpah, a biblical reference to a stone tower that symbolized the Lord's watchful care. She also came up with the name for Tonopah, the settlement that grew up around the mine, by combining two Shoshone words meaning "greasewood spring."

Tonopah was a curiously modern sort of mining town, with a brick hotel, telephone exchange, and automobiles in the streets. The Mizpah reached a peak production of $9.5 million in 1907, but began to decline afterwards. Tonopah has managed to hold onto the county seat, though, possibly because it is the only town in the county.

✳ **Location:** Tonopah is at the crossing of U.S. 6 and 95, about 210 miles northwest of Las Vegas. ✳ **Events:** Parade, barbecue, miner competitions, Old West entertainment, chili cook-off, catfish fry, stock car races. ✳ **Contact:** Tonopah Chamber of Commerce, P.O. Box 869, Tonopah, NV 89049, (702) 482-3859.

New Mexico

CARLSBAD

❖ Bat Flight Breakfast: Second Thursday in August.

It was bats that led to the discovery of Carlsbad Caverns in 1901. So it is appropriate that the community which has grown up around the National Park sets aside one day each summer in tribute to the nocturnal winged mammals.

A cowboy named Jim White was first drawn to the cave entrance by a bat swarm he observed at sunset. Descending into the underground blackness, he found himself in a fantastic world of fanciful rock formations and vast subterranean rooms. White emerged and devoted the rest of his life to publicizing the wonders he had seen. His efforts were rewarded twenty-two years later when Carlsbad Caverns was made a National Monument and White was hired as a ranger and guide. The caverns were elevated to National Park status in 1930.

The bat population of the caverns numbers in the millions, most of them of the Mexican free-tail variety. One of the park's most spectacular sights is the sunset swarm of bats during the warm months. They come flying out of the caverns in search of insects to feed on, then at dawn they return. There may be as many as half a million in the air at one time, taking half an hour or more to pass through the cave mouth.

✳ **Location:** The breakfast is held near the bat cave entrance. The way is marked from the entrance to the park, 23 miles southwest of Carlsbad by way of U.S. 62 and 180. ✳ **Events:** Community breakfast and observation of bat flights. Park rangers also give lectures all through the summer at dusk as the bats fly out of the cave. ✳ **Contact:** Administration Offices, 3225 National Parks Highway, Carlsbad, NM 88220, (505) 785-2232.

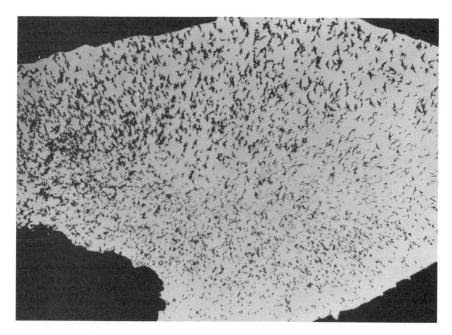

The sight of thousands of hungry bats swarming from this spot at dusk led a curious cowboy to discover the wonders of the Carlsbad Caverns. (Courtesy of National Park Service)

CIMARRON

◈ **Cimarron Days:** Labor Day weekend.

Kit Carson loved this place and intended to settle down on a ranch here. Buffalo Bill organized his first Wild West show in the town's historic St. James Hotel and returned for many winters to spend Christmas. Lucien Maxwell, at one time the richest man in New Mexico, built the town in the midst of his 1.7 million acres of land.

Near the mouth of a canyon at the edge of the magnificent Sangre de Cristo range of the Rockies, Cimarron often has been as untamed as the meaning of its Spanish name (the English translation of *cimarron* is wild or unruly). A ranching center, it is one western town that actually lived up to the pulp fiction images. Restless cowboys, gamblers working the Santa Fe Trail inns, dancehall girls, and gunmen—they all came to Cimarron in the 1870s.

Maxwell, the town founder, could compare to any of the West's larger-than-life characters. A scout with John Fremont's exploring expeditions, he married into New Mexico's Beaubien family, which was then engaged in a dispute over title to a Spanish land grant. It would drag on for forty-one years, and when it was finally resolved Maxwell was left as the owner of this massive territory, which extended into southern Colorado. Maxwell built a hotel and a bank in the town and saw it prosper. Then his investments went sour, he sold his land at a panic price, and died in obscurity in 1875.

Cimarron is one of the best preserved old towns in the West, and many of the buildings from its wild years are still standing, including the St. James Hotel and the mill that Maxwell built here in 1864.

✳ **Location:** Cimarron is on U.S. 64, about 35 miles west of Interstate 25. ✳ **Events:** Arts and crafts fair, entertainment, frontier crafts and skills demonstrations. ✳ **Contact:** Cimarron Chamber of Commerce, P.O. Box 604, Cimarron, NM 87714, (505) 376-2417.

EIGHT NORTHERN PUEBLOS

◈ Artist and Craftsman Show: Third weekend of July.

The eight pueblos of northern New Mexico combined in 1965 to run several social welfare programs. Out of this informal administrative arrangement grew the concept of an annual art fair, to showcase the deep traditions and artistic heritage of these independent communities. The first fair was held in 1972, and it has grown into the largest such Native American event in America.

The eight pueblos range from Tesuque, which is just north of Santa Fe, to Taos. In between, going from south to north, are Pojoaque, Nambe, San Ildefonso, Santa Clara, San Juan, and Picuris. At the show's inception, the intent was to rotate the event among all the pueblos, because each has its own artistic traditions. But as the crowds grew, only a few of the pueblos could accommodate them. So the show now rotates among some of the pueblos on an irregular basis and visitors must check in advance for the location from year to year.

San Ildefonso, especially, has made a reputation as the artistic center of the region. This was the home of Maria Martinez, whose black-on-black pottery became nationally famous in the early years of the twentieth century. She was inspired by shards found on the nearby Pajarito Plateau, where her ancestors had lived. And she in turn trained younger generations in the technique. Many members of this pueblo have exhibited at the Museum of Modern Art, in New York, and a local museum also shows off their work.

✳ **Location:** San Ildefonso is on New Mexico 4, west of U.S. 84 and 285, about 20 miles north of Santa Fe. ✳ **Events:** Art and crafts fair, Native American foods, dances, traditional games. ✳ **Contact:** Eight Northern Indian Pueblo Council, P.O. Box 969, San Juan Pueblo, NM 87566, (505) 852-4265.

GALLUP

❖ Inter-Tribal Indian Ceremonial: The five days after the second Tuesday in August.

This town grew up along the Santa Fe Railroad just as it approached the huge Navajo reservation. Enterprising members of that tribe soon realized that by locating at the railroad station, they had a good chance of selling their wares to eastern tourists who probably were encountering Native Americans for the first time. They sold some rugs, posed for photographs, and Gallup developed a reputation as a center of Indian culture.

A group of local businessmen decided that they could build on that. In 1922 they met with representatives of several southwestern tribes to organize a celebration that would feature their combined cultures and crafts. The Native Americans responded enthusiastically, and the first Inter-Tribal Ceremonial was held that summer at the county fairgrounds.

It has grown into the largest and best-known such event in the country, with more than fifty tribes from across the West and Canada participating. It soon outgrew its first home and a natural amphitheater was developed for it at Red Rock State Park. The original date was the last week in August. But according to local lore, that coincided with a Hopi ceremonial in Arizona which prominently featured rain dances. The Gallup event kept getting doused by the thunder called up to the west. Rather than fight it, the date here was switched.

✳ **Location:** Gallup is on Interstate 40 at U.S. 666. Red Rock Park is 10 miles east of the city, along the interstate. ✳ **Events:** Ceremonial dances, parade, rodeo, traditional games, Native American crafts, visual and performing art. ✳ **Contact:** Inter-Tribal Ceremonial Association, P.O. Box 1, Church Rock, NM 87311, (800) 233-4528.

MESCALERO

◈ Apache Maidens' Dances: July 4.

This branch of the Apache family got its name from the plant on which its desert life was based. Mescal was used for food, as clothing, as an intoxicant, even as thread. It was so bound up with this nomadic people's existence that the Spanish simply called them Mescalero.

A wrong-headed experiment by the U.S. government in the 1860s resulted in seventeen years of intermittent warfare with the tribe. Uneasy about having a potentially hostile Navajo nation on its flank when the Civil War began, the army transported most of the tribe from ancestral land in Arizona to a reservation near Fort Sumner, New Mexico. Then to make things worse, the Navajo were thrown onto this land with their ancient enemies, the Mescalero. The Navajo went on a hunger strike, refusing to plant any crops until they were returned to Arizona. The Mescalero, appalled at conditions there, simply left the reservation in 1866, realizing that if they were pursued the restive Navajo would be left unguarded. They then took up a life of raiding along the Mexican border country.

They would cross the border to get horses and weapons, then swoop back into New Mexico miles from where they had originally disappeared. They eluded the U.S. Cavalry for years, until it began to stake out the waterholes, the one resource which compelled the Mescalero to come to a specific place. They finally made peace in 1883, and this reservation was established for them.

It has been one of the great Native American success stories. The land had rich timber resources and also was suited for grazing, and tribal enterprises were set up to take advantage of that. In addition, the Mescalero have developed attractive recreational facilities, including a ski resort. These traditional dances, associated with the puberty rites for young girls, attract the largest crowds of the year to reservation headquarters. No cameras are allowed at the dances.

✳ **Location:** Mescalero is on U.S. 70, about 90 miles northeast of Las Cruces. ✳ **Events:** Pre-dawn maidens' ritual, Mountain Spirits dances at dusk, rodeo. ✳ **Contact:** Mescalero Apache Tribe, P.O. Box 227, Mescalero, NM 88340, (505) 671-4494.

SANTA FE

◈ **Indian Market:** Third weekend in August.

◈ **Santa Fe Fiesta:** Weekend following Labor Day.

Many American cities claim a certain uniqueness—a look, a texture that is only and unmistakably theirs. Santa Fe may be the only city where the claim is justified. There is no place else in the country like this blend of Spanish, Native American, and Anglo cultures, all mixed in with knock-out scenery and one of the country's liveliest artistic communities. Santa Fe has developed into a top destination, a place so popular that it sometimes seems in danger of losing the qualities that set it apart. The shops that once encircled the Plaza, the center of the community's life, have now been replaced almost entirely with art galleries and specialty stores. It is a pleasant stroll for visitors, but the old-time residents mark the change with a certain degree of sadness.

This is a city that isn't fond of change. It was a capital before any Pilgrim had landed in Plymouth. Its Palace of the Governors is the oldest public building in the country, parts of it dating to the founding of the city in 1610. Much of the Plaza area doesn't look much different than it did when it was the end of the Santa Fe Trail.

Santa Fe was the administrative center of Spain's empire north of Mexico, covering a territory that stretched from the Mississippi River to the Pacific and north to uncharted regions. A rich civilization grew up around the city, churches and haciendas reflecting the glory of the empire. But it was also a cruel place. Indian labor was exploited and religious persecutions were common. Officers of the Inquisition were frequent visitors. Finally, in 1680 a leader arose among the Pueblo tribes. Po-pe made an alliance with the Apaches and they combined to drive the Spanish out of New Mexico in a bloody uprising. But they withdrew only as far as El Paso, and twelve years later Don Diego de Vargas returned with an army of 300 men. Santa Fe surrendered peacefully.

On the twentieth anniversary of the reconquest, in 1712, the governor at the time, Marques de la Penuela, decreed a fiesta be held in celebration. The Santa Fe Fiesta has been observed every year since, making it the oldest historic festival in the United States.

Santa Fe's festivals reflect its Native American heritage: here, Pueblo dancers celebrate a traditional feast day. (Photo by Mark Nohl, courtesy of Santa Fe Convention and Visitors Bureau)

The appreciation of the artistic accomplishments of the Pueblo cultures came much later. The Spanish dismissed these Native peoples as little more than savages to be worked and converted. The idea that they had an artistic vision to offer was not considered. By the late nineteenth century, however, a small group of American and British writers and painters were coming under the spell of this land. In the 1890s, they started arriving in Santa Fe and Taos, to paint the land and allow its mystery to permeate their own works. In return, they began to understand the achievements of the Pueblo people as artists in their own right.

By the 1920s, a thriving market in Southwestern Indian art had grown up and the first museums were being organized to display it. The first Indian Market for jewelry, pottery and other crafts was organized in Santa Fe in 1922. It has since grown into the most prestigious juried show of its kind and has expanded into a celebration of all facets of Pueblo culture.

✳ **Location:** Both festivals are centered around the Plaza, the historic heart of Santa Fe. ✳ **Events:** The Indian Market has juried competition, entertainment, traditional Native American music and dances, food booths. The Santa Fe Fiesta features religious processions and pageantry, folk dancing, fireworks, art shows. ✳ **Contact:** Indian Market, 509 Camino de los Marques, Santa Fe, NM 87501, (505) 983-5220. For Santa Fe Fiesta, contact the Convention and Visitor's Bureau, P.O. Box 909, Santa Fe, NM 87504-0909, (800) 777-CITY; or the Santa Fe Fiesta Council, (505) 988-7575.

❖ While You're There:

The Museum of Indian Arts and Culture and the Wheelwright Museum of the American Indian are outstanding collections of Native American works, from archaeological sources to contemporary artists. The museums are on adjoining lots along Camino Lejo, off the Old Pecos Trail, on the southeastern approach to the city.

SANTO DOMINGO

❖ Green Corn Dance: August 4.

This is the largest and most colorful of all the Pueblo celebrations in New Mexico. More than 500 people participate every year, taking the roles of singers, dancers, clowns, and drummers. Santo Domingo is a farming community, and the cycle of agricultural festivals is of primary importance.

A summer celebration of the corn is a feature of dozens of Native American farming cultures throughout the Midwest and South as well as in the pueblos of the Southwest. It usually takes the form of a new year festival. It is a mixture of solemnity and carnival, where old sins are cast away amid a spirit of ceremonial mockery.

Because this is a celebration of intense religious significance, no photography, sketching, or recording devices are permitted. A few of the pueblos have closed their ceremonials completely to outsiders because of violations of these bans. Basically, the Pueblo people are quite friendly. But they expect their traditions to be respected.

Santo Domingo is also noted for its fine work in silver and turquoise and its shell decorations.

✴ **Location:** Santo Domingo is north of Interstate 25, at New Mexico 22, about 30 miles southwest of Santa Fe. ✴ **Events:** Religious ceremonies. ✴ **Contact:** Santo Domingo Community Center, (505) 465-2214.

TAOS

◆ San Geronimo Feast Day: September 29–30.

The best-known and the most haunting of the New Mexico pueblo settlements, the five-and six-story apartment structures of Taos look just as they did when the first Spanish explorers arrived in 1540. Even then, they were old. Taos is believed to have been settled in the fourteenth century by people of the older Chaco culture to the southwest, which was then breaking up. The buildings face each other across a central plaza, with Taos Creek running through the center. The dark slopes of the Sangre de Cristo rise in the background. The sense of permanence, serenity, and harmony is realized in few American places more than this.

Taos occupies the frontier between the Pueblo and the Plains cultures. It was heavily influenced, through raids and trade, by the Apache and Comanche. It was a Taos man, Po-pe, who led the Pueblo rebellion against Spanish rule in 1680 (see Santa Fe), and after the Mexican War, when an insurrection arose against the newly imposed American rule, it was Taos that directed it.

It remains one of the most conservative of the New Mexico pueblos. There is no electricity or running water, by choice. Religious observances are frequent, and the pueblo may be closed to visitors at anytime with little advance warning. It is also a place that has inspired Anglo writers and artists for generations. D. H. Lawrence lived and worked nearby, as did Willa Cather and Georgia O'Keeffe.

This best-known of the pueblo's celebrations is its patron saint's feast day, a time for merry-making and traditional games.

✳ **Location:** Taos Pueblo is about 75 miles north of Santa Fe. ✳ **Events:** Sundown dance, greased-pole climb, traditional races and games. ✳ **Contact:** Tourism Information, P.O. Box 1846, Taos, NM 87571, (505) 758-1028.

❖ While You're There:

In the nearby town of Taos are a number of places associated with the Anglo historic and cultural development of the area. Here is the famed mountain man and guide Kit Carson's home and museum, the Millicent Rogers Museum of locally crafted art, and the Ernest L. Blumenschein Home, honoring one of the first great artists who made this area his studio and home.

Oregon

❖ **Chief Joseph Days:** Last full weekend in July.

The land of the Wallowa Valley was promised to the Nez Perce by federal treaty in 1855. But that was before they found gold on it. That changed things. Just eight years after the treaty was signed, Washington drew up a new agreement, reducing the tribe's holdings by three-quarters and restricting them to reservation lands in Idaho.

The Nez Perce, led by Chief Joseph, protested and even made some allies in the U.S. Senate, which refused to ratify the new treaty. But in 1875 the government ruled that since the Nez Perce were a migratory people they had no special claim on the Wallowa. The tribe was then ordered to Idaho. So began one of the longest and strangest battles in the history of the Indian wars. It ran across 1,500 miles, lasted an entire summer, and didn't end until the vastly outnumbered Nez Perce were forced to surrender, just forty miles short of sanctuary in Canada.

The fight began in June 1877, when young men of the tribe, angry at their treatment, began raiding white settlements while being transported to Idaho. Chief Joseph knew their punishment would be severe, so he decided to make a run for it. With a fighting force that never numbered above 200 men, and an additional 500 noncombatants to protect, the Nez Perce still managed to elude their pursuers for three months as they dashed across Idaho and into Montana. They bloodied an attacking force of U.S. Cavalry at Big Hole Battlefield and escaped once more. But after crossing the Missouri River, Chief Joseph inexplicably slowed down. Some historians feel he thought that the river was the international

Under Chief Joseph's leadership, a small band of Nez Perce resisted the federal government's orders to relocate to Idaho and made an extraordinary attempt to escape to freedom in Canada.

(The Bettman Archive)

border; others think he could not move the wounded and the sick any further.

At Bear's Paw on September 30 he was finally surrounded and out-gunned. He made his famous speech of surrender, which concluded: "From where the sun now stands, I will fight no more forever." Chief Joseph's father, who was known as Old Joseph, is buried near this town named for the Indian leaders. This annual celebration is a reminder of the Native American people who were dispossessed from this valley.

* **Location:** Joseph is about 70 miles east of Interstate 84 from the La Grande exit, by way of Oregon 82. * **Events:** Rodeo, Native American dances, cowboy breakfast, parade, carnival. * **Contact:** Joseph Chamber of Commerce, P.O. Box 13, Joseph, OR 97846, (503) 432-1015.

MEDFORD

◈ **Pear Blossom Festival:** Second weekend in April.

The first fruit-growers in Oregon arrived in 1847, with 800 seedlings carried beneath the canvas of their covered wagons. Early reports had indicated that the soil and climate in the western valleys of Oregon were ideally suited to any kind of crop, and they were determined to put that claim to the test. When they were able to sell four boxes of apples in San Francisco for $500, they knew they were on to something. But it was pears that turned out to be the most profitable crop.

The Rogue River Valley which surrounds Medford is filled with pear trees. The area was transformed in the first decade of the twentieth century, when it quadrupled in population. Just as industrial workers flocked to Detroit in that era, fruit-growers migrated to Medford, hoping to buy in while the land was still inexpensive. Most of the orchards were planted in that period.

Mail-order houses have made Medford pears the best known, and most widely traveled, in the country. But until you see the springtime vistas of blossoming trees, or smell the aroma of fruit prepared for packaging in the fall, you cannot appreciate the impact that this single fruit has on the city.

✳ **Location:** Medford is on Interstate 5, about 30 miles north of the California state line. ✳ **Events:** Parade, food booths, street entertainment, 5K run, Mayor's walk, stamp show, pageants. ✳ **Contact:** Pear Blossom Festival Office, P.O. Box 335, Medford, OR 97501, (503) 734-PEAR.

PENDLETON

◈ **Roundup:** Second full week in September.

The cattle drives from Texas north to the railheads on the Great Plains were long hard pulls for cowboys and livestock alike. While the Pendleton cattle drives didn't cover quite as great a distance, they may have been even more difficult, because a good part of their course was uphill, across the passes of the Rockies.

Pendleton was the center of a vast cattle empire in eastern Oregon throughout the 1880s. The herds had to be driven to railroad towns in Montana and Wyoming for shipment east. It was a hazardous trip, and a certain camaraderie developed among the cowboys who made it. The drives ended in 1889 when the railroad finally reached Pendleton, and shortly afterwards the country began changing to an agricultural base. But the legacy of the old drives lived on among the old-timers, and in 1910 the town held its first roundup.

It was meant to be part community rodeo and part celebration of the past. It was so well received, however, that in 1912 it became an annual event. Native Americans from the adjacent Umadilla Reservation joined in enthusiastically from the start, and Jackson Sundown, a member of that tribe, was one of the first winners of the all-around cowboy award. The Roundup has become one of the best-attended events in the West and even runs its own hall of fame.

✳ **Location:** Pendleton is at the junction of Interstate 84 and U.S. 395. The Roundup is held at the Round Up Grounds at the western edge of town. ✳ **Events:** Rodeo, covered wagon parades, Indian encampment and traditional dances, Old West entertainment and costumed reenactments. ✳ **Contact:** Pendleton Roundup Offices, P.O. Box 609, Pendleton, OR 97801, (800) 524-2984.

PORTLAND

 Rose Festival: Thursday after Memorial Day through mid-July.

Exactly how Portland's fixation on roses began is uncertain, but it has been going on for a very long time. The Rose Festival, one of the largest urban celebrations in America, traces its origins back to 1889 and the first major exhibit of the Portland Rose Society. For the record, that was six months before Pasadena, California, held a parade on New Year's Day 1890 for the first Tournament of Roses.

Portland also claims to be the first city to have a motorized floral parade. That happened in 1904, when four automobiles were strewn with roses and paraded through town. But the Rose Festival didn't officially begin until three years later when the first queen was chosen.

As an adjunct to the festival, Portland has also developed the International Rose Test Gardens. Started in 1917, these gardens in Washington Park cover four acres and include 10,000 plantings of 400 varieties of rose. Cuttings from all over the world are sent here and grafted to develop new types of rose. The gardens are at the peak of color during the festival.

Illuminated floats light up Portland's Rose Festival. (Courtesy of Dick Powers)

✱ **Location:** The celebrations are citywide and in some of the smaller communities in the area. ✱ **Events:** Floral parade, rose shows, band competitions, Indy car races, air show, hot air balloon show, a children's parade billed as the largest in the country, live entertainment, waterfront fair and exhibition area. ✱ **Contact:** Portland Rose Festival Association, 220 N.W. Second Ave., Portland, OR 97209, (503) 227-2681.

Utah

◆ Peach Days: Weekend after Labor Day.

The first symbolic act performed by the Latter Day Saints after reaching Salt Lake City was to till the soil. It was a commitment to sustain themselves from the land, to make the desert bloom.

They found soil conditions to be good in the valleys west of Wasatch Range. This land had been part of a prehistoric lake and was a fertile alluvial basin, rich in nutrients. Still, it was a far different setting from the well-watered farmlands of the Midwest, growing conditions to which the newcomers were accustomed. But they adjusted to the rainfall shortages, and Mormons have become some of the most adept dry-land farmers in the world.

The fruit orchards in the northern section of the state are the prime example of how they prospered. The former route of U.S. 89, which parallels Interstate 15 on the east, is known as the Golden Spike Fruitway and is lined with orchards and produce stands. Every September since 1904, Brigham City has celebrated its top local agricultural product with this festival. The town was originally called Box Elder but was renamed to honor Brigham Young after the church leader made his final public speech here in 1877.

✳ **Location:** Brigham City is on Interstate 15, about 20 miles north of Ogden. ✳ **Events:** Parade, carnival, flower shows, musical entertainment, art show. ✳ **Contact:** Brigham Chamber of Commerce, 6 North Main St., Brigham City, UT 84302, (801) 723-3931.

PROMONTORY

◈ Driving of the Golden Spike: May 10.

Several historians have called it the end of the beginning. When crews from the Union Pacific and Central Pacific Railroads met at this windswept point in the Utah desert in May 1869, the first transcontinental railroad was completed and an historical era was coming to an end. The time of isolation, lonely wagon trains, Pony Express riders, and jolting stagecoaches was almost over.

This epic struggle, a mixture of extraordinary heroism and titanic greed, was a classic American adventure. As soon as California was joined to the Union by a bond of gold, it was evident that it had to be connected to the rest of the country by rail. The first surveying parties began scrambling across the Sierra Nevada and the Great Plains as early as 1852. Debates raged in Congress over the course of the route because sectional politics figured deeply in the decision. Jefferson Davis, who was then secretary of war, did everything he could to steer the proposed railroad into the South, even engineering the Gadsden Purchase of Mexican land in southern New Mexico and Arizona to accommodate it. When the Civil War began, the question was still unsettled.

Or, rather, the war settled it once and for all. Now there was no question that the northern route would be followed, and in 1862 President Lincoln authorized the start of construction. The Union Pacific would build west from Omaha; the Central Pacific east from Sacramento. Tremendous subsidies were granted to the railroads in the form of land grants and bonuses. Still, the project bogged down until the war was over. The resources to man and equip the work gangs could not be mustered until then.

In 1866, the rails finally started to move towards each other. The Central Pacific was faced with the greater task of building across the Sierra. The railroad, which received higher bonuses for mountain work, managed to stay financially afloat only by moving the mountain range twenty-five miles west on paper to speed up payment of the extra money. The Union Pacific, led by Maj. Gen. Grenville Dodge, who was on leave from the army, saved his company by bullying and cajoling the crews to reach Cheyenne by the end of 1867, increasing its bonus payments. There were fortunes to be made with every mile of track and the work crews, predominantly Irish on the UP and Chinese on the CP, were driven relentlessly.

There had been no stipulation on where the two lines should join, and by early 1869 they were laying track right past each other. There were even instances of the competing lines setting off dynamite charges near their rival's tracks, blowing several workers on either side into the here-

The first transcontinental railroad was completed with the driving of the golden spike in Promontory, Utah, an event that joined a nation and heralded the end of the Wild West.

(*Ewing Galloway*)

after. Finally, a truce was worked out and this desolate spit of land was selected for the great meeting. As the golden spikes were driven into the last track by the presidents of the two railroads, telegraphers tapped out the message to a jubilant America. The country had been joined. A total of 1,775.5 miles of track had been laid at a cost of $165 million.

Promontory's moment at the center was brief. The place was simply too remote to serve as a permanent junction point, and the terminal was soon moved to Ogden. In 1903, the main line of the railroad was shifted to another route, and the transcontinental trains no longer came through. Promontory was reduced to being placed upon a spur. But the moment at which a continent was joined is re-created each May at the place it happened. The Golden Spike National Historic Site features a permanent museum at the place, with displays on the history of the railroad.

✷ **Location:** Promontory is about 35 miles west of Interstate 15, from Brigham City, by way of Utah 83 and county roads. ✷ **Events:** Reenactment of the Golden Spike ceremony using vintage railroad equipment, with costumed participants. ✷ **Contact:** Golden Spike Historic Site, P.O. Box 897, Brigham City, UT 84302, (801) 471-2209.

BELLINGHAM

❖ Lummi Stommish Festival: In June, dates vary according to tides.

The seafaring traditions of the Native American peoples of the Pacific Northwest come alive at this annual celebration on the Lummi Reserve. The Lummi were a branch of the Salishan people, ranging all the way from Washington's San Juan Islands to the Fraser River of British Columbia.

By 1849, with their numbers depleted by disease and years of warfare with neighboring tribes, the Lummi were resettled on this reservation. It is a spectacular site, occupying a peninsula opposite the port city of Bellingham, with the peaks of the Cascades rising behind it.

The Lummi have built up a strong commercial fishing fleet, which is the spine of the tribal economy. There is also a thriving tourist industry. The tribe is expert at preparing barbecued salmon, and it operates a restaurant, with a spectacular water view, that specializes in the dish. This festival is derived from the custom of potlatch, annual gatherings in which leaders distributed gifts to enhance their own status.

✳ **Location:** The reservation is reached from Bellingham by way of northbound Interstate 5, then west on county roads from the Marietta exit. ✳ **Events:** War canoe races, salmon bake, traditional dances, arts and crafts exhibits. ✳ **Contact:** Lummi Casino, 2559 Lummi View Dr., Bellingham, WA 98226, (360) 758-7559.

SEQUIM

◈ **Irrigation Festival:** First weekend in May.

A few miles west of this town on the northern shore of the Olympic Peninsula is some of the rainiest terrain in North America. Rain forests that average more than 140 inches of precipitation annually can be found throughout Olympic National Park.

But Sequim gets about one-tenth of that amount. Clouds are drained of their moisture as they come in off the Pacific, and by the time they reach this area they are bone dry. Sequim has become a retirement haven because it is one of the sunniest places in the state. But that did present certain agricultural problems.

The irrigation programs of eastern Washington, centered around the massive federal program at Grand Coulee Dam, are nationally known. But it is in tiny Sequim (the word means "quiet water"), with its rather modest dry-farming program, that the community actually turns out to celebrate the wonders of irrigation.

✳ **Location:** Sequim is on U.S. 101, about 15 miles east of Port Angeles. ✳ **Events:** Parade, community picnic, flower show, art displays. ✳ **Contact:** Sequim Chamber of Commerce, P.O. Box 907, Sequim, WA 98382, (206) 683-6197.

SUQUAMISH

 Chief Seattle Days: Third weekend in August.

The great city directly across Puget Sound bears his name. But Chief Seattle rests for eternity at this place, on the Port Madison reservation, to which the Suquamish people were restricted by treaty after 1855.

Seattle seems to have been a very practical man. He first regarded the white settlers as potential allies in his tribe's ongoing struggles with the Cowichan, a powerful people who lived on Vancouver Island and periodically raided the Suquamish for slaves. But as he began to comprehend the numbers that were coming into his lands, Seattle realized that the only possible course was accommodation.

He was born in this area in around 1788. The outlines of the 520-foot cedar longhouse which was his birthplace are still visible on the beach. His grave is on an adjacent hillside. He did enjoy something of a final triumph, however. For many years his descendants were paid a tax for use of his name by the City of Seattle. The settlers had chosen the name as a way of maintaining amicable relations with the Indians. Seattle, however, pointed out that tribal beliefs taught that to mention a dead man's name disturbs his spirit. So the city paid well for the privilege. This celebration invokes the spirit of the Suquamish and their cultural legacy.

✳ **Location:** Suquamish is north of the Winslow Ferry station to downtown Seattle, by way of Washington 305. ✳ **Events:** Canoe races, salmon bake, traditional dancing, art show. ✳ **Contact:** Suquamish Tribe, P.O. Box 498, Suquamish, WA 98392, (206) 598-3311.

Wyoming

❖ Frontier Days: Last full week in July.

Cheyenne had barely emerged from its actual days as a frontier settlement when it began celebrating them during Frontier Days. This is regarded as the oldest western festival in the country, held every year since 1897. Wyoming had been in the Union only seven years and its capital city had been existence for only thirty when Frontier Days began.

Cheyenne, actually, was founded as a result of the enterprise that led to the end of the frontier. Maj. Gen. Grenville Dodge, head of the transcontinental rail project for the Union Pacific, camped there while looking for the best route across the Laramie Mountains. He platted a town on his old campsite when the rails came through in 1867. When the Wyoming Territory was formed two years later, Cheyenne was its largest town and so became its capital.

The first Frontier Days was simply held out on the plains near town. Starting as a rodeo, it has grown into one of the great Old West spectacles. It features a cast of thousands: cowboys, Indians, rodeo stars, country music stars. It draws crowds about six times as large as the city's usual population of 50,000, so special accommodation has to be made to take care of them. Pancake batter, for example, is customarily made in a cement mixer. It is a vision of what Buffalo Bill's Wild West show must have been like a century ago. But his show was on the road, and Cheyenne's always is held in one place.

✳ **Location:** Events are held citywide. ✳ **Events:** Parades, rodeo, chuckwagon races, street entertainment, Indian dancing, theatrical presentations, Air Force flying shows, pancake breakfast. ✳ **Contact:** Frontier Days, (307) 778-7200; Cheyenne Area Convention and Visitors Bureau, 309 West Lincoln Way, Cheyenne, WY 82001, (307) 778-3133.

Chuck wagon races draw crowds at Cheyenne's Frontier Days, the oldest western festival in existence. (Courtesy of Frontier Days)

DOUGLAS

◈ Jackalope Day Celebration: Third full weekend in June.

It is fairly easy to understand how the story of the jackalope got started. Jack rabbits have outsized ears that, from a distance, could look a little like antlers. They share the attribute of speed and are among the fastest creatures on the Plains. There is even a species of jackrabbit that is known as the antelope jackrabbit in the southwestern states.

But the jackalope is an invention peculiar to Wyoming and it has become part of the state's folklore. Souvenir stores and taxidermy shops throughout Wyoming display them, with tiny antlers mounted on a rabbit's body. Gullible visitors from the East were told for years about the existence of this fantastic creature. If they expressed doubts, well, here it was, mounted right before their eyes. How could they argue with that? Douglas, for reasons lost in obscurity, was where the legend of the jackalope originated. There is even a monument to it in the middle of town.

The town grew up near the old frontier outpost of Fort Fetterman when the railroad arrived in the vicinity. It was originally called Tent

Douglas, Wyoming, celebrates the mythical jackalope with its own festival. *(Courtesy of The Douglas Budget and Douglas Area Chamber of Commerce)*

Town because of the preferred method of shelter among its first residents, but was soon renamed for Stephen A. Douglas. Since this occurred in 1886, a full twenty-six years after he lost the presidential election to Abraham Lincoln, it was quite a magnanimous gesture. Situated on the North Platte River, it is a livestock center and serves the surrounding oil and gas region.

✳ **Location:** Douglas is on Interstate 25, about 50 miles east of Casper.
✳ **Events:** Jackalope hunt, carnival, bicycle races, 5K run, volleyball competition, street dance, barbecue, bed races, parade, Little Miss Jackalope contest. ✳ **Contact:** Douglas Area Chamber of Commerce, 318 First St. West, Douglas, WY 82633, (307) 358-2950.

MEDICINE BOW

 Medicine Bow Days: Fourth weekend in June.

He gave Gary Cooper one of the classic lines in movie history. "When you say that, smile," he said in the film made from Owen Wister's western novel, *The Virginian*. The book, published in 1902, was set in the town of Medicine Bow, on the plains at the edge of the Wyoming Rockies.

Wister was a Harvard graduate who had studied music and intended to be a composer. But he fell ill while touring Europe in 1882 and, much like a college classmate, Teddy Roosevelt, went west to regain his health. Wister later wrote a biography of Roosevelt, who did his ranching in North Dakota.

Wister eventually bought property near the Teton range in the western part of the state. But he was a frequent visitor to Medicine Bow, a picture-book Old West cowboy town, and used it as the setting for his novel. The Virginian Hotel, however, was not part of that setting. It wasn't built until 1911 and was named for Wister's hero. The rail depot, built two years later, now houses a museum of the town's past. *The Virginian* was later turned into a stage play and several movies, and it was the basis for a popular television series in the 1960s. This festival incorporates parts of the Medicine Bow's actual past and the fictitious events written by Wister.

✳ **Location:** Medicine Bow is on U.S. 30, about 55 miles northwest of Laramie. ✳ **Events:** Rodeos, foot races, games, street entertainment, Old West-themed shows, picnic, parade, craft show. ✳ **Contact:** Medicine Bow Museum, 405 Lincoln Hwy., Medicine Bow, WY 82329, (307) 379-2383.

PINEDALE

 Green River Rendezvous: Second weekend in July.

The system was developed by William Ashley, head of the Rocky Mountain Fur Company. Instead of restricting his agents to fixed trading posts, the method used by the rival Hudson Bay Company, he allowed them to roam wherever the hunt might take them. The only stipulation he placed on them is that on a given date each year they would rendezvous with company agents to turn in their pelts and receive their trade goods for the next season.

It was perfect for the free spirits of the mountain men, who hated being tied down to any system that limited their mobility. Ashley's men began penetrating the long-hidden valleys of the Rockies and beyond in the 1820s, and starting in 1832 the rendezvous was a regular part of the year's cycle.

The Green River Rendezvous was the biggest, in the heart of the great trapping territory that lay between the Teton and Wind River ranges of Wyoming. This is where the legends came: Jim Bridger, for whom the adjacent national forest is named, and William Sublette, whose name is now on the county. Jedediah Smith was another of the great scouts who learned the business under Ashley and attended rendezvous.

Historian Bernard DeVoto, in his book *Across the Wide Missouri,* described the rendezvous as "the annual season of supply, trade and saturnalia." It was a time to swap stories, take whatever pleasure these men had in human companionship, enjoy the marginal joys of civilization. Bridger was proud of the fact that after going into the wilderness in 1822 until the breakup of the rendezvous system in 1838, he had never tasted bread.

Changing management, the passing of Ashley's company, the increasing difficulty in finding pelts, the opening of the Oregon Trail— they all combined to end the rendezvous system. Its end was as sure a closing of an era as was the transcontinental railroad. Pinedale, the community closest to the actual Green River site, re-creates the look of a typical 1830s rendezvous in this annual celebration.

❋ **Location:** Pinedale is on U.S. 191, about 100 miles north of Interstate 80. The Rendezvous site is 6 miles west of town. ❋ **Events:** Reenactment of the trappers, traders and Indians meeting in this annual event; frontier competitions and crafts. ❋ **Contact:** Museum of the Mountain Man, P.O. Box 909, Pinedale, WY 82941, (307) 367-4101.

Selected events that are either commemorated or played an important role in the festivals in this book.

1450	Iroquois Confederacy formed in New York.
1492	Columbus discovers Americas.
1539	Hernan DeSoto lands near Bradenton, Florida.
1565	Spanish settle St. Augustine, Florida, the oldest European community in the United States.
1621	First Thanksgiving celebrated at Plymouth, Massachusetts.
1623	First fishing boats put to sea from Gloucester, Massachusetts.
1680	Indians accompanying the Spanish retreat from New Mexico found the pueblo at Ysleta, Texas.
1682	First Pennsylvania Dutch arrive in America.
1690	Elfreth's Alley built in Philadelphia, Pennsylvania.
1692	Witchcraft trials at Salem, Massachusetts.
1698	D'Iberville lands at Biloxi Bay, Mississippi.
1700	Mission San Xavier del Bac founded near Tucson, Arizona.
1712	First Fiesta celebrated at Santa Fe, New Mexico.
1741	Moravians arrive at Bethlehem, Pennsylvania, on Christmas Eve.
1754	Azaleas first imported to Mobile, Alabama.
1763	British garrison at Fort Michilimackinac, Michigan, overwhelmed in Pontiac's Rebellion.
1769	Daniel Boone enters Kentucky through the Cumberland Gap.

1772	British patrol boat *Gaspee* seized by irate colonials near Warwick, Rhode Island.
1773	Tea dumped in Boston Harbor at the Boston Tea Party.
1774	Chestertown, Maryland, holds its own tea party in sympathy.
1774	Flora MacDonald joins the Highland Scot colony in North Carolina.
1775	Minutemen rout the British at Concord, Massachusetts.
1775	Battle of Bunker Hill, Charlestown, Massachusetts.
1776	Continental Congress adopts Declaration of Independence.
1776	Mission of San Juan Capistrano founded in California.
1776	British evacuate Boston.
1776	George Washington crosses the Delaware to surprise the British at Trenton, New Jersey.
1777	Hurley becomes temporary capital of New York.
1777	Battle of Bennington, Vermont.
1777	Battle of Germantown, Pennsylvania.
1778	Captain James Cook lands in Hawaii.
1779	George Rogers Clark captures the British fort at Vincennes, Indiana.
1779	First group of Cajuns arrive from Canada in Louisiana.
1781	Lord Cornwallis surrenders at Yorktown, Virginia.
1782	Spanish settlers arrive at Santa Barbara, California.
1784	Gasparilla turns pirate along the Florida Gulf coast.
1784	The "lost state" of Franklin is created.
1787	U.S. Constitutional Congress drafts new Constitution.
1789-97	George Washington serves as the first U.S. president.
1796	Zane's Trace becomes the first overland route into Ohio.
1797-1801	John Adams serves as U.S. president.
1801-09	Thomas Jefferson serves as U.S. president.
1803	Louisiana Purchase approved.
1804	Lewis and Clark stop at St. Charles, Missouri, on their westward voyage.

1805	Rappites settle Harmony, Pennsylvania.
1806	National Road opens to the West.
1806	Zebulon Pike Expedition sees and names Pikes Peak in the Rocky Mountains.
1807	Shaker Colony established at South Union, Kentucky.
1809-17	James Madison serves as U.S. president.
1817-25	James Monroe serves as U.S. president.
1817	Rush-Bagot Agreement delineates U.S.-Canada border along the Great Lakes.
1819	Cahawba becomes Alabama's first capital.
1819	Vandalia named capital of Illinois.
1825-29	John Quincy Adams serves as U.S. president.
1825	Opening of Erie Canal in New York.
1825	Kansa sign treaty assuring safe passage for travelers on the Santa Fe Trail, at Council Grove, Kansas.
1828	American Fur Company founds Fort Union, North Dakota.
1829-37	Andrew Jackson serves as U.S. president.
1830	Head of the Santa Fe Trail moves to Independence, Missouri.
1830	First westbound wagon train leaves on the Oregon Trail.
1832	First Green River Rendezvous at Pinedale, Wyoming.
1835	First shots of the Texas rebellion fired at Gonzales.
1836	Republic of Texas formed at Washington, Texas.
1836	Lockport, Illinois, becomes headquarters of Illinois and Michigan Canal.
1837-41	Martin Van Buren serves as U.S. president.
1837	German colonists arrive in Hermann, Missouri.
1838	Pottery industry established at East Liverpool, Ohio.
1839	Mormons settle at Nauvoo, Illinois.
1839	New Cherokee capital built at Tahlequah, Oklahoma.
1840	Marble quarries open at Jasper, Georgia.
1840	Miami sign land treaty at Forks of the Wabash, Indiana.
1841-45	John Tyler serves as U.S. president.

1845-49	James K. Polk serves as U.S. president.
1845	Johnny Appleseed buried near Fort Wayne, Indiana.
1845	German colonists settle Frankenmuth, Michigan.
1846	Fandango massacre at Alturas, California.
1846	Dutch colonists arrive at Holland, Michigan.
1846	Swedish Janssonists found community at Bishop Hill, Illinois.
1846	German settlers arrive at Fredericksburg, Texas.
1848	First womens' rights convention at Seneca Falls, New York.
1849-50	Zachary Taylor serves as U.S. president.
1849	Lummi Reservation set aside in Washington.
1849	James Whitcomb Riley born in Greenfield, Indiana.
1850-53	Millard Fillmore serves as U.S. president.
1850	Chesapeake and Ohio Canal opens to Cumberland, Maryland.
1853-57	Franklin Pierce serves as U.S. president.
1853	Grateful citizens of a new Illinois county seat name the town after their attorney, Abraham Lincoln.
1854	German settlers come to New Ulm, Minnesota.
1855	Chief Seattle signs treaty and obtains reservation lands for Suquamish in Washington.
1857-61	James Buchanan serves as U.S. president.
1857	Mystic Krewe of Comus organized for Mardi Gras in New Orleans.
1858	Buena Vista Winery opens at Sonoma, California
1858	Gold strike at Idaho Springs, Colorado.
1859	Comstock Lode comes in, resulting in the population of Nevada.
1860	Pony Express starts its run.
1860	Annie Oakley born near Greenville, Ohio.
1861-65	Abraham Lincoln serves as U.S. president.
1862	Gold strike at Wickenburg, Arizona.
1863	First land grant under the Homestead Act, near Beatrice, Nebraska.

1863	Thanksgiving proclaimed a national holiday.
1863	Henry W. Longfellow writes *Tales of a Wayside Inn*.
1864	Battle of Pleasant Hill, Louisiana.
1864	Battle of New Market, Virginia.
1864	Battle of Olustee, Florida.
1864	First Memorial Day observed at Boalsburg, Pennsylvania.
1865-69	Andrew Johnson serves as U.S. president.
1865	Mark Twain publishes "The Celebrated Jumping Frog of Calaveras County."
1865	Battle of Natural Bridge, Florida.
1867	American flag raised at Sitka, Alaska.
1867	First cattle drive leaves Texas on the Chisholm Trail.
1868	Navajo Reservation established.
1868	Jesse James raids Russellville, Kentucky.
1869-77	Ulysses S. Grant serves as U.S. president.
1869	Transcontinental railroad completed at Promontory Point, Utah.
1869	Mardi Gras re-established at the start of Lent in Mobile, Alabama.
1871	First silver strike comes in at Silverton, Colorado.
1872	Nebraska proclaims the first Arbor Day.
1873	Chester Greenwood invents earmuffs in Farmington, Maine.
1873	Running of the first Preakness Stakes, Baltimore, Maryland.
1873	General George Custer takes command of 7th Cavalry at Fort Abraham Lincoln, North Dakota.
1873	W. C. Handy born in Florence, Alabama.
1874	Custer expedition finds gold in South Dakota's Black Hills.
1875	First Kentucky Derby held at Louisville.
1875	Elberta peach developed near Fort Valley, Georgia.
1876	James and Younger gang wiped out after raid at Northfield, Minnesota.
1876	Mark Twain publishes *Tom Sawyer*.

1876	Battle of the Little Big Horn, Montana.
1876	Wild Bill Hickok gunned down at Deadwood, South Dakota.
1877-81	Rutherford B. Hayes serves as U.S. president.
1877	Rugby School and community established in Tennessee.
1877	Nez Perce rebel at being moved to Idaho and start their run for the Canadian border.
1878	Cheyenne raid on Oberlin, Kansas.
1879	Will Rogers born near Claremore, Oklahoma.
1880	Charles Russell arrives in Montana to paint the Old West.
1881-85	Chester A. Arthur serves as U.S. president.
1881	Gunfight at the O.K. Corral, Tombstone, Arizona.
1881	Chinese community celebrates first Bok Kai Festival in United States, at Marysville, California.
1881	First national tennis championship, at Newport, Rhode Island.
1882	First Bach Festival at Bethlehem, Pennsylvania.
1882	First performance of Handel's *Messiah* at Lindsborg, Kansas.
1883	Mescalero Apache reservation formed in New Mexico.
1883	Theodore Roosevelt arrives in North Dakota as a rancher.
1885-89	Grover Cleveland serves as U.S. president.
1885	Winterthur built near Wilmington, Delaware, by Colonel Henry F. du Pont.
1885	Thomas Edison opens his laboratory at Fort Myers, Florida.
1885	Winter Chautauqua first held at De Funiak Springs, Florida.
1886	First Winter Carnival at St. Paul, Minnesota.
1887	Lilac trees first planted in Highland Park, Rochester, New York.
1889-93	Benjamin Harrison serves as U.S. president.
1889	Oklahoma Land Rush.
1889	Oil strike at Sistersville, West Virginia.
1890	First Tournament of Roses, Pasadena, California.
1891	Circus opens winter quarters at Peru, Indiana.
1891	First Fiesta at San Antonio, Texas.

1892	Corn Palace first erected at Mitchell, South Dakota.
1893-97	Grover Cleveland serves his second term as U.S. president.
1893	Waldensian colonists arrive in North Carolina.
1893	Cherokee Strip opened to settlement in Oklahoma.
1894	Corn flakes introduced at Kellogg Sanitorium, Battle Creek, Michigan.
1897-1901	William McKinley serves as U.S. president.
1897	Scott Joplin publishes "Maple Leaf Rag."
1897	First Frontier Days festival held in Cheyenne, Wyoming.
1900	Jim Butler finds silver at Tonopah, Nevada.
1901-09	Theodore Roosevelt serves as U.S. president.
1901	Discovery of Carlsbad Caverns, New Mexico.
1901	Mummers hold first organized parade in Philadelphia, Pennsylvania.
1902	Owen Wister's *The Virginian* is published.
1903	Wright Brothers make their first successful flight.
1903	Chocolate town of Hershey, Pennsylvania, is built.
1905	Yamato colony of Japanese settlers established at Delray Beach, Florida.
1905	Greek sponge divers arrive at Tarpon Springs, Florida.
1905	W. C. Handy writes "The Memphis Blues."
1907	Japanese cherry trees imported to Washington, D.C.
1909-13	William Howard Taft serves as U.S. president.
1911	Danish settlers arrive in Solvang, California.
1911	First "500" race run at Indianapolis, Indiana.
1913-21	Woodrow Wilson serves as U.S. president.
1917	Jazz performances first recorded in New Orleans, Louisiana.
1918	Choctaw win right to a reservation in Mississippi.
1921-23	Warren G. Harding serves as U.S. president.
1921	First Miss America Pageant at Atlantic City, New Jersey.
1922	First Inter-Tribal Festival at Gallup, New Mexico.

1923-29	Calvin Coolidge serves as U.S. president.
1924	First Macy's Thanksgiving Day Parade, New York City.
1925	Grand Ole Opry goes on the radio in Nashville, Tennessee.
1927	Carter Family makes its first recording.
1929-33	Herbert Hoover serves as U.S. president.
1931	First national broadcast of Lum n' Abner.
1931	Ernest Hemingway arrives in Key West, Florida.
1933-45	Franklin D. Roosevelt serves as U.S. president.
1945-53	Harry S Truman serves as U.S. president.
1947	Offshore oil strike near Morgan City, Louisiana.
1953-61	Dwight D. Eisenhower serves as U.S. president.
1953	Elvis Presley cuts his demo record in Memphis, Tennessee.
1959	St. Lawrence Seaway dedicated.
1961-63	John F. Kennedy serves as U.S. president.
1963-69	Lyndon B. Johnson serves as U.S. president.
1969-74	Richard M. Nixon serves as U.S. president.
1971	London Bridge reopens at Lake Havasu City, Arizona.
1971	Orville Redenbacher begins to market his gourmet popcorn at Valparaiso, Indiana.
1974-76	Gerald R. Ford serves as U.S. president.
1976	Last log drive down the Kennebec River to Skowhegan, Maine.

◈ April

◈ May

❖ June

July

◈ August

 November

December

flower festivals

food festivals

Historic Communities

Historic Eras

Historic Events

Historic Persons

Industry-Local

Music Festivals

Native American Celebrations

Parades

Reenactments

Traditions-Local